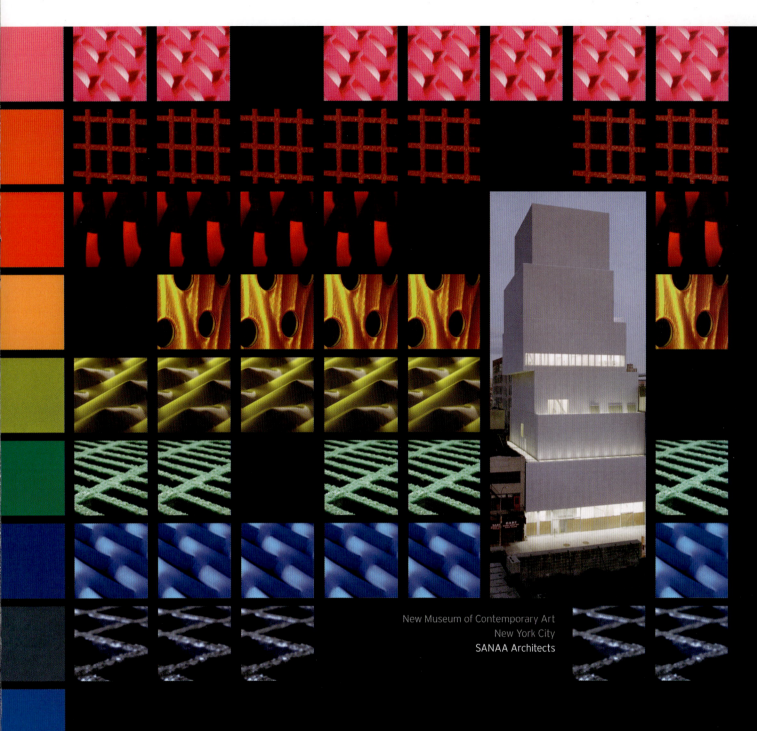

New Museum of Contemporary Art
New York City
SANAA Architects

AMICO   A GIBRALTAR INDUSTRIES COMPANY

BoOk LaMp

Martí Guixé

presented by

luján + sicilia

NEW CATALOGUE 2012 AVAILABLE

Brookview TECHNOLOGIES

Visualplanet *touchfoils*™ are large format projected capacitance films that can be applied to glass and other surfaces to add *interactive* touch capabilities with LCD/LED monitors or projected images. They are *touchable* through *glass* and can be used inside display cases and enclosures, through windows, in kiosks and tables, and many more applications.

Already in use at these locations and more:

Grammy Museum — Los Angeles

Walt Disney Family Museum — San Francisco

Natural History Museum of Utah — Salt Lake City

Bata Shoe Museum — Toronto

International Civil Rights Museum — Greensboro

For more information contact

Michael Gaffney

(239) 642-5772

mikeg@brookviewtechnologies.com

www.brookviewtechnologies.com

We are the manufacturer designated Wholesale Distributor in North America. Solutions Partner inquiries are encouraged.

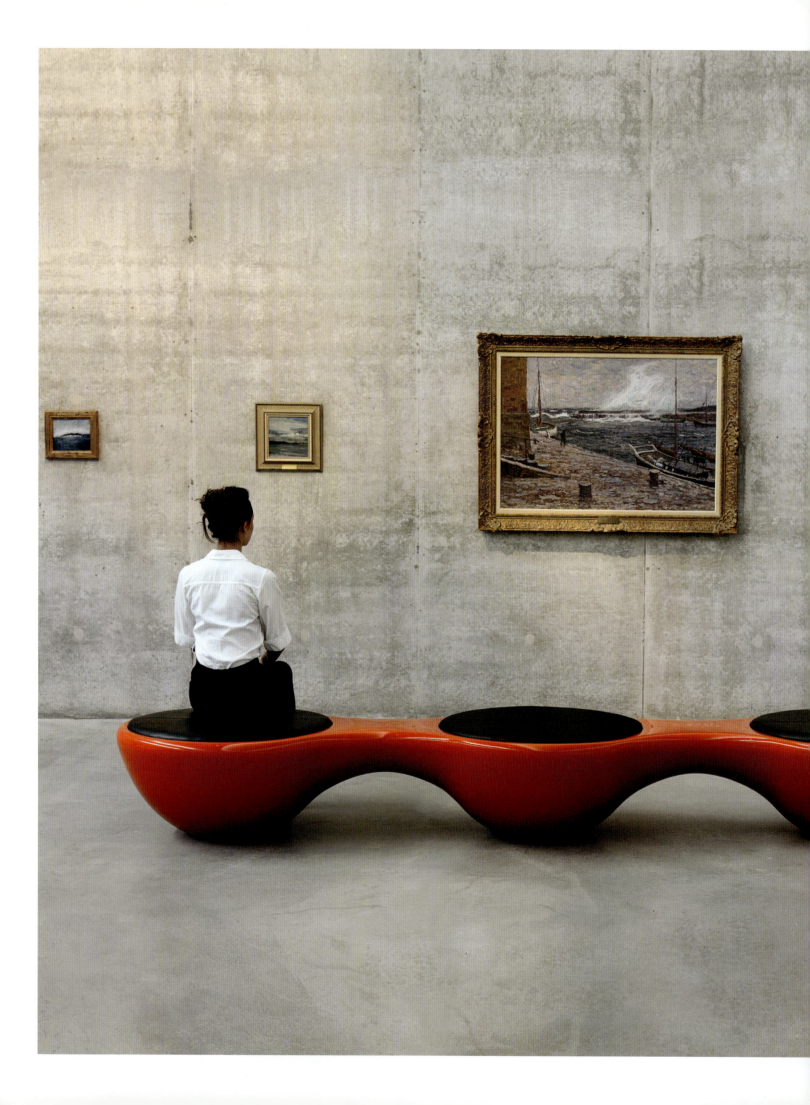

unionbench™
panorama

The newest addition to Jangir Maddadi's pivotal Union Bench Collection, the Panorama brings
sophistication to a whole new level. Modern and organic, this bench seats 12 people,
offers two integrated tables and occupies a width of only 90 cm (35.4 in).
Clean. Perfect. Panorama.

JANGIR MADDADI
DESIGN BUREAU

www.jangirmaddadi.se

unionbench™

yacht

. . . .

Bring the pleasures of boating back to the land with our Yacht Bench. With its fiberglass base and certified teak seats inspired by yacht decking, this bench is the essence of style. Place it indoors or outdoors and the Yacht Bench will always add an exclusive nautical taste.

. . . .

JANGIR MADDADI
DESIGN BUREAU

. . . .

WWW.JMDB.SE

COMPOUND
COLLECTION

Spaces are most comfortable when the furniture in them molds to your needs. People can adapt to their surroundings with ease. Conversation sets in, thinking and reflecting abound. Our new Compound Collection was created to be a seating product that encourages dynamics, innovation and opportunity. This collection is comprised of a series of four compounds offered in five separate materials. The product itself is easy and fun to re-shape and re-design at will. The space changes with the needs of the people.

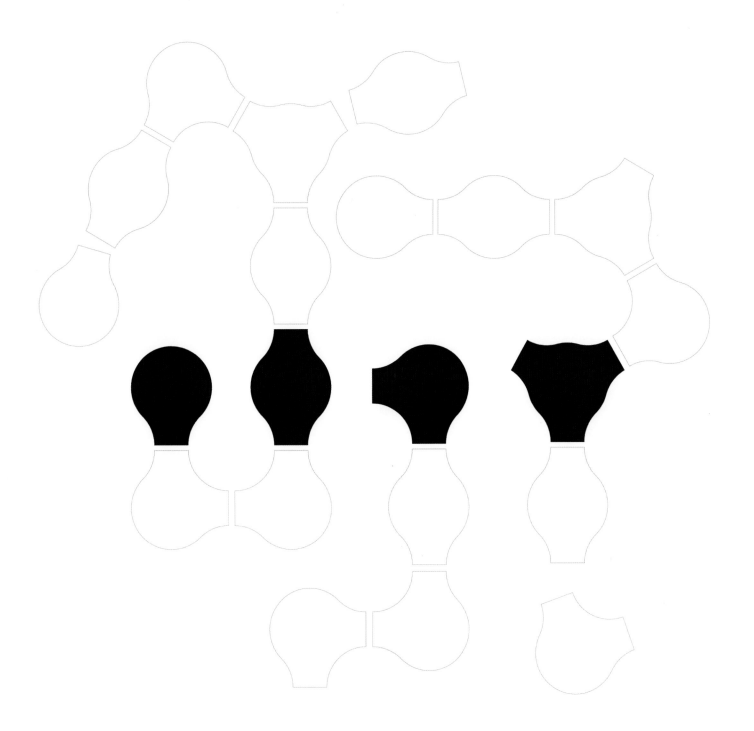

Compound Collection – *Endless possibilities*

JANGIR MADDADI
DESIGN BUREAU

WWW.JMDB.SE

meet:
the extraordinary common acapulco chair

thecommonproject.
www.thecommonproject.net

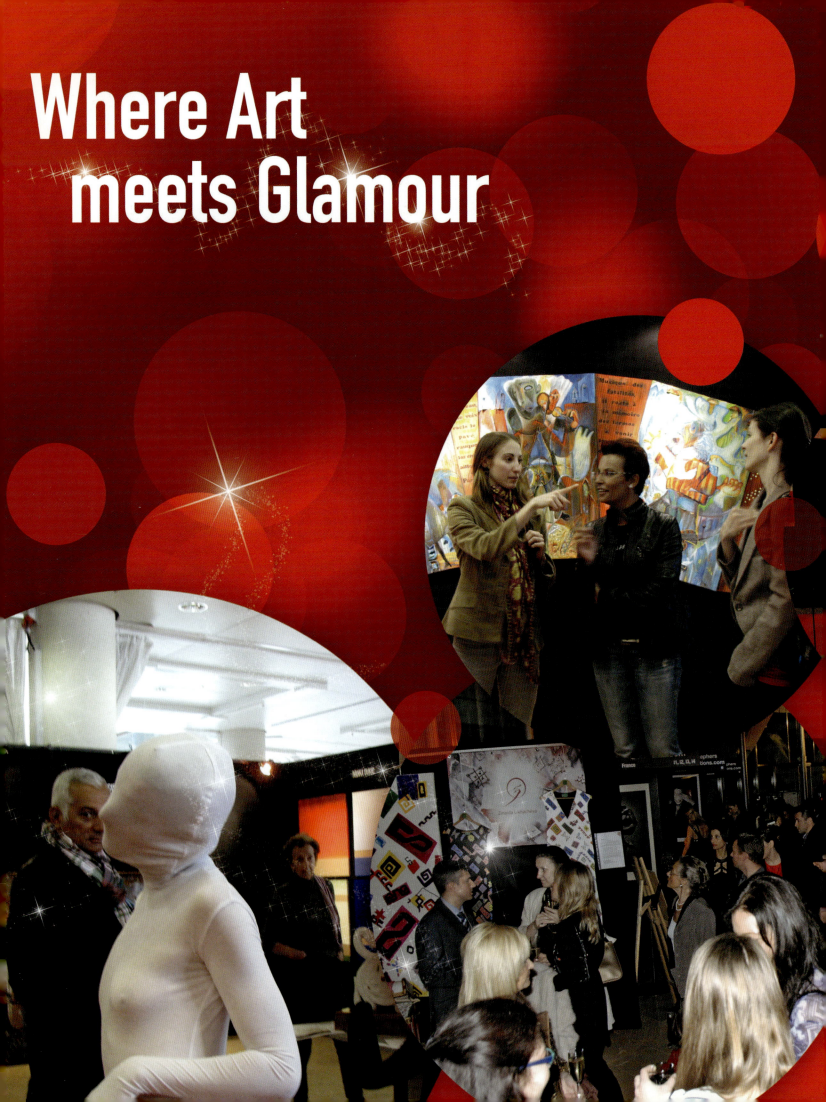

Where Art meets Glamour

ARTMONACO'12

Salon d'Art Contemporain | Côte d'Azur

ArtMonaco is the international art fair that brings together art collectors, galleries and art lovers from all over the world. We facilitate interaction, networking, and generate sales opportunities and new partnerships.

Continuing our search for quality exhibits, and following our commitment in becoming the artistic meeting point for excellence on the French Riviera, we are increasing ArtMonaco this year to include and welcome the leading galleries in the Fine Art, Antiques and Design sectors.

5 – 8 April, 2012

monaco.
visitmonaco.com

GRIMALDI FORUM

OPUS·EVENTI

Events coming soon

Art Armenia
Արվեստ - Հայաստան
Yerevan'12

Art 2013 Marseille contemporain
Capitale Européenne de la Culture

www.monu-magazine.com

shop.Archinect.com

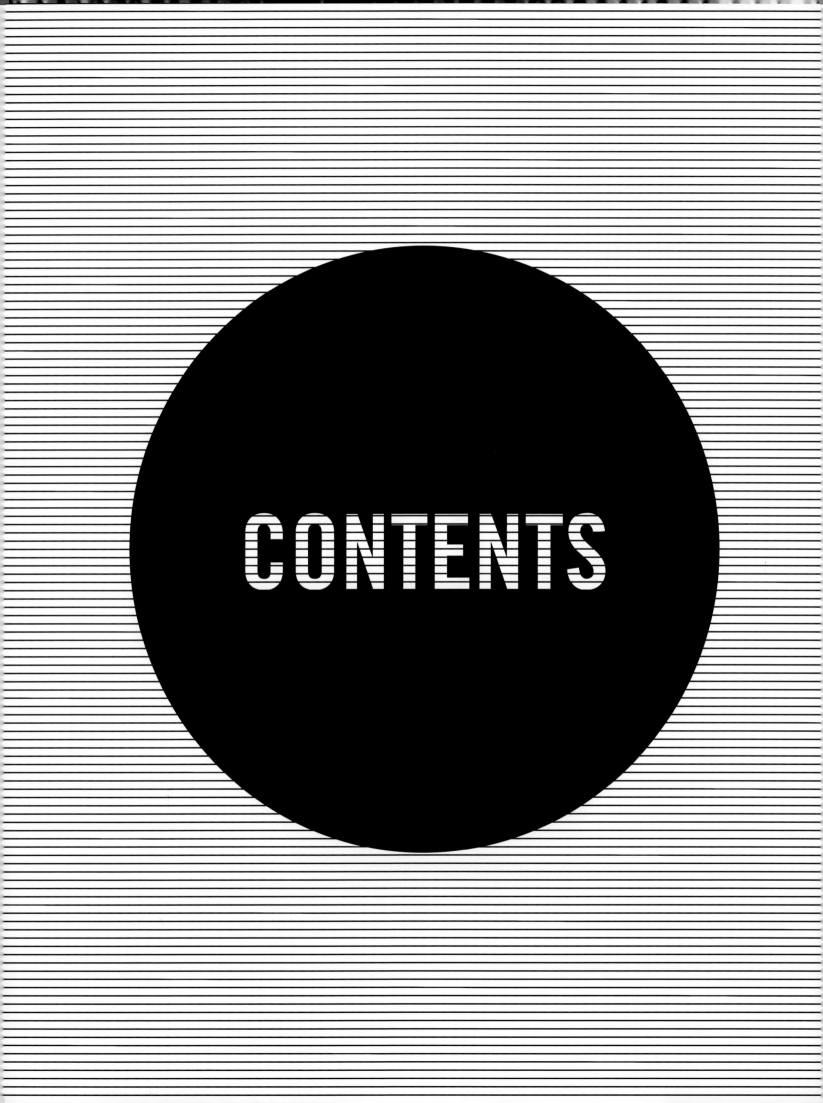

CONTENTS

CREDITS

EDITORIAL

Editor-in-chief / Creative Director	Carlo Aiello
Editors	Paul Aldridge
	Noémie Deville
	Anna Solt
	Jung Su Lee
Contributors	Brian Ahmes
	Vincent Callebaut
	Daniel Carper
	Danielle del Sol
	Heidi Druckemiller
	Elie Gamburg
	Arvin Garay-Cruz
	Lidija Grozdanic
	Fumio Hirakawa
	Kurt C. Hunker
	Jason Levy
	Dennis Lynch
	Bridgette Meinhold
	Andrew Michler
	Chad Porter
	Paul Preissner
	Beatriz Ramo
	Benjamin Rice
	Emmanuel Ruffo
	Marina Topunova
	Eugene Tssui
	Christopher Warren
Graphic Design	HI (NY) Design
	www.hinydesign.com
Printing	Asia Pacific Offset
	Printed in China
Cover	China Comic and
	Animation Museum
	/ MVRDV

eVolo is published by:	Evolo, LLC
	570 West 204 Street, 1B
	New York, NY 10034
	magazine@evolo.us
	www.evolo.us
Subscriptions	magazine@evolo.us
	www.evolo.us
Advertising	magazine@evolo.us
	www.evolo.us
**Distribution	Retail Sales**	Export Press
	dir@exportpress.com
	www.exportpress.com
eVolo 04	
ISSN: 1946-634X	
Summer 2012	

PUBLISHING

EDITORIAL

by CARLO AIELLO

The architecture for performance and exhibition, being museums, galleries, music halls, pavilions, etc., has been in the leading edge of architectural innovation throughout the history and evolution of the discipline. Architects and designers experiment on new aesthetics, concepts, and ideas with projects that tend to have a flexible program and a large budget. In many cases, the main requirement of such structures is not only to accommodate a specific program but also to inspire the imagination of its users and challenge the current state of architectural design. Some examples, such as the Guggenheim Museum Bilbao by Frank Gehry or the Sydney Opera House by Jørn Utzon are considered design masterpieces of the 20th Century. Gehry's Museum transformed the city of Bilbao from a small industrial Spanish city into a world destination, while Utzon's Opera House become the symbol of Sydney and Australia.

This issue of eVolo studies the most innovative examples of performance and exhibition architecture today. These are projects that revolutionize architecture on many levels, including sustainability, aesthetics, technology, and urban design. It is interesting to point out that these works are not concentrated in one specific region, but are located in every corner of the globe; from MVRDV's Comic and Animation Museum in China, to the new Broad Museum in Los Angeles by Diller Scofidio + Renfro, or Kengo Kuma's Victoria and Albert Museum in Dundee, Scotland.

The variety of programs is as diverse as their location. Steven Holl's Museum of Ocean and Surf in Biarritz, France creates awareness of the oceans' fragile state and emulates the kinetic sensibility of water through sweeping walls and carefully articulated volumes. Holm Architecture's circular Samaranch Olympic Museum in Tianjin, China is a study on framing and juxtaposing artificial and natural landscapes to generate a continuous exhibition loop. X-TU Architects' Prehistory Museum in Jeongok, South Korea was parametrically designed as a futuristic vessel erected as a bridge atop hills along the Hantan River preserving the untouched historic landscape. Among other projects, Diller Scofidio + Renfro's Museum of Image and Sound in Rio de Janeiro, Brazil, is an interface between exhibition spaces and the city. Other smaller scale projects are WORD's Holocaust Memorial for Atlantic City's Boardwalk, which acts as an inscriptive apparatus, which etches the history of the Holocaust in our memory, and the America's Cup Pavilion by Daniel Carper, which functions as an epicenter for various activities. The design is based on the tectonic and function qualities of high-end sailing vessels.

For this issue we had the opportunity to interview one of the most promising architects of Mexico: Fernando Romero, who recently completed the Soumaya Museum in Mexico City. The museum has been praised by the critics as one of the most outstanding works of architecture in the country this decade. Fernando also shares with us the his experience in practicing architecture in Mexico, the United States, Europe, and China — an interesting insight on the major differences, challenges, and advantages of working in different cultures and economies.

The Opinion section includes essays on morphogenetic computational design and zero-energy buildings. Emmanuel Ruffo from the Graz University of Technology explains structural patterns formation and the digital tools utilized to explore these geometries and their potential use in architecture. On the other hand, Dr. Eugene Tssui, from the University of Science and Technology in Guangzhou, China, proposes the first true zero-energy building based on studies of the Termite's nest of central Africa. Dr. Tssui's "Evolutionary Architecture" is an in-depth study of living organisms and their natural processes. Finally, Beatriz Ramo, from Tilburg's Architecture Academy exposes the abuse by architects, designers, writers, politicians, etc., of the so-called "green" sustainable architecture, which in many cases is just an advertising gimmick and not true environmentally responsible designs.

In the News section Kurt C. Hunker from the New School of Architecture in San Diego examines the consequences and changes in high-rise architecture since 9/11. In this section we also present the winners of the 2011 eVolo Skyscraper Competition. The contest recognizes outstanding ideas that redefine skyscraper design through the implementation of new technologies, materials, programs, aesthetics, and spatial organizations. Studies on globalization, flexibility, adaptability, and the digital revolution are some of the multi-layered elements of the competition. It is an investigation on the public and private space and the role of the individual and the collective in the creation of dynamic and adaptive vertical communities.

eVolo – to study, to develop, to evolve, to fly away…

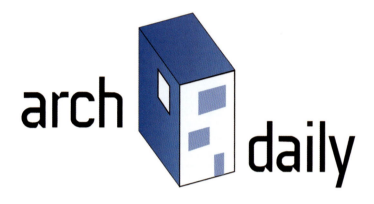

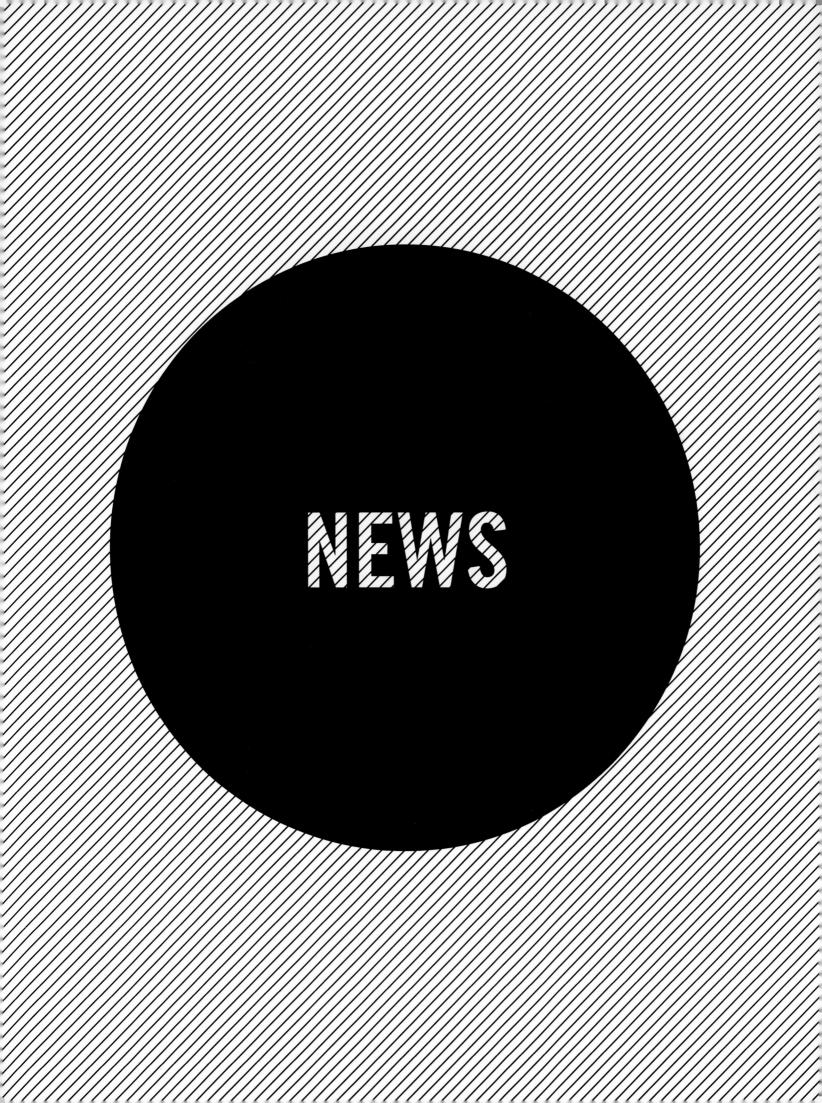

eVolo | Issue 4 | 2012

THE TALL OFFICE BUILDING ARTISTICALLY CONSIDERED

CRITICAL EVENTS SINCE 9/11

Text:
Kurt C. Hunker

"The trouble with skyscrapers is that we cannot make up our minds about them."
- Deyan Sudjic

The American architecture critic John King surely echoed the sentiments of many some years ago when he wrote, "Everything's different after 9/11"[1]. In one sense, everything is different. If there was any doubt, it is abundantly clear now that Asia and the Middle East have eclipsed the big cities of the United States as the urban laboratories for cutting-edge high-rise design that gets built. New materials have given architects new possibilities of expression. Parametric modeling and increasingly sophisticated computer software have likewise expanded the range of expression. And the iconic potential of the tall building as the "legitimizer" of a New World Order—for better or for worse—is on the minds of architects, urbanists, clients, writers and, of course, critics.

Curiously, however, some things have not changed. Some critics still debate the relative merits of building tall in dense urban conditions or in historically-sensitive environments. Many discussions continue about the engineering limits of skyscrapers, and how tall is "tall enough." There is, too, the invariable recognition that it is economics above all that drives high-rise architectural design. Finally, the pervasive (but not always articulated) fear that tall buildings in a post-9/11 world would forever after serve as "targets" for extremists does not seem to have materialized into any kind of significant factor. As a matter of fact, in an online interview critic Blair Kamin has stated, "The self-inflicted damage from our over-reaction to the terrorist threat has been particularly lamentable"[2].

So where does this paradox leave us? *Former New York Times* architecture critic Ada Louise Huxtable, in her 1982 book *The Tall Building Artistically Reconsidered: the Search for a Skyscraper Style*, set forth the history of high-rise design as a progression of four phases: functional, eclectic, modern and postmodern[3]. It would appear we have long since passed through her postmodern phase, concerned as it was with a revivalist approach to skyscraper design, so we must be in a "fifth phase". The changes and challenges since

eVolo | Issue 4 | 2012

30 Mary Axe Street
London, UK
Foster + Partners

9/11 mark a definitive break. One might, in fact, argue that we have entered something of a new "functional" phase, an updated retelling of the "skyscraper story" in twenty-first century language, with a distinctly new emphasis.

In the so-called first, or functional, phase "architecture was the servant of engineering." Aesthetics were, in Huxtable's words, a "subordinate function" to the economic and technical pragmatics of building tall. Architects were focused on the application of novel technologies—the passenger elevator and steel skeleton obviously among the most critical—that made the skyscraper a reality in the first place. At the present we see, once again, an intense interest in the mechanics of building tall, of the potentials of new materials and systems. That much is indeed similar. But in other respects, things are not the same.

THE SPECTACLE OF THE TECHNICAL

What is truly unique in our situation is that the market-driven determinism that fueled Huxtable's first phase and established the eternal conflict between innovation and economics has been replaced by what we might term The Spectacle of the Technical. Issues informed observers thought might dominate the next great phase—iconography, third-world urbanism, cultural sensitivity, even sustainability, to a degree—have given way, at least momentarily, to a fascination with technology's impacts on high-rise building and on us. The sense of wonderment that surrounds much current critical writing on tall buildings is an acknowledgement of the presence of spectacle in skyscraper design today. The fascination is not limited to professionals; critics, students, even the lay public share in it.

Wes Jones, in his 2010 essay, *Big Forking Dilemma*, argues that contemporary architecture has been confronted with two "forks in the road" of theory and practice. There is, on one hand, the distinction to be made between the "authored", or theoretically-charged work, and the "automatic", which Jones defines as the kind of program-heavy, performative practice often associated with the Dutch School. The other fork, and the dilemma that concerns us here, consists in what Jones calls "...*the profound divergence today of sense and sensation—between work that appeals traditionally to the intellect and that which appeals only to the senses*" [4]. It is just a short conceptual hop from architecture of the senses, that is, of "sensation" to the idea of spectacle.

ARCHITECTURE AS SPECTACLE

Numerous writers have made the connection between architecture in the new global economy and the concept of spectacle, none with the impact perhaps of Rem Koolhaas in *S,M,L,XL* and later *Content*. For him, architecture of spectacle is not solely one of novel form (the Seattle Public Library, for example) or inventive programming (as at his Maison Bordeaux) or even size (Congrexpo), it is also rhetorical: *"I want to kill the traditional idea of the skyscraper—it has run out of energy,"* he says in describing the CCTV tower in Beijing [5].

Criticism has broached this condition extensively over the past decade. For writer/editor Luis Fernandez-Galiano, the new architecture is actually "architainment", integral to the new "landscape of wealth" that consists of sprawl and "spectacle". Architecture in support of consumerism resorts to its own forms of drama—its own spectacle—to induce people to buy. In his preface to *Commodification and Spectacle in Architecture*, editor William Saunders confirms that it is spectacle to which contemporary architecture responds: *"...along with every other cultural production...the design of the built environment has been increasingly engulfed in and made subservient to the goals of the capitalist economy..."* [6].

SENSATION AND AFFECT

If spectacle provides the setting for the architectural "Wow!" factor, sensation gives it material form. Farshid Moussavi and Michael Kubo argue that buildings relate to culture through the creation of sensation vis-a-vis "affect." They suggest that architects respond to contemporary conditions by reconsidering the ways in which they create "building expressions" [7]. There is an increasing emphasis on the building skin—the very place where "spectacle" may register most directly. Whereas postmodernism gave us undecipherable codes of symbolic communication in the form of "decor", they argue, new architecture responds nimbly with an aesthetic we can sense.

Coupled with sensation is "affect", lucidly defined by Robert Levit (in an essay critical of aspects of Moussavi's and Kubo's book The Function of Ornament) as *"The impression made on the senses through the effects of material, light, color, reflection, and presum-*

Burj Khalifa
Dubai, UAE
Adrian Smith / SOM
Photo: ©Goran Bogicevic

8 Spruce Street
New York City, USA
Gehry Partners
Photo: ©Sean Pavone Photo

ably pattern…"[8]. That book, which proposes ornament as a replacement for failed forms of communication, is a catalogue of affects ranging from the "dematerialized" to the "random" to the "cinematic." Affects may be applied to any kind of building, including high-rises; the authors include Norman Foster's 30 St. Mary Axe Street of 2004 and the Torre Agbar Headquarters (Jean Nouvel, also 2004) in their inventory.

CRITICAL CONCERNS

Architectural critics and writers have reinforced the preoccupation with spectacle and sensation in their coverage of new high-rise buildings. Blair Kamin, writing last year in *Architectural Record* about the Burj Khalifa in Dubai, introduces early on the sustainability argument:

"In the Great Recession, when sustainability

supposedly has supplanted spectacle as architecture's guiding principle, the bling of the Burj Khalifa offers a convenient target for those eager to consign the pre-Crash Age of Excess to the ash heap of history".

But then goes on to expound on the Burj's surreal appearance, technological bravura and stupendous height—in other words, the sheer *spectacle* of it [9].

New York Times architecture critic Nicolai Ouroussoff focuses his review of Frank Gehry's new residential high-rise 8 Spruce Street, which he considers New York's best skyscraper in decades, on its "rumpled" metal skin. To be sure, there are discussions about the building's sitting and program, but it is clear Ouroussoff wants us to share his fascination with the skin ("*10,500 individual steel panels, almost all of them different shapes…*") and with the digital-age processes that made it possible. The surfaces appear to

have been "etched by rivulets of water"; they are "constantly changing" and "endlessly shifting." He favorably compares Gehry's design to Cass Gilbert's nearby Woolworth Building of 1913, itself a potent combination of technology and handicraft. New Yorkers have been watching its construction "with a mix of awe and trepidation"—surely the kinds of emotions one associates with spectacle [10].

Other recent literature, often unrelated to traditional architectural criticism per se, reinforces the pervasive fascination with The *Spectacle of the Technical*. Consider these representative outtakes from winning entries in the annual eVolo design competitions for the "Skyscraper for the XXI Century" [11]:

• "The Genotower05 was an investigation of the potential of 7+ dimensional digital space-time, established through

Aqua
Chicago, USA
Studio Gang

Photo: Courtesy of Studio Gang

Menara Mesiniaga
Kuala Lumpur, Malaysia
Ken Yeang

Photo: ©Daniel Ryan

an ever-changing search space which uses a stratification of sculpted numeric and geometric randomness in a resonant eugenic single-celled generative automaton." ("The Genotower 05", Nicholas Pisca, USA, 2006).

• "The structural net has 2 (sic) main reactive behaviors derived from the typological hybridization..." ("Chimera", Paula Tomisaki, USA, 2007).

• "...the units are individually controlled by each inhabitant, who can direct them via several shape-memory epoxy 'hot spots' on the 'carbon isogrid' tube from a PC to any desired location." ("Flyscraper", Paul Burgstaller, Ursula Faix and Michael Kritzinger, Switzerland, 2008).

Many entries include staggeringly tech-

nical narratives, signs of a widespread interest in the technical as a manifestation of the spectacle in high-rise design today.

Thus, four key themes emerge in the literature of skyscrapers today, constructed around issues of sensation and affect: Extreme forms of iconography, structural daring, materiality, and change and adaptation.

EXTREME ICONOGRAPHY

Studio Gang Architect's 2009 high-rise "Aqua," with its sinuous facade of balconies, has been labeled "Among the most arresting new forms on Chicago's skyline" by Blair Kamin on ArchDaily [12]. Indeed, we can surely sense the building's daring sculptural qualities, even appreciate them, without wondering too deeply about the cultural rele-

vance of such an approach: it's the spectacle that counts.

STRUCTURAL DARING

Rem Koolhaas's CCTV is a virtuoso piece of structural engineering. As the architect himself has made clear (despite unconvincing protests that it's simply responding to the program) the point of the form is to make structure sensational. In describing the engineering processes used by his consultant Arup, Koolhaas tells us, *"I was elated and horrified by the sheer outrage of the problem that we had set them. Why do they never say NO?"*

MATERIALITY

The current attention to materials, orna-

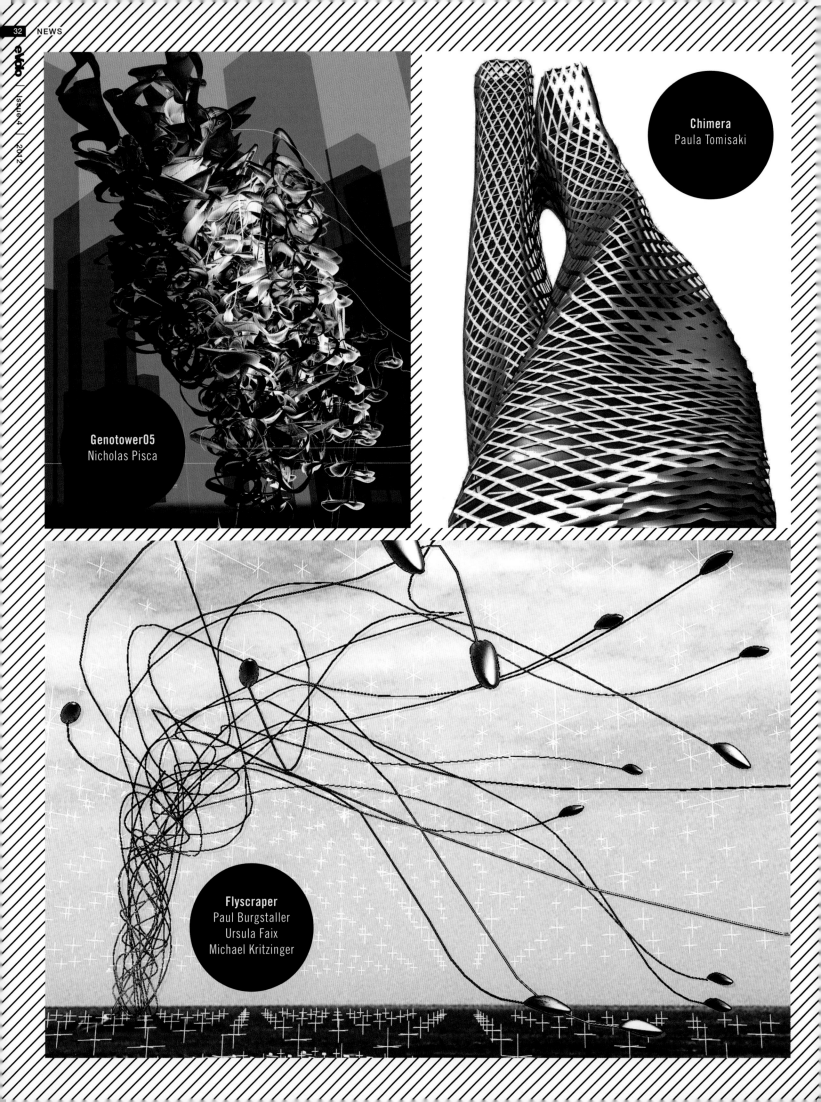

eVolo

issue 4 2012

Genotower05
Nicholas Pisca

Chimera
Paula Tomisaki

Flyscraper
Paul Burgstaller
Ursula Faix
Michael Kritzinger

ment, patterns and their effects—materiality—seems consistent with phenomenology, critical regionalism and other movements emphasizing "tactility" as an undervalued but significant attribute of building. In the highrise building, by contrast, the potential is in stunning visual effects such as those achieved by Gehry in his New York commission.

CHANGE AND ADAPTATION

Architecture's long fascination with buildings that move, or facades that can change, is manifest in much new work. Projects such as those exhibited in the eVolo competitions demonstrate architects' interest in the possibilities. What could be more spectacular than the truly "animate" building? There may be, in all of this, the rise of a tendency one critic, Andrew Payne, labels "biomorality" [13]. If in the global economy success is defined in *biological* terms, as some suggest, skyscrapers that take on biological characteristics, that are "organic" or "animate" or "living", are therefore inherently successful.

CONCLUSIONS

Clearly, something different is happening in the world of high-rise design. Despite all the misgivings, skyscrapers today are a hot topic. Critics such as Peter Buchanan see their very existence, in the not-so-distant future, tied to sustainability: *"...ironically, the green agenda and quest for sustainability...might reinvent and reinvigorate the tall building"* [14]. A decade or two ago, many thought sustainability would indeed become the Next Big Thing for highrises, that Ken Yeang's bioclimatic Menara Mesiniaga was a harbinger of buildings to come. Despite a few notable examples, this is a worthy phenomenon still waiting to happen.

The rapid rise of Asian economies at a global scale, most importantly China's, might have signaled an interest in evolving localized concepts of symbolism and iconography. This, too, has not come to pass. Critics have commented unfavorably on the tendency to commission western architects, often from the US, to design not "Asian" skyscrapers" but "western" ones. The received symbolism is that of the modern, post-industrial society that has arrived—exactly what these clients wish for. The leveling effects of globalization are surely at play. If everyone has the same symbol, does it really mean anything significant anymore, at a cultural level? Furthermore, is there any point in trying to make

buildings mean anything to societies that don't seem to care?

At the moment, the focus seems to lie elsewhere. Architects armed with advanced parametric modeling programs and digital skills have the tools to create unprecedented forms and see them get built. Designers have at their disposal a vast array of new materials, including composites and systems, which allow for eye-catching effects. The general public, consumers now of buildings as well as everything else, want to be entertained. The delight in affects, the willingness to surrender to sensation, is indicative of a changed sensibility collectively wary, perhaps, of post-modernist/post-structuralist intellectual argument and obscure theorizing. The University of Toronto's Andrew Payne is clear on this point in his 2009 *Harvard Design Magazine essay:*

"My own sense is that current appeals to pleasure, affect, and sensation are keyed to...a desire to re-engage the aesthetic dimensions of architecture and its experience..."

So what do we make of this curious situation? As with most things, there is both good and bad to be found. Clearly, the interest in spectacle presents a distraction from sustainable problem-solving and from the deeper debates about the very worth of tall buildings in urban environments—that is indeed unfortunate. Skyscrapers make their indelible mark on cities: why not consider what this means to our future?

On the other hand, there is at least some good to be had in this state of affairs. First off, it is not likely to last: too much "affect" simply may be numbing. At the same time, and reminiscent of the very earliest days of the skyscraper age, the widespread fascination with what is essentially an intensive application of engineering suggests that people do, after all, care. Architecture has their attention. Tall buildings allow practitioners to put their unique skills on very public display in a way no other building type allows. For a profession struggling against becoming marginalized, this is good news: architects are truly needed. Who better to create the *Spectacle of the Technical?*

(1) King, John. "Everything's different after 9/11." SFGate.com. September 12, 2006 http://articles.sfgate.com/2006-09-12/entertainment/.

(2) Kamin, Blair. "The Indicator: A Critic's Terror and Wonder". Online interview with Guy Horton. October 22, 2010 http://www.archdaily.com/84060/the-indicator-a-critic%e2%80%99s-terror-and-wonder/.

(3) Huxtable, Ada Louise. The Tall Building Artistically Reconsidered: The Search for a Skyscraper Style. New York: Pantheon Books, 1982.

(4) Jones, Wes. "Big Forking Dilemma: Contemporary Architecture's Autonomic Turn." Harvard Design Magazine 32, Spring/Summer 2010, pages 8-17.

(5) Koolhaas, Rem with OMA and others. Content. Koln: Taschen, 2004.

(6) Saunders, William, ed. Commodification and Spectacle in Architecture. A Harvard Design Magazine Reader. Minneapolis and London: University of Minnesota Press, 2005.

(7) Moussavi, Farshid and Michael Kubo, eds. The Function of Ornament. Barcelona: Actar, 2006 for the Harvard University Graduate School of Design.

(8) Levit, Robert. "Contemporary 'Ornament': The Return of the Symbolic Repressed." Harvard Design Magazine 28, Spring/Summer 2008, pages 70-85.

(9) Kamin, Blair. "Burj Khalifa, Dubia." Architectural Record, August 2010, vol. 118, no. 8, pages 78-85.

(10) Ouroussoff, Nicolai. "Downtown Skyscraper For the Digital Age." The New York Times, February 10, 2011, pages C1 and C8.

(11) Aiello, Carlo. Skyscrapers for the XXI Century. New York: eVolo Publishing, 2008.

(12) Kamin, Blair. "Fall architecture preview: Tall towers at center stage as the 'Year of Big' goes on." Chicago Tribune, September 11, 2009.

(13) Payne, Andrew. "Sustainability and Pleasure: An Untimely Meditation." Harvard Design Magazine 30, Spring/Summer 2009, pages 68-83.

(14) Buchanan, Peter. "The Tower: An Anachronism Awaiting Rebirth?" Harvard Design Magazine 26, Spring/Summer 2007, pages 5-14.

eVolo | Issue 4 | 2012

VINCENT CALLEBAUT ARCHITECTURES

BIONIC-ARCH, A SUSTAINABLE TOWER

TAICHUNG ECOPOLIS, TAIWAN

For the hundredth birthday of the creation of "Taiwan R.O.C.", the main aim of the Taichung City Government is to honour the local building traditions and symbolize the new Taiwan dynamics into economic, political, social and cultural achievements.

International model of the green building of the 21st century, the innovative and pioneering design of the Bionic Arch is part of the new master plan "Taichung Gateway – Active Gateway City", the future urban oasis for lifestyle, innovation, culture and biodiversity in the heart of Central Taiwan.

The green tower combines and surpasses the nine major indicators defining a green building by law, and intensifies the relation between the building site and the surrounding Taichung Gateway Park, including an environmental integration of the park and the green land, the integration of green vertical platforms, sky gardens and living façades, interaction between human and natural environments. It actively contributes to the development of the use of new sustainable energies (solar and wind generated power, coupled with botanical and bio-technologies), emphasizes cohabitation and respectful attitude in order to reach even higher standards than regular green buildings.

Raising awareness of climate changes and the need for environmental protection, Taiwan Tower will become the new landmark of sustainability, 100% self-sufficient with CO_2 zero-emission, therefore contributing to the government's policies in terms of energy saving and carbon emission reduction.

AERIAL VIEW

AERIAL VIEW ▲

VIEW FROM
GATEWAY PARK ▲

AERIAL VIEW ▼

SKY GARDEN ▼

THE SITE

The Project site is included in the Taichung Gateway City. The Taiwan Tower is centred at the intersection of the two main axis of the new master plan. The concept of the tower is the development of a vertical landscape in the continuity of the park, like a green double ogive arch, keeping the perspective views clear between the main districts. This Bionic Arch integrates directly all sustainable technologies and its design presents an aerodynamic geometry inspired by Nature in the axis of dominant winds.

TAIWAN TOWER

With its 380 meters above ground level (490 meters high above sea level), the Bionic Arch will become the highest building and the most important visual focus in Central Taiwan, including sightseeing and recreational functions. The observatory is higher than the Dadu Mountain in order to give to visitors a panoramic view on the Taiwan Strait and Taichung Harbour. Besides its sightseeing functions, the tower will also embody a telecommunication base.

MUSEUM OF TAICHUNG CITY DEVELOPMENT

The Taiwan Tower experience starts from the Museum of Taichung City Development on the ground floor, which will feature exhibitions on the city's development including history, urban and rural tug-of-war, urban design and planning, industrial development, telecommunication, sewerage, fire prevention, flood and disaster control transportation, etc.

The museum's operation will integrate civil participation, cultural recreation and ecological practice to exemplify the energy and dynamism of the new Taichung Ecopolis.

DESIGN CRITERIAS

The structural concept "exoskeleton" and the design of the structure takes into consideration the earthquakes factors, typhoons and also reviewing the September 11 attack.

The space structure of the building itself, which has the longer lifetime period, considers the possibilities of enhancing its flexibility.

All the suspended gardens are very flexible platforms designed to evolve with time. In fact, the interior planning offers a maximal flexibility to respond to future changes in functional and spatial requirements. The double deck system also participates to this maximum potential of flexibility for the maintenance and replacement of wire/line equipment of water, electrical utilities and air conditioning in order to extend the building's overall lifetime usage.

The Bionic Arch has the ability to resist to the largest earthquakes in the future within elastic range. The ends of the main beams are made of resin, designed with plasticization in order to prevent the building from damage.

The structural strength is assured by seismic technologies as isolator floor, viscoelastic dampers, bracing frame structure, etc.

The bionic and aerodynamic shape of the tower is specially designed to reduce wind impact and to accelerate it in the direction of the three vertical wind turbines in order to minimize structural vibration. The design of the structure includes the addition of a damper device to prevent typhoons or strong winds from generating an uncomfortable situation similar to seasickness.

GREEN ARCHITECTURE

In 2003, the Taiwan government began implementing the "Green Architecture Promotional Project" in conjunction with the Green Silicon Island policies, to assiduously attempt with a green architectural plan to preserve the ecological environment.

As a pre-condition to the application of the building permit, the project requires first to obtain a Certificate of Green Building Candidate. The goal is to respect and to largely exceed the nine major indexes for green architectural compliance audits in order to reach the Diamond level certification referring to the criteria of LEED: "minimization of earth resources use, to produce architecture with the least waste".

The Bionic Arch presents pro-active ob-

jectives to answer to these nine major indexes:

1. PLANTING GREEN: Encouraging more production of Oxygen, greater absorption of CO_2, cleaning the air, achieving the homeostasis for urban climate warming effects

2. WATER CONSERVATION: Improve the capacity of the land to store water, to provide the ground with a rich microbial environment able to support organic life and to reduce the need of drainage.

3. DAILY ENERGY EFFICIENCY: Reduce the amount of energy needed by the air conditioning system and lighting, Encourage re-use applications of waste energy.

OFFICES

WIND TURBINES

DIAGRAM OF RENEWABLE SYSTEMS
▼

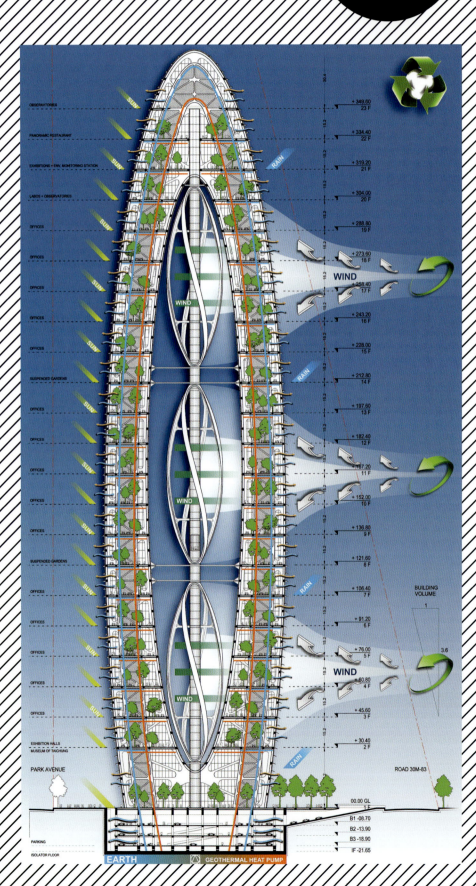

4. CARBON DIOXIDE REDUCTION: Use the design and construction processes to achieve improvements whereby reductions in CO2 emissions result, and by lightweight minimized architecture, resiliency, and re-usability of materials to accomplish reduces CO2 emissions.

5. WASTE REDUCTION: Refers to the production during the construction process of Cut and fill non-Balancing Design, wasted soil, building materials waste, and easily dissipated dust particles.

6. WATER RESOURCE: Refers to the ratio of the building's actual water use to an average water use, or the "water consumption conservation ratio".

7. WASTEWATER AND GARBAGE IMPROVEMENTS: Establish tools to certify a hygienic environment control and improve impact assessment.

8. PROTECTION OF THE BIODIVERSITY: Improve the ecological quality with porous environment encouraging ecological ponds, water ponds, permitting multi-scaled biodiversity, protecting native species and flora. This index is organized into 5 thematic categories: "Ecological Network", "Microorganism Resting Place", "Vegetation Diversity", "Soil Ecology", "Ecologically Symbiotic Architectural Design".

9. REFINEMENT OF THE INTERIOR ENVIRONMENT: Refers to evaluating the indoor environmental quality for noise protection, ambient lighting, air flow, interior design, air quality, and environmental factors which may impact on occupant health or comfort.

Thanks to its suspended gardens, real bioreactors for purification, the tower becomes a pro-active architecture built respecting its environment, recycling air, water and wastes and giving a new symbiotic ecosystem for the sub-tropical multi-scaled biodiversity of Taiwan. The architecture interacts completely with its context climatically, chemically, kinetically and socially to better reduce our ecological footprint in urban area.

The Bionic Arch is a didactic prototype of ecological experimentations using the most advanced technologies in terms of self-sufficient energy construction, in order to better reveal its applications in the contemporary society.

The design is based on the integration of all the renewable technologies with its crystalline glass skin made of heat insulation solar glass and photovoltaic cells, and with its three vertically superposed wind turbines. Its energetic results are positive and enable to assure not only the self-functioning of the tower but also the nocturnal lighting of the Gateway Park.

▶

1ST FLOOR

3RD FLOOR

▶

22ND FLOOR

▶

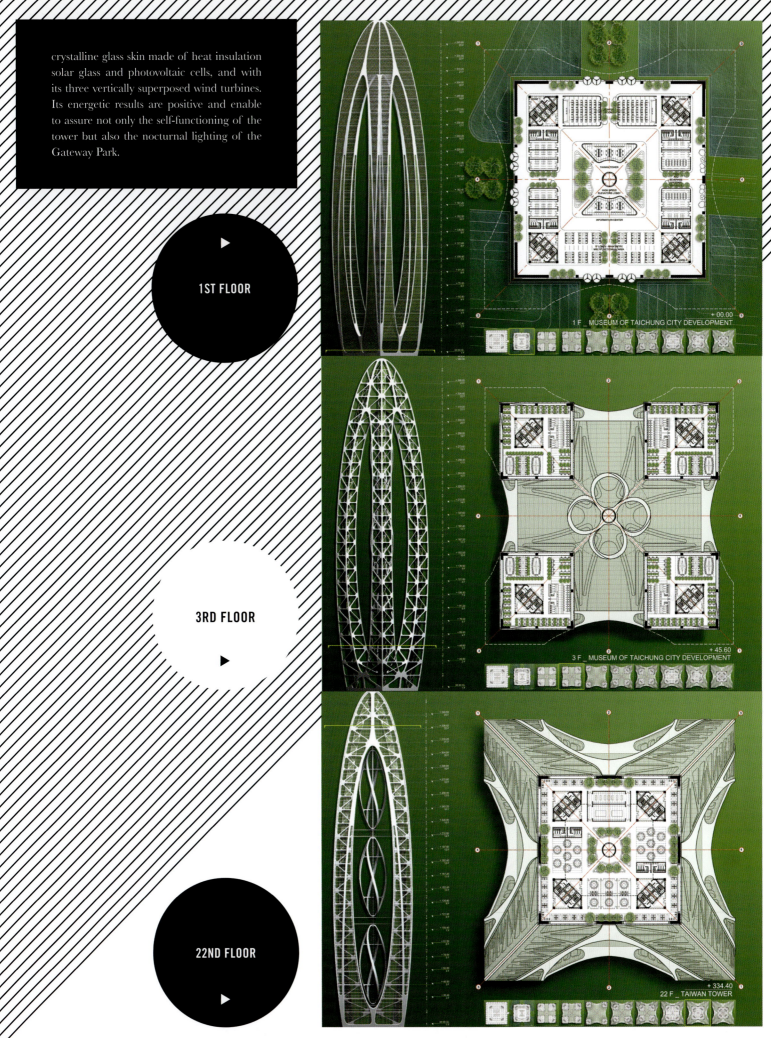

1 F _ MUSEUM OF TAICHUNG CITY DEVELOPMENT.

3 F _ MUSEUM OF TAICHUNG CITY DEVELOPMENT

22 F _ TAIWAN TOWER

eVolo | Issue 4 | 2012

2011

SKYSCRAPER COMPETITION

eVolo | Issue 4 | 2012

LO2P-DELHI RECYCLING CENTER
FIRST PLACE

FRANCE

ATELIER CMJN | JULIEN COMBES | GAËL BRULÉ

AERIAL VIEW

▶

The LO2P-Delhi Recycling Center takes the main source of Delhi, India's pollution – vehicles for transportation – and turns them into the mechanism that can cleanse the world's fourth most polluted city by constructing a recycling center from recycled cars.

Traffic is the main source of pollution in Delhi, causing widespread health problems and an estimated 8,000 deaths a year. With pollution increasing and natural resources being depleted, the designers of the LO2P project anticipate that cars will soon become obsolete, replaced by public transportation in a world where gas is no longer affordable.

When this happens, instead of seeing all of the unused cars as waste, a dramatic paradigm shift will help the public realize that "waste is no longer waste: its resources." Thus, cars, which are composed of 74 percent metal (making them good material for construction), will be used to construct the new center, which is shaped like a ring to symbolize "cycles," as in reusing waste and restoring the health of the environment by using something that once hurt it.

The center uses and recycles all of its energy. The operating model imagines that adding waste to pollution and carbon dioxide will yield resources and oxygen. It combines state of the art separation procedures with the ability to purify the air through natural processes, use renewable energies and produce renewable fuel for vehicles. The whole ring cleans the city's most pressing environmental hazard by capturing suspended particle matters from the air and further purifying it with greenhouses located throughout the structure. Mineralization baths, CO2 enrichment, exhaust filters, biofuel production and carbonate and particle recycling are other features of the structure. The ring itself is one giant wind turbine with blades in the center. It is 175 meters tall.

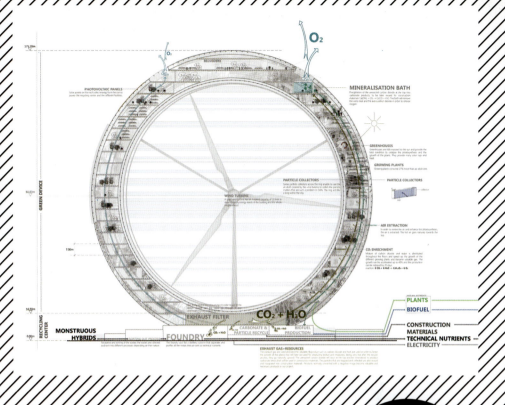

LONGITUDINAL SECTION ▲

STREET VIEW ▼

eVolo | Issue 4 | 2012

FLAT TOWER
SECOND PLACE

FRANCE

PAUL-ERIC SCHIRR-BONNANS | YOANN MESCAM | XAVIER SCHIRR-BONNANS

COURTYARD
▶

AERIAL VIEW
▶

▼ NIGHT VIEW

▼ INTERSECTION WITH CITY GRID

In a medium sized metropolis with a low rise built urban fabric, a "Flat Tower" is proposed that matches the height of the Burj Khalifa building in Dubai, one of the world's tallest at 800 meters, but does so horizontally in an arcing dome. The world is racing to build the tallest skyscrapers, say the designers of the "Flat Tower for Medium Sized Metropolis" project, but that paradigm is neither allowed nor desired in more modestly sized cities. The dome design can preserve the beauty and functionality of the existing environment by wrapping around it instead of overwhelming it.

The dome is comprised of a dense network of programmatic cells surrounded by large skylights that provide light to the cells and the field located inside the structure on the ground floor.

The building houses facilities in the basement on either end. As the dome arcs up, residential units fill the structure on its south side and offices fill space to the north. On the top there is a roof with pedestrian access. On the ground floor inside the dome, the base of the structure is a large urban park.

An automated transport system runs on the surface of the dome to take resi-dents or workers to units above. The offices and apartments are all differently shaped, though the general design follows a cylindrical shape that features a skylight well on top. Walking between the differently shaped units gives people in the building the experience of "a labyrinthical and ever changing journey."

The structure's shape makes it particularly suited for sustainability, as the large surface area can be covered in solar collectors and can also allow for rainwater collection.

EXISTING SITUATION

HEIGHT REGULATION MAX 120 M HIGH

RESIDENTIAL AREA RAIL TRACKS RAIL TRACKS WARE HOUSES AREA RESIDENTIAL AREA

◄ CONCEPT DIAGRAMS

PROPOSAL

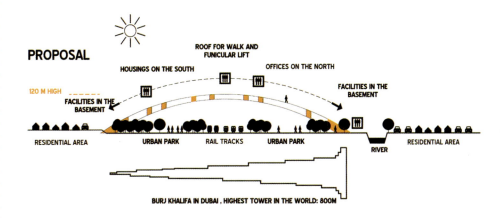

ROOF FOR WALK AND FUNICULAR LIFT

HOUSINGS ON THE SOUTH OFFICES ON THE NORTH

120 M HIGH

FACILITIES IN THE BASEMENT

FACILITIES IN THE BASEMENT

RESIDENTIAL AREA URBAN PARK RAIL TRACKS URBAN PARK RIVER RESIDENTIAL AREA

BURJ KHALIFA IN DUBAI , HIGHEST TOWER IN THE WORLD: 800M

eVolo | Issue 4 | 2012

TOWER IN A DAM
THIRD PLACE

UNITED KINGDOM

YHEU-SHEN CHUA

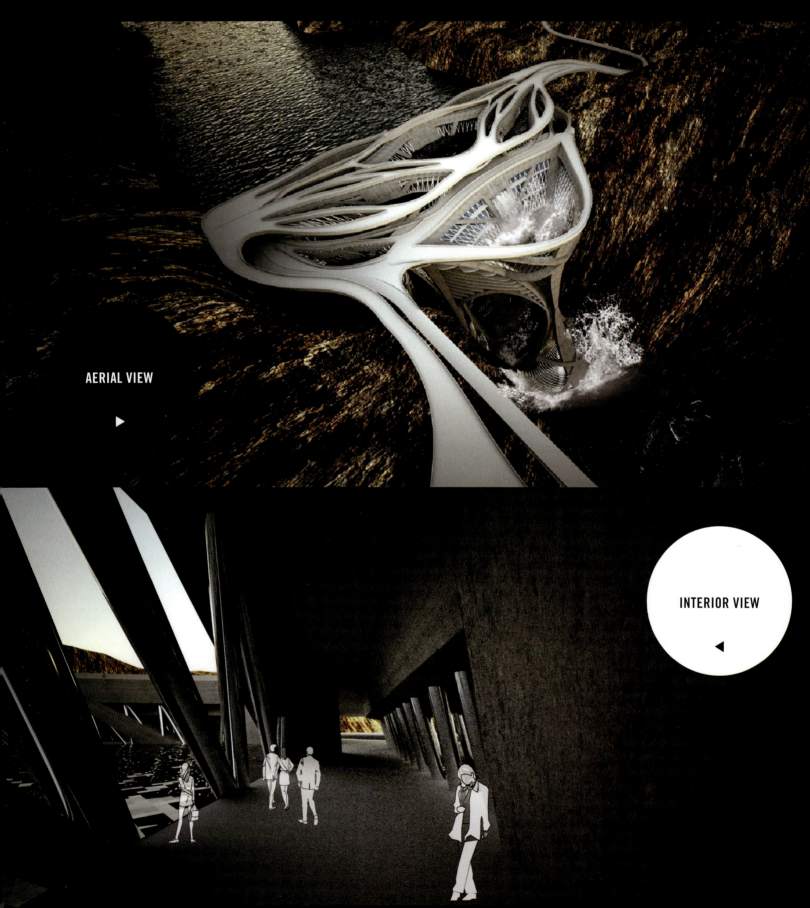

AERIAL VIEW
►

INTERIOR VIEW
◄

The "Tower in a Dam" project proposes inserting a hanging tower that will house gallery and exhibition space inside the Hoover Dam outside of Las Vegas, Nevada.

The project is implemented in three phases. The first redirects how water flows down the dam. "Containers," or folds in the concrete of the dam over which the water flows, are created to channel the water in specific locations.

The second phase involves the insertion of a tower in the underside of the peaks of these containers, between the penstock. The supporting arches transfer the weight down to the penstock, allowing the tower to hang between. The tower is then used as an exhibition and gallery space. The turbines of the dam still function below.

Finally, the highway that runs across the dam is streamlined by dedicating lanes to specific vehicle type and length to avoid traffic crunches. One lane is given specifically to bicycles, another to small and mid-sized cars, a third to vans, and the last to trucks. Three lanes are also divided for vehicles that require inspection – a proposal that was made after the September 11 attacks – one for trailers, another for recreation vehicles and motor homes, and a final lane for buses and rental trucks.

The structure as a whole is 260 meters tall, putting the height on par with the Canary Wharf tower in London, and the CCTV building in Beijing.

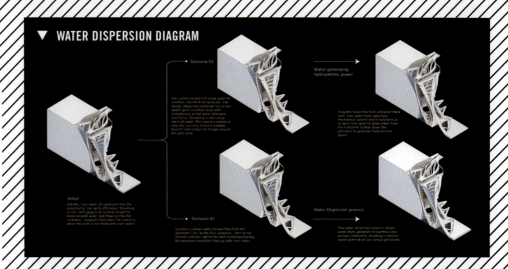

▼ WATER DISPERSION DIAGRAM

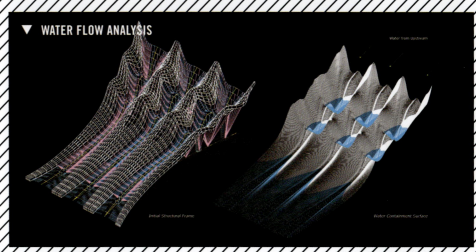

▼ WATER FLOW ANALYSIS

SECTION - MECHANICAL SYSTEMS
▼

PROGRAM DIAGRAMS
▼

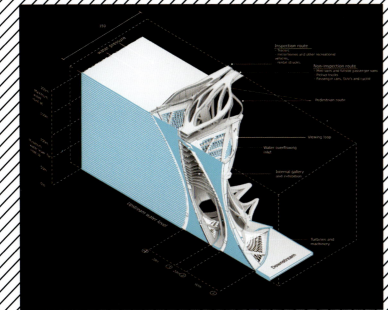

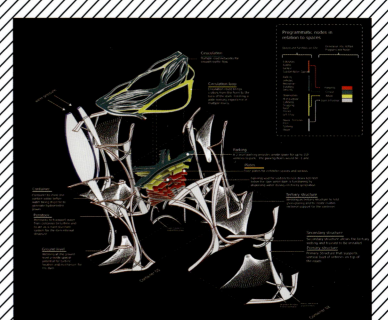

eVolo | Issue 4 | 2012

FLOATING OLYMPIC COMPLEX

ANDREW CHOW WAI TAT | XUE LIANG ZHANG | TAO HUANG

VIEW FROM THE BEACH
▶

The Flutante Olímpico or Floating Olympic project proposes the construction of an inverted pyramid-shaped skyscraper to solve several urban planning problems within the context of the Olympic Games. Past Olympic structures that cost millions to build are utilized for two and a half weeks and then abandoned, leaving cities with deserted expanses of urban land and vacant stadiums and buildings. By designing structures that are shaped like mushrooms with narrow bases that branch into wide platforms in the sky, space for density of spectators and activity is maximized while the structure's footprint on the ground is minimized.

This design initially serves its host city by contributing to growth with minimal disturbance to the ecology of the land below. In the long term, though, its creation continues to feed the city as the skyscrapers, built along a coastline, grow into a mini city of their own right, expanding vertically so as not to disturb the existing density below.

The Floating Olympic can test its plans for an inverted skyscraper during the 2016 Olympic Games in Rio de Janeiro. By locating a sports complex on the top of a skyscraper that is surrounded by levels of spectator viewing, but also residential units, fans can enjoy competitions from a setting with the comfort level of their choosing. After the Olympic Games have ended, the complex then can retain its residential use and expand development on the area used for the sporting event.

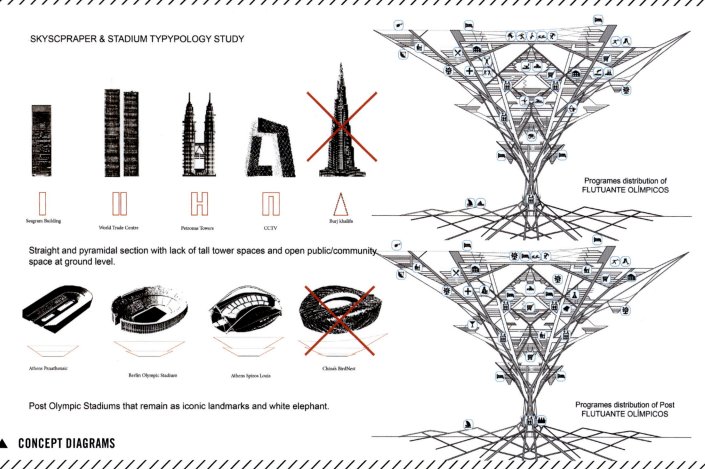

SKYSCPRAPER & STADIUM TYPYPOLOGY STUDY

Seagram Building

World Trade Centre

Petronas Towers

CCTV

Burj khalifa

Straight and pyramidal section with lack of tall tower spaces and open public/community space at ground level.

Athens Panathenaic

Berlin Olympic Stadium

Athens Spiros Louis

China's BirdNest

Post Olympic Stadiums that remain as iconic landmarks and white elephant.

Programes distribution of FLUTUANTE OLÍMPICOS

Programes distribution of Post FLUTUANTE OLÍMPICOS

▲ CONCEPT DIAGRAMS

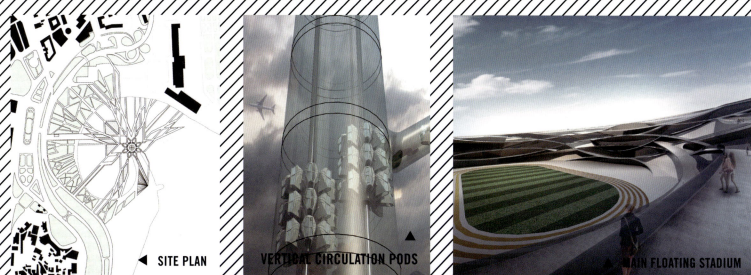

◀ SITE PLAN

VERTICAL CIRCULATION PODS ▲

▲ MAIN FLOATING STADIUM

NEO TAX: 3D CITY

STUDIO DMTW | MARC ANTON DAHMEN | RENE LIERSCHAFT | ANNA-MARIA WIEDEKIND

VIEW FROM THE PARK ▶

UNITS AGGREGATION ▼

3D GROWTH OF THE ORGANISM IN A CUBICAL GRID

 → → → →

▼ **VERTICAL AND HORIZONTAL CIRCULATION**

MODULE TRAFFIC SYSTEM / LOCAL PUBLIC INFRASTRUCTURE

1. MACRO SCALE

2. MESO SCALE

3. MICRO SCALE

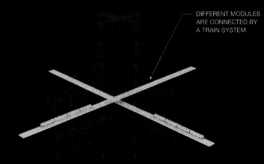

DIFFERENT MODULES ARE CONNECTED BY A TRAIN SYSTEM

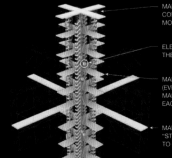

MAIN VERTICAL "STREET" & CONNECTION TO OTHER MODULES ABOVE

ELEVATORS CONNECT THE MAIN PLATFORMS

MAIN PLATFORM (EVERY 20M THERE IS A MAIN PLATFORM MAKING EACH UNIT ACCESSIBLE)

MAIN HORIZONTAL "STREET" & CONNECTION TO OTHER MODULES

EACH UNIT HAS ITS OWN MICRO INFRASTRUCTURE

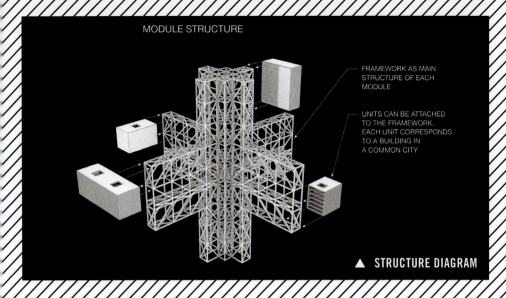

MODULE STRUCTURE

FRAMEWORK AS MAIN STRUCTURE OF EACH MODULE

UNITS CAN BE ATTACHED TO THE FRAMEWORK. EACH UNIT CORRESPONDS TO A BUILDING IN A COMMON CITY

▲ **STRUCTURE DIAGRAM**

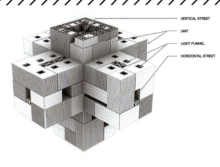

VERTICAL STREET
UNIT
LIGHT FUNNEL
HORIZONTAL STREET

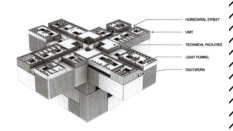

HORIZONTAL STREET
UNIT
TECHNICAL FACILITIES
LIGHT FUNNEL
DUCTWORK

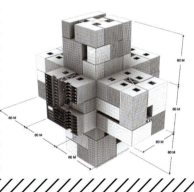

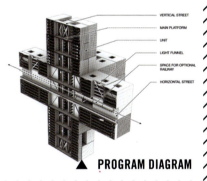

VERTICAL STREET
MAIN PLATFORM
UNIT
LIGHT FUNNEL
SPACE FOR OPTIONAL RAILWAY
HORIZONTAL STREET

▲ **PROGRAM DIAGRAM**

BUILDING SERVICES

SUPPLY KNOT / TECHNICAL FACILITIES (HEAT, WATER, ENERGY SUPPLY & DISTRIBUTION) THE MODULE ITSELF IS CONNECTED TO A GLOBAL SUPPLY NET

DUCTWORK (POSSIBLE CONNECTION TO OTHER MODULES)

▲ **INFRASTRUCTURE**

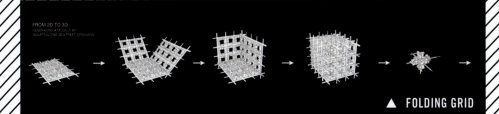

FROM 2D TO 3D
GENERATING A MODULE BY
SQUATING ONE 3D STREET CROSSING

▲ **FOLDING GRID**

The designers of the Neo Tax 3D City see a problem with the world's ever-expanding population: traditional city layouts, which address density by building vertically in separate towers, create a grid of dead ends that waste surface area and disturb the ground's ecological health. To sustainably develop for the future, the designers suggest bending the street grid up at all four corners to create a box, or a 3D horizontal and vertical landscape.

Instead of being defined by intersections and blocks, the 3D city is grouped into "cubical grids," or modules, that are self-sustaining frames that individual units or buildings attach to. Each module then connects to surrounding modules to create one large, functioning city. On the micro level, each module has its own infrastructure that is enclosed within a "supply knot" that houses heating, water and energy supply mechanisms.

Main vertical "streets," essentially elevators, connect the platforms within a module that define the vertical street grid. Platforms are spaced every 20 meters. This 3D design gives residents short connection paths between destinations and holds a higher urban density, which allows for increased neighbor interaction.

Vertical main streets within modules also provide access to other cubes within the modular complex; they are also connected horizontally by a train system. Constant communication between different modules is essential to avoid traffic and other related problems, but is made simple thanks to infrastructure and proximity.

Light funnels are carved as openings on the outside modules to bring natural illumination to inner modules. Modules are based on a framework that units can attach to. By expanding communities in the sky, conditions of the earth's terrain become irrelevant, allowing for complete flexibility in site selection.

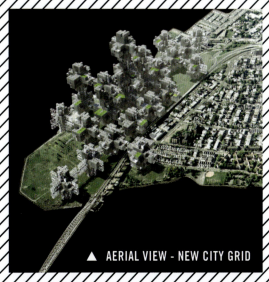

▲ **AERIAL VIEW - NEW CITY GRID**

ON DEMAND SKYSCRAPER

BENJAMIN FEENSTRA | JELMER FRANK WIJNIA

▶ CONCEPT DIAGRAM

▲ ON DEMAND SKYSCRAPER

▼ OFFICE AND GOLF   ▼ MULTI-LAYERED ON DEMAND PROGRAMS

◀ ORDERING A SPECIFIC PROGRAM

The apartment
"There's a box for that"

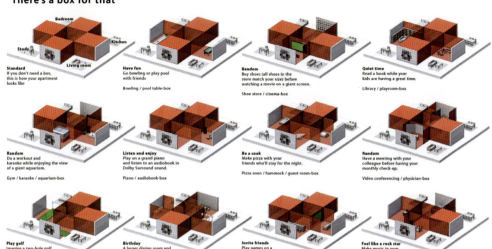

Standard
If you don't need a box, this is how your apartment looks like

Have fun
Go bowling or play pool with friends.
Bowling / pool table-box

Random
Buy shoes (all shoes in the store match your size) before watching a movie on a giant screen.
Shoe store / cinema-box

Quiet time
Read a book while your kids are having a great time.
Library / playroom-box

Random
Do a workout and karaoke while enjoying the view of a giant aquarium.
Gym / karaoke / aquarium-box

Listen and enjoy
Play on a grand piano and listen to an audiobook in Dolby Surround sound.
Piano / audiobook-box

Be a cook
Make pizza with your friends who'll stay for the night.
Pizza oven / hammock / guest room-box

Random
Have a meeting with your colleague before having your monthly check-up.
Video conferencing / physician-box

Play golf
Imagine a two-hole golf course in your house
Golf-box

Birthday
A larger dining room and more space to store your presents.
Birtday / dining room-box

Invite friends
Play games on a super-sized screen. Use the bar to celebrate your victory.
Game / bar-box

Feel like a rock star
Make music in your music studio. Enjoy the jacuzzi like a true rock star.
Study / music studio / jacuzzi-box

APARTMENT TRANSFORMATION ◄

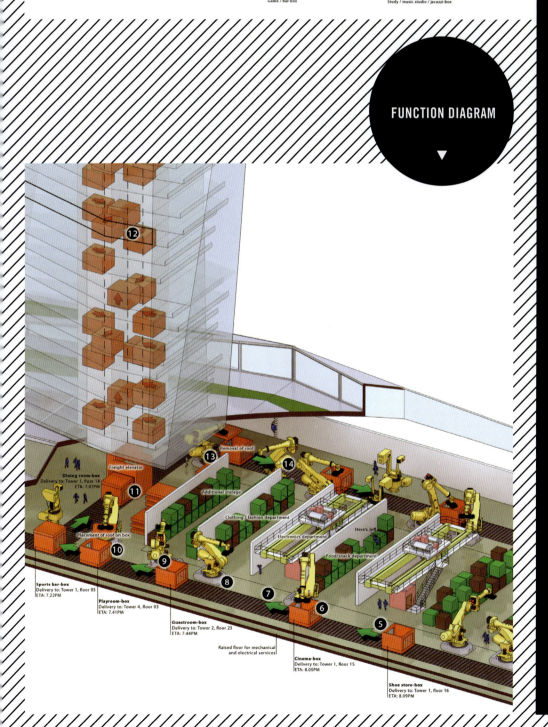

FUNCTION DIAGRAM ▼

The On Demand skyscraper answers every resident's potential need with a single slogan: "There's a box for that." The plan imagines a series of skyscrapers that are all connected to one large distribution warehouse. The warehouse is an assembly shop for boxes, or rooms with specific purposes that residents living in the connected skyscrapers can order. The boxes serve all of the possible needs a resident might have, rendering the need to leave home to do any shopping or errand useless.

Box types range from the practical, such as physician, grocery, gym, video conferencing, home school, laundry and more to the purely enjoyable: golf course, sauna, bowling, music studio, cinema, karaoke and basketball. Residents can order whatever box they'd like via their hand-held devices; boxes are assembled at the nearby warehouse and then transferred, fully ready and furnished, to each individual apartment via large freight elevators.

In a typical On Demand complex, four skyscrapers will share one warehouse, which is located underneath the buildings (and the roof of which is landscaped as a park for residents of the skyscrapers to enjoy). Once a box order is received in the warehouse's control room, an empty box is sent down an assembly line. It first receives floors and wall color, and then furniture is added to aid the function and aesthetic of the box. Then the amenities that fit the box's theme are added, whether they're decorations, clothing, food, sports equipment, electronics, etc. Once the room is properly outfitted, a roof is added, and the box is transported via elevator. Residents enjoy the boxes in the allotted timeslot they have chosen; they are then returned to the warehouse for emptying, cleaning, and to start life anew as a different box.

PORO-CITY

eVolo | Issue 4 | 2012

INDIA

KHUSHALANI ASSOCIATES | RAJIV KHUSHALANI | THOMAS KARIATH | MIHIR SANGANEE

BAY VIEW ◀

SITE ANALYSIS AND STRATEGY ▶

S I T E   S T R A T E G Y

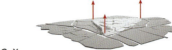

01

the site

dharavi, a triangualar sector covering 216 hectares is spread between 2 main suburban lines - western railway and central railway in mumbai city.

02

strategy

to lift the volume upwards along the southern end and inclining the northern plane by restructuring and organizing the existing development.

03

restructuring

subtracting evenly scaled fractals of the larger volume to create the missing porosity in the existing site.

04

circulation

the structure binding the volumes together becomes the circulation member at all levels comprising of travelators, elevators, escalators.

05

reorganizing

the main volume is reorganized by providing the smallest fractals towards the north front, river facing and gradually increasing the scale of each fractal to create porosity and accomodate existing industrial programs at different levels.

The "Poro-City" plan imagines the restructuring of Dharavi, Mumbai, a city with extremely high density of 376,000 people within a small site. By reorganizing Dharavi into an integrated, 3-dimensional city that ad dresses climate, environmental, sustainability, community and public services issues, its residents can live better lives, say designers.

The site is 216 hectares large and triangular in shape. By lifting the site vertically, the existing development is restructured into a tall triangular structure. From there, "evenly scaled fractals of the larger volume" are subtracted from the structure as a whole to create "the missing porosity of the site."

The structure's smallest units are three meter by three meter "habitable cubes" that can serve as residences, community spaces or home-based industries. These units have north-facing terraces to avoid the harsh tropical sunlight, expanding the living space for use even during the day. Six by six meter units can house the same types of units, but also clinics, medical stores, small grocery stores, nurseries and more. Units that are 12 meters by 12 meters can hold hospitals, schools, libraries, and industries like paper recycling, pottery, leather tanning and garment manufacturing. Units that come in 24 by 24 and 48 by 48 meter sizes are used as large community gathering spaces.

Inside the structure, circulation is integrated within the structural trusses, transporting people vertically, horizontally and diagonally via elevators, moving walkways, escalators and funiculars. It is a car-free environment.

The open-ended nature of the system allows different structures to be "plugged in" over time so that the structure can grow if needed. It is imagined to be almost 1,600 meters tall.

▼ INTERIOR VIEW

▼ GEOMETRIC ANALYSIS

POROSITY STUDY

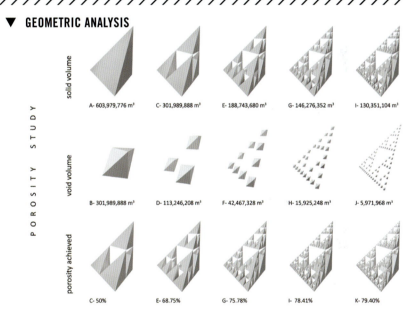

solid volume

A- 603,979,776 m³ C- 301,989,888 m³ E- 188,743,680 m³ G- 146,276,352 m³ I- 130,351,104 m³

void volume

B- 301,989,888 m³ D- 113,246,208 m³ F- 42,467,328 m³ H- 15,925,248 m³ J- 5,971,968 m³

porosity achieved

C- 50% E- 68.75% G- 75.78% I- 78.41% K- 79.40%

HOUSING UNITS

▼

▼ LONGITUDINAL SECTION

PART SECTION

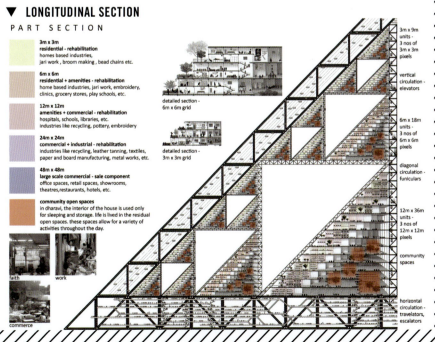

3m x 3m
residential - rehabilitation
homes based industries,
jari work , broom making , bead chains etc.

6m x 6m
residential + amenities - rehabilitation
home based industries, jari work, embroidery,
clinics, grocery stores, play schools, etc.

12m x 12m
amenities + commercial - rehabilitation
hospitals, schools, libraries, etc.
industries like recycling, pottery, embroidery

24m x 24m
commercial + industrial - rehabilitation
industries like recycling, leather tanning, textiles,
paper and board manufacturing, metal works, etc.

48m x 48m
large scale commercial - sale component
office spaces, retail spaces, showrooms,
theatres,restaurants, hotels, etc.

community open spaces
in dharavi, the interior of the house is used only
for sleeping and storage. life is lived in the residual
open spaces. these spaces allow for a variety of
activities throughout the day.

faith   work

commerce

detailed section -
6m x 6m grid

detailed section -
3m x 3m grid

3m x 9m
units -
3 nos of
3m x 3m
pixels

vertical
circulation -
elevators

6m x 18m
units -
3 nos of
6m x 6m
pixels

diagonal
circulation -
funiculars

12m x 36m
units -
3 nos of
12m x 12m
pixels

community
spaces

horizontal
circulation -
travelators,
escalators

TOWER OF THE DEAD

ISRAEL LÓPEZ BALAN | ELSA MENDOZA ANDRÉS | MOISÉS ADRIÁN HERNÁNDEZ GARCÍA

UNDERGROUND
CEMETERY ENTRANCE
◄

SKY-WELL
►

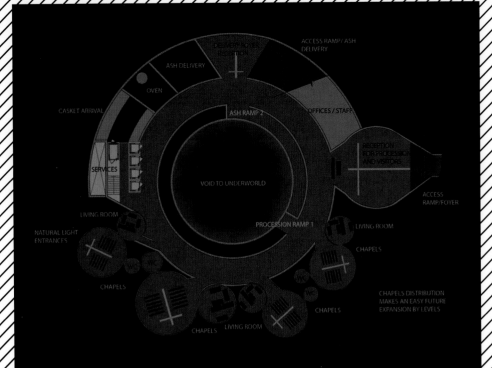

▲ **PLAN**

The Tower of the Dead considers the typical sprawling configuration of a cemetery with two realities in mind, the present and the future. Over the next four decades, the elderly population is due to increase exponentially worldwide. Also, metropolises are, by their very nature, dense with little room left for development. Considering these two facts, and thinking about how dense Mexico City is, the designers asked themselves: Where will people go for their final rest in Mexico City after 2050? The answer is down.

The Tower of the Dead is an underground skyscraper that pierces the earth like a screw, winding and leading grieving friends and families down as they carry or follow the corpse of their loved one to a depth of 250 meters into the ground.

This design is meant to foster a healing psychological environment in a time of duress; every level the visitor reaches represents a new level in the stages of grief. At 10 meters depth the members of the funeral procession are still in shock. By the time they reach 40 meters, they have begun to feel the pain of their loss and have entered the "emotional release" phase. They descend into "crisis" at 75 meters and experience "symptoms of distress" at 100. By 125 meters there may even be hostile reactions. Along the way they may stop at chapels and reception areas to commiserate and grieve. Guilt hits at 155 meters, depression at 200 meters and withdrawal at 220 meters. But by the time they leave their loved ones at 250 meters depth, in the "Good-Bye Space," grieving parties feel acceptance, resolution and readjustment. They ascend back to the surface feeling reborn and healed.

SCENARIO 1

Over the next four decades, the concentration of older persons in the less developed regions will intensify. The number of people aged 60 years or over living in the less developed regions is expected to increase more than threefold, passing from 473 million in 2009 to 1.6 billion in 2050. In contrast, the number of older persons in the more developed regions is projected to increase by about 60 per cent, passing from 264 million in 2009 to 416 million in 2050.

Since the older population has grown faster than the total population, the proportion of older persons relative to the rest of the population has increased considerably. At the global level, 8 per cent of the population was at least 60 years of age in 1950, and 5 per cent was at least 65 years of age. By 2009, those proportions had increased to 11 per cent and just under 8 per cent, respectively. By 2050, 22 per cent of the world population is projected to be 60 years or over, and 16 per cent will likely be 65 years or over.

POPULATION PYRAMIDS; MEXICO, 2000 AND 2051

Source: CONAPO (2002)

SCENARIO 2

Mexico City urban area is nowadays scarce, there is no way to grow anymore except towards the outskirts with the consequent loss of agricultural land that becomes part of the city everyday; in addition longer trips to destinations increase pollution deteriorating inhabitants life quality. This is how water subsoil infiltration areas are being lost resulting in developed areas growth, microclimate and climate changes that contributes to global warming effects. Hence the only coherent and pertinent possibility of the city is to go upwards.

DESIGN CONCEPT

1. The typology of cemeteries until early XXI century have been developed in a horizontal way increasing by the time their footprint and creating "Cities for the Dead", which usually are seen as sites for "rest" where people remember their loved ones. The grieving process begins with the burial where family and friends back home feeling as dead as the corpse they just bury.

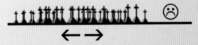

2. The growth process is reversed by focusing on a point of the cemetery that allows the gradual release of space of the graves area for its transformation into green areas. Gravestones become trees.

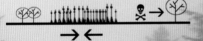

3. Over time the cemetery grows in a vertical way into the ground; transforming its relation with the environment and creating a "Tower for the Dead". Family and friends not only bury their dead, but they accompanying hundreds of feet underground and starting a psychological and sensory experience of the grieving process due to architecture. They return home reborn after a trip to the underworld.

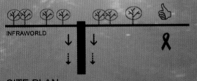

INFRAWORLD

SITE PLAN
Mexico City
19°24' N 99°12' W
Dolores Cemetery

SCENARIO 3

With all this in mind the question is:

WHERE WILL PEOPLE REST WHEN THEY DIE IN MEXICO CITY AFTER 2050?

▲ CONCEPT DIAGRAM

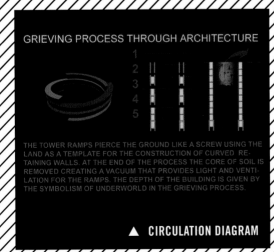

GRIEVING PROCESS THROUGH ARCHITECTURE

THE TOWER RAMPS PIERCE THE GROUND LIKE A SCREW USING THE LAND AS A TEMPLATE FOR THE CONSTRUCTION OF CURVED RETAINING WALLS. AT THE END OF THE PROCESS THE CORE OF SOIL IS REMOVED CREATING A VACUUM THAT PROVIDES LIGHT AND VENTILATION FOR THE RAMPS. THE DEPTH OF THE BUILDING IS GIVEN BY THE SYMBOLISM OF UNDERWORLD IN THE GRIEVING PROCESS.

▲ **CIRCULATION DIAGRAM**

VIEW FROM THE OCEAN

▶

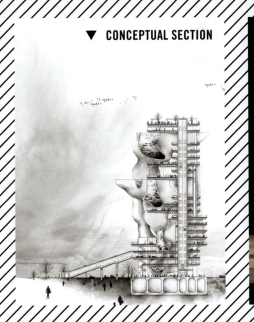

▼ CONCEPTUAL SECTION

▼ MODEL

▼ MODEL

The designers of the Fish Tower have designed a skyscraper to heed the warnings of a Canadian ecologist who claims that, if overfishing continues at the speed that it is today, there will be no fish left to eat by 2048. The tower, which rises from the sea, creates an urban fish-farming prototype that has space for visitors and a fish market, but is mainly comprised of space to farm fish and space for new technology.

The tower's 20 levels hold the equivalent of 600 fish farms today, the designers say. In the fish farm section of the skyscraper, different rooms create ideal habitats for different species. The rooms take the speed and typical movement of a species, as well as their typical swimming depth. They are shaped organically into pools that simulate the natural shape and craggy depths of each species' true environment.

The technological portion of the Fish Tower introduces special equipment that will allow for an increase of the density of the fish 30-fold. The pools form nebulous, bulging vertical masses that run the length of the tower. Interspersed at set levels are flat, steel platforms that house attractions for visitors or allow workers to access the tanks.

The ground floor is designed for visitors and will feature, in addition to main gathering and exhibition areas, shops, a recreation space, a coffee shop, a media center and a garden. Visitors can travel up several levels to view the fish farms and shop at the fresh markets. At the very top of the tower there is a restaurant to enjoy the building's bounty. Species raised in the building include blue fin tuna, grouper, and freshwater eel.

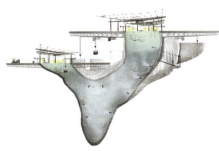

▲ FISH FARM

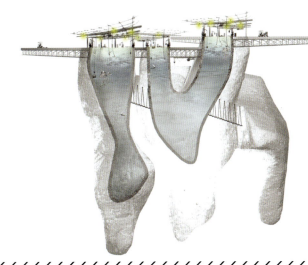

▲ FISH HABITAT

▲

RESEARCH FACILITY AND FISH FARM

WASTE COLLECTOR SKYSCRAPER

eVolo | Issue 4 | 2012

POLAND

AGATA SANDER | TOMEK KUJAWSKI

STREET VIEW ▶

CONCEPT DIAGRAM ▶

sorting
compression
storing
distribution
transformation

transmission   attraction   support   domination   transformation   elevation   recycling

The Waste Collector skyscraper is a giant waste processing facility located in Shanghai's most densely populated neighborhood, the Huangpu district of Shanghai, China. With an emphasis placed on recycling, the tower is a sustainable solution to urban waste abundance in the country that is the world's largest municipal solid waste generator and carbon dioxide emitter.

Located on the waterfront, the skyscraper's ground level is for waste intake only; there, the ground floor waste collector can carry 30,000 tons of solid waste. After intake, objects are sorted, glass, plastic, metal and paper all go to separate parts of the building to be prepared and processed. In the metal section, magnetic devices separate aluminum from steel and the two are melted separately of each other. They are then poured into "ingots" for distribution. Paper is manually sorted into brown, white and other, compressed and bundled for distribution. Plastics and glass also sorted and prepared for reuse. Once all of the products are readied for reuse, they are sent to an underground level directly beneath the ground floor, where they are prepared for distribution and sent off.

The top half of the skyscraper holds space for several functions. Solar heat collectors capture the Sun's rays and redistribute them through heating pipes that run throughout the building. Areas for gas storage and ventilation allow for gasses to be created, used and released in a non-industrial way.

Gasses are created mainly through the building's collection and fermentation of solid waste. Two hundred tons of organic matter arrive every day to the skyscraper and ferments in a silo within the building for 3 months, making its constant volume or organic matter 20,000 tons. The building's porous skin allows combustion gasses to seep out of the building rather than funneling them through industrial chimneys.

THE SKIN
A porous covering enabling the building to "breathe" in the upper part of the structure, letting out combustion gases without dominating forms of industrial chimneys and filters.
It is correlated with a solar heating installation consisting of a net of pipes filled with liquid.
Accumulated heat is transferred to municipal infrastructure.
Construction part of skin serves as an additional support of main construction.

CONSTRUCTION REINFORCEMENTS
The waste collector is a heavy installation, estimated to carry a weight of up to 30'000 tons of pure waste - not mentioning the structure's own weight.

OTHER WASTE SILO
All waste which cannot be processed in the Waste Collector is sent to a separate silo and distributed later to specialised facilities where it can be treated and recycled.

METALS PROCESS
The first step of the processing of metal waste is magnetic sorting which seperates ferrous metals from non-ferrous metals.
Most popular are alluminium and steel and it is only these two that the Waste Collector or the "other" silo for more specialised recycling while alluminium and steel are cleaned and compressed and moulded into ingots.
Alluminium and steel melt in different temperatures therefore they require separate technological lines although the process is identical for both. The ingots are stored in seperate silos waiting to be distributed.

PAPER PROCESS
The only process requiring human engagement in the whole recycling process which takes place in the Waste Collector (after the manual sorting line in the reception base) is the stage of specialistic paper sorting. After being manually sorted into, brown, white and other paper it is cleaned, compressed and bailed and sent to the silos.

GAS TANK AND POWER PLANT
Collection, utilisation and distribution of byproducts: heat, methane and carbon dioxide used for heating and fuel both within the Waste Collector and distributed to the ubran infrastructure.

ORGANICS SILO
Anaerobic digestion of organic waste: the discharge is compressed under it's own weight. It undergoes pulping and methanization with the use of heat and fresh water, both come from the recycling process itself. It is a self sustainable process. The organic waste takes ca. 3 months from the day it is delivered to the Waste Collector to the moment when it is recycled into compost, heat, water and methane all either distributed to new users or used within the Collector.
There are 200 tonnes of organic waste arriving each day. With a 3 month cycle of the fermentation process it makes 20000 tons in constant motion - with everyday intake and weekly distribution.

ORGANICS CONVEYOR BELT
Organic waste makes up 50% of the total waste produced in Shanghai daily. Therefore it is placed in the end of the sorting line. Vertical elevation of the waste uses little energy. The benefit of it is that it enables more effective anaerobic digestion of the waste because of vertical concentration. There are place and energy saving benefits as well. Along it's trip upwards the organic waste undergoes a series of preparatory treatments, that is volume breakdown and moisture absorption among others.

PLASTICS SILOS
Different types of plastics are stored ready for distribution in the form of clean, raw ground material ready for direct use in various industries as components of new materials and products.

GLASS SILOS
Cullet is the intermediate product from the recycled glass in the Waste Collector - it is the most universal and requiring least space form of glass for further production. The silos for glass cullet have the capacity to store incoming waste for up to 90 days.

PLASTICS VOLUME DECREASE
After being divided into different material categories the plastics are shredded, cleaned and ground into the smallest possible "grain" whilst still being maximally effective as an intermediate product - this means a very big decrease in volume of the most space consuming compound of MSW.

GLASS GRINDING
The last step of the process of preparing glass cullet is grinding it in a mill

INFRARED SORTING OF PLASTICS
After passing through the manual sorting line on reception, the various plastics undergo mechanical sorting with the use of infrared technologies into six categories:
•HDPE •LDPE •PET •PP •PVC •PS

INFRARED SORTING OF GLASS
Initially sorted glass undergoes mechanical sorting with the use of infrared into three categories: white/ brown/ green. Any other types of glass are seperated in the first step of manual sorting as other waste. The glass is also cleaned and ground here after being divided into 3 seperate technological lines.

WASTE RECEPTION AND PRELIMINARY MANUAL SORTING
It is here where all processes share one common starting point. Here all municipal solid waste is manually divided into the following categories: •metals •papers •plastics •glass •organics •others (unrecycleable matter , e.g. electronics requiring more specialized processes)

● **DESCRIPTION OF COMPONENTS AND PROCESSES**

▲
PROGRAM ANALYSIS

SITE
▼

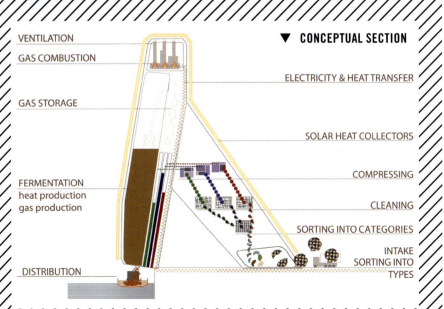

▼ **CONCEPTUAL SECTION**

VENTILATION

GAS COMBUSTION

ELECTRICITY & HEAT TRANSFER

GAS STORAGE

SOLAR HEAT COLLECTORS

COMPRESSING

FERMENTATION
heat production
gas production

CLEANING

SORTING INTO CATEGORIES

INTAKE
SORTING INTO
TYPES

DISTRIBUTION

● **SHANGHAI - COLLECTION AREA**

● **HUANGPU - BUILDING SITE**

● **WATERFRONT - LOCATION**

3D GREEN SKYSCRAPER

YIQING JIANG | YING TAO

AERIAL VIEW ◀

Form	Main Structure	Protective Mesh	Vegetable Grown	Transportation & Wind Turbines	Final Appearance

▲ COMPONENTS DIAGRAM

The 3D Green skyscraper proposes breaking the monotony of concrete and glass in dense, urban Shanghai, by inserting vertical farmland within the existing built environment of skyscrapers.

The 3D Green concept proposes the construction of a high-rise structure that is comprised of rows and rows of farmland, and then wrapping the structure around an existing office building. It is twisted onto the building so as to best capture sunlight. This placement will vary from building to building, as in a metropolis the buildings surroundings will dictate sun exposure.

This placement of high-rise agriculture onto a downtown office building has many benefits for workers inside of the building and in surrounding buildings: they can look onto green vistas, buy fresh vegetables grown on their own office building, and they are able to enjoy various public green spaces that are open within the farmland, known as "voids," that can be used for sports activities or relaxation. There is also the natural added benefit of creating cleaner air, thanks to the plants intake of carbon dioxide and output of oxygen.

After the green structure is wrapped around the existing skyscraper, wind turbines are placed on top of the building to generate energy for self-use and surrounding structures. Gray water is recycled from the surrounding buildings to meet the irrigation needs of the urban farmland.

Plans imagine the structure being over 350 meters tall and featuring a protective mesh between the structure itself and the space for agricultural growth. At 250 meters, a large reservoir for water storage holds a mass of fluid to disperse in case of fire.

Forming

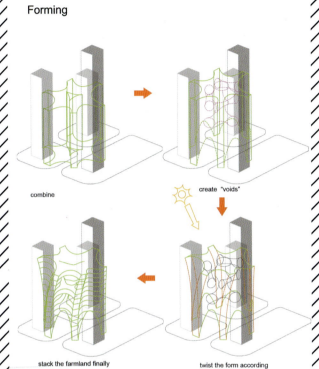

combine

create "voids"

stack the farmland finally

twist the form according to the sun direction

▲ GEOMETRY ANALYSIS

EXTERIOR VIEWS
NEW BUILDING ATTACHED
TO EXISTING ONES
▼

Perspectives inside vertical farmland

▲ INTERIOR VIEWS - GARDENS

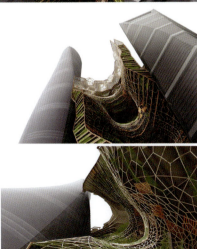

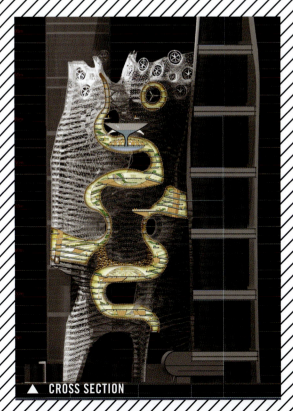

▲ CROSS SECTION

SEEDS OF LIFE

EGYPT

OSAMA MOHAMED ELGHANNAM | KARIM MOHAMED ELNABAWY | MOHAMED AHMED KHAMIS
NESMA MOHAMED ABOBAKR

RESIDENTIAL UNITS

illustration plan

PLAN

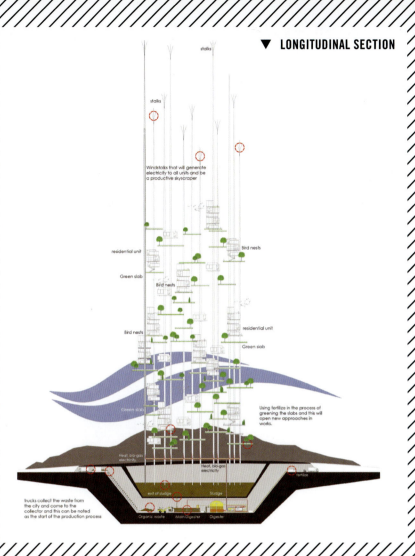

▼ **LONGITUDINAL SECTION**

stalks

stalks

Windstalks that will generate electricity to all units and be a productive skyscraper

residential unit

Bird nests

Green slab

Bird nests

Bird nests

residential unit

Green slab

Using fertilize in the process of greening the slabs and this will open new approaches in works.

Green slab

Heat, bio-gas electricity

Heat, bio-gas electricity

fertilize

trucks collect the waste from the city and come to the collector and this can be noted as the start of the production process

exit of sludge

Sludge

Organic waste

Main Digester

Digester

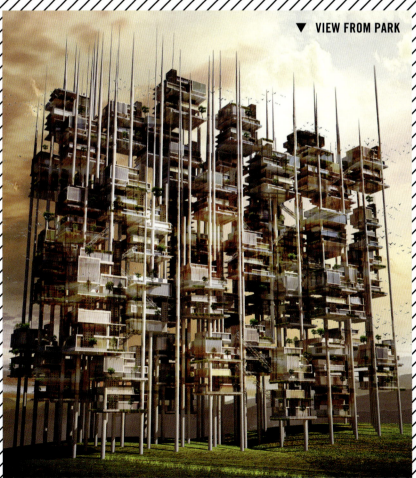

▼ **VIEW FROM PARK**

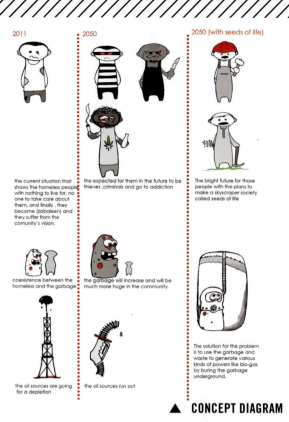

2011

2050

2050 (with seeds of life)

the current situation that shows the homeless people with nothing to live for, no one to take care about them, and finally, they become (zabaleen) and they suffer from the comunity's vision.

the expected for them in the future to be thieves, criminals and go to addiction

The bright future for those people with the plans to make a skyscraper society called seeds of life

coexistence between the homeless and the garbage

the garbage will increase and will be much more huge in the community

the oil sources are going for a depletion

the oil sources run out

The solution for the problem is to use the garbage and waste to generate various kinds of powers like bio-gas by buring the garbage underground.

▲ **CONCEPT DIAGRAM**

The "Seeds of Life" project looks at the slums of Cairo, Egypt and their problems with waste collection. Slums in Egypt and elsewhere can, with the steady compilation of trash, turn into garbage cities. Trash piles high and the impoverished and homeless residents who have nowhere else to go must learn to live amongst the filth, suffering from the diseases and pollution it brings.

This problem can be remedied by putting both the polluted conditions and the homeless residents to work for a positive end. The trash is moved underground into a giant pit and a skyscraper is built on top. As the trash continues to be stored underground, facilities above ground in the first floor of the skyscraper use the biogas and organic matter to generate energy and fertilizer. Trash itself becomes the solution to pollution, creating new jobs for the homeless and allowing them to be productive to their communities.

The skyscraper itself is comprised of many metal tubes that provide structures for the units built in between. The tubes, in addition to being skeletal for the structure, provide power to the tower's units through wind energy as they splay at the top and turn into "windstalks" that generate power.

The skyscraper's units are used for residential, cultural and entertainment purposes. The structure also features garden slabs interspersed amongst units in an attempt to foster agricultural growth. This allows the building to be self-sustaining and non-polluting.

Holes of varying size puncture the exterior of the units. Their intent is to connect the people inside the building with the nature outside; some holes are used as birds' nests, and others provide natural lighting to the interiors.

eVolo | Issue 4 | 2012

TREE OF LIFE

UKRAINE

SVIRID DENIS | GUDZENKO ANASTASIYA

AERIAL VIEW
▶

▼ SUSTAINABLE SYSTEMS

Greenhouse ▽

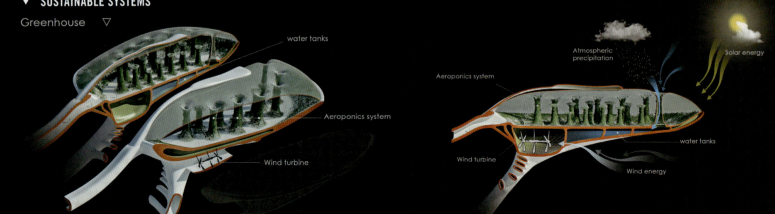

water tanks

Aeroponics system

Wind turbine

Atmospheric precipitation

Solar energy

Aeroponics system

water tanks

Wind turbine

Wind energy

1. The quarry Kennecott Bingham Canyon Mine, Utah, USA. Copper mining. Depth-1km, width-3 .5km

2. The quarry `Diavik', Canada, Lake Las de Gras. Diamond mining.

3. The Kimberley diamond-pipe 'Mir', Yakutia, Russia. Outer diameter- 1200m, depth — 525m

4. Kimberly City ,SAR. Nonworking diamond mine, area- 17 hectares, width -463m, perimeter -1,6 km.

5. Chuquicamata, Chile. Every day water is pumped out in large quantities turning this place into one of the most arid areas on Earth.

▼ CONCEPT DIAGRAM

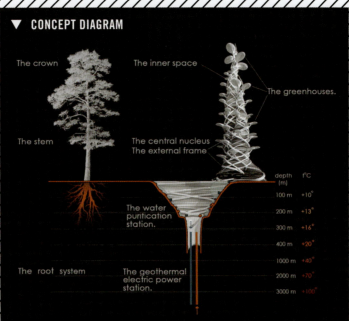

The crown
The inner space
The greenhouses.
The stem
The central nucleus
The external frame
The water purification station.
The root system
The geothermal electric power station.

depth (m)	t°C
100 m	+10°
200 m	+13°
300 m	+16°
400 m	+20°
1000 m	+40°
2000 m	+70°
3000 m	+100°

Floor at the elevation +250.0 m

▲ TYPICAL FLOOR PLAN

▼ CROSS SECTION

Section 1-1

Geothermal electric power station

Water purification station

▼ HOUSING UNITS AND GREEN TERRACES

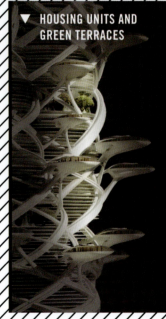

"Tree of Life" towers are constructed to heal the Earth in places where open extraction is taking place. Open extraction (mining) is a process that damages soil and vegetation layers, pollutes the water and the ground and disturbs animal and plant ecosystems of an area. By pairing the open damaged earth with the roots of a "Tree," the Earth can be healed.

Tree of Life towers are autonomous ecosystems where inhabitants live and work inside to produce ecologically sound products for themselves and for export.

The root system, the main system feeding the tower, features a geothermic electric power station that has limbs that extend 3,000 meters into the earth. The process is both ecologically sound and inexpensive. The roots also house a water purification station that collects and cleans groundwater for use and recycles wastewater.

The carrying structure, or the "stem," is a system of structural parts that comprise the nucleus and the external frame of the tower. The building is designed as two interlacing stems for additional support. High-speed, direct lifts and floor-to-floor lifts are operated with vacuum suction and transport people vertically in the tower.

The inner space is the crown of the tree, and it resembles the structure of a city.

Large parks for recreation separate the different levels, each having its own function. The public sector has restaurants, offices, clinics, schools, entertainment and trade centers. Above the public sector there a three different residential areas, a scientific research area and a geometeorological station with a planetarium. "Streets" are defined as small greenways that run along the outer perimeter of the building.

The outer greenhouses are the fruits of the tree, and they grow various crops by aeroponic methods.

HYDRA TELSA SKYSCRAPER

eVolo | Issue 4 | 2012

SERBIA

MILOS VLASTIC | VUK DJORDJEVIC | ANA LAZOVIC | MILICA STANKOVIC

BUILDING DURING THUNDERSTORMS

▶

"Electric power is everywhere present in unlimited quantities and can drive the world's machinery without the need of coal, oil, gas, or any other of the common fuels."

Nikola Tesla

1/ LIGHTNING
2/ CONDUCTIVITY
3/ BATTERY
4/ ELECTROLYSIS
5/ HYDROGEN PRODUCTION
6/ STORAGE
7/ TRANSPORT AND DISTRIBUTION

▲ **CONCEPT DIAGRAM**

▲ **AERIAL VIEW**

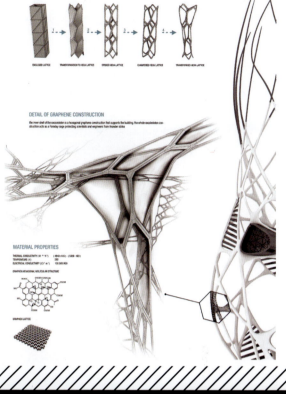

▼ **GEOMETRY ANALYSIS**

CONSTRUCTION FORM ANALYSIS

ENCLOSED LATTICE — TRANSFORMATION TO HEXA LATTICE — OPENED HEXA LATTICE — CHAMFERED HEXA LATTICE — TRANSFORMED HEXA LATTICE

DETAIL OF GRAPHENE CONSTRUCTION

the inner shell of the exoskeleton is a hexagonal graphene construction that supports the building. the whole exoskeleton construction acts as a Faraday cage protecting scientists and engineers from thunder strike.

MATERIAL PROPERTIES

GRAPHENE HEXAGONAL MOLECULAR STRUCTURE

GRAPHEN LATTICE

▼ **ENERGY COLLECTION SYSTEMS**

GRAPHENE CORE
the basic structural element of some carbon allotropes including graphite, charcoal, carbon nanotubes and fullerenes

GRAPHENE COATING
graphene has the greatest thermal and electrical conductivity ever measured yet. its also one of the strongest materials ever tested. It has a breaking strength 200 times greater than steel.

CONTROL ROOM

ELEVATOR SHAFT

FARADAY CAGE

LABS

COMMAND ROOM

RESEARCH FACILITY
the place where all the scientific research regarding the hydra project occurs. A part of the research facility is represented as a maintenance unit. Engineers and scientist work in this part of the unit.

SECURITY

MAINTENANCE

ELEVATOR SHAFT

VENTILATION HATCH

HIVE
residential place of the whole facility. the hive is directly connected with the mega-battery and the electrolysis facility.

STORAGE
storage of large quantities of hydrogen underground

MEGA-BATTERY
used as storage of electric charge which is later used for electrolysis of water during periods of poor storms

HOUSING
there are 3 housing units providing accommodation for the scientists and engineers

TRANSPORT
the transportation is used for both employees of the facility and hydrogen distribution

POOLS FOR ELECTROLYSIS

SECTION

0 — 50m

The "Hydra Tesla Research Facility" poses a question that would make many energy companies nervous: What would happen when the ultimate source of energy became free for all people? By designing a skyscraper that harnesses energy from lightening and uses the power to generate hydrogen for use as renewable fuel, the Hydra tower pulls double energy duty.

The tower's mechanical functions use an electrical discharge shell for hydrogen production through a process called "electrolysis of water," where water molecules are broken down to obtain the hydrogen particles. The designers see hydrogen as the best possible fuel source because of its low production costs and attainability. Lightening is also a logical and ideal energy source as more than 16 million lightening storms light up the sky with electricity across the world each year.

Not all areas experience lightening strikes evenly, however, so this project is therefore implemented in one of the areas of the world where lightening occurs most frequently tropical regions like in the Congo, Venezuela or Florida. The tower is constructed with "tentacles" that are used to harness the electric power from lightening.

The tower's form is called a "transformed hexa lattice," and is coated in graphene, which has the greatest thermal and electrical conductivity ever measured. It is also one of the strongest materials ever tested, with a breaking strength 200 times greater than steel. The core is also comprised of graphene.

A mega-battery near the building's base helps store energy when storm frequency is low. The structure has three housing units for scientists and engineers working within. The tower is positioned like a strong tree, with roots anchored it to the ground underneath for stability.

The tower is named after the hydra creature, a genus of a simple freshwater animal that possesses radial symmetry.

eVolo | Issue 4 | 2012

SPORTS TOWER

UKRAINE

SERGIY PROKOF`YEV | OLGA PROKOF`YEVA

VIEW FROM RIVER -
HABITABLE BRIDGE

▶

AERIAL VIEW

▶

Sports can unite people in powerful ways, and as such, the grouping of all sports in a region into one grand facility poses a unique opportunity, say the designers of the "Sports Tower."

Located on the Dnepr River in the Ukraine, the Sports Tower complex uses the riverbanks and an island in between to anchor multiple sports facilities and a sky-scraper on top. The structure is comprised of three parts: the first, located on an island in the river, is the structure's anchor and houses the largest of the sports arenas, in-cluding the soccer stadium. The second portion of the structure is a stair-stepping mass that spans the river and sits on top of the first part of the building. It serves as a pedestrian bridge, linking both sides of the river, but also has public gardens and smaller sports facilities, such as tennis and basketball courts and an ice hockey rink. The third portion of the complex rises into the sky and houses nine hotels for athletes and tourists, restaurants and an observation deck.

The structure will allow people to move freely between stadiums, even during events, and will thus always be full of life and activity. Capable of holding thousands of spectators, the Sports Tower can hold anything from small matches to the world's largest sporting events. Its unifying impact will create a new "type and quality of sport society," bringing together people from all segments of society in one exciting atmo-sphere. Transparent walls allow people from the outside to glimpse at the excitement of the sport and the energy of the crowd.

▼ AERIAL VIEW

PROGRAM SECTION
▼

▲ EXTERIOR VIEW

▼ PROGRAM DIAGRAM

functional diagram

Structure. The "Sports tower" will be located on the bank of the Dnepr river and will consist of three main blocks.

Block 1 will be located on an island along the river bank and will consist of the biggest sport facilities, i.e. 4 soccer stadiums.

Block 2 will be located across the river and will have three supports: right bank, Block 1, left bank. It will accommodate smaller stadiums: tennis courts, ice-hockey stadium, swimming pool, basketball and volleyball stadiums. Block 2 will also serve as a pedestrian bridge-public garden, connecting two banks of the river.

Block 3 – multistory – will include 9 hotel blocks for teams of participants. The two blocks on the top of this tower will include restaurants and observation platform.

restaurant

Hotel

lift

block 3

exit

block 2

lift

exit

block 1

lift

stairs

square

entry exit

seat

info

ice rink

pool

play field

play field

play field

entry exit

stairs

square

seat

soccer field

soccer field

soccer field

parking

parking

parking

parking

WATER CIRCLE

SOUTH KOREA

YOUNG WAN KIM | SUE HWAN KWUN | JUN YOUNG PARK | JOONG HA PARK

RE-ENVISIONED
OIL RIGS
◀

RESEARCH FACILITY
▶

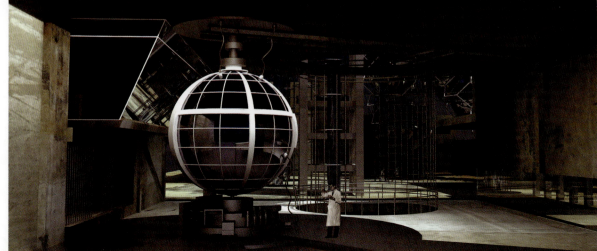

The "Water Circle" project imagines the reuse of oilrigs once fossil fuels have been depleted and the massive structures are rendered obsolete. These platforms, essentially used to deplete the world's resources and contribute to the destruction of its environment, are recycled to help restore it and save the Earth from further damage.

The drill pipes of the oilrigs are repurposed to vertically pull up and store water in spherical tanks. The water is desalinated and treated, and once the tanks are full of fresh water, they are then transported to countries in need of drinking water or water for use in agricultural irrigation. If used to grow trees and green vegetation, it further helps the environmental cycle, as the plants will help process carbon dioxide out of the air. The water is drawn into the structures without the use of energy, as long and narrow capillary tubes can automatically raise water vertically. As water is pulled up in the tubes the movement turns screws that help generate energy. This energy is used for marine research centers and relevant management facilities. Out of use oilrigs can also be used, according to this plan, as labs, lodges and management ships for exploring marine ecosystems.

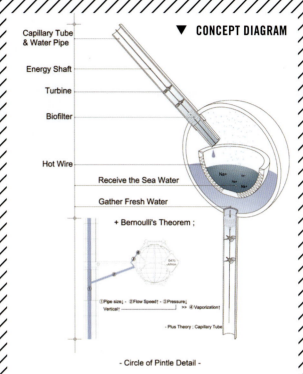

▼ CONCEPT DIAGRAM

Capillary Tube & Water Pipe

Energy Shaft

Turbine

Biofilter

Hot Wire

Receive the Sea Water

Gather Fresh Water

+ Bernoulli's Theorem ;

①Pipe size↓ - ②Flow Speed↑ - ③Pressure↓
Vertical↑ >> ④Vaporization↑

- Plus Theory ; Capillary Tube

- Circle of Pintle Detail -

▲

SHIPPING FRESH WATER

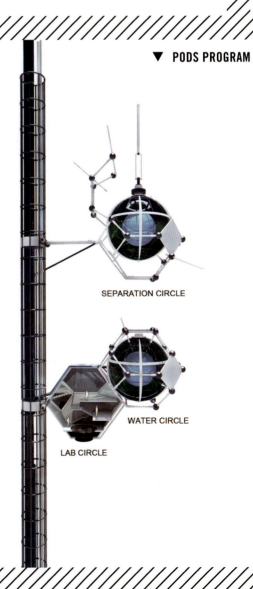

▼ PODS PROGRAM

SEPARATION CIRCLE

WATER CIRCLE

LAB CIRCLE

▼ CONCEPTUAL SECTION

TENSILE TOWER

DAVID GULL | JIN YOUNG SONG

UNITED STATES

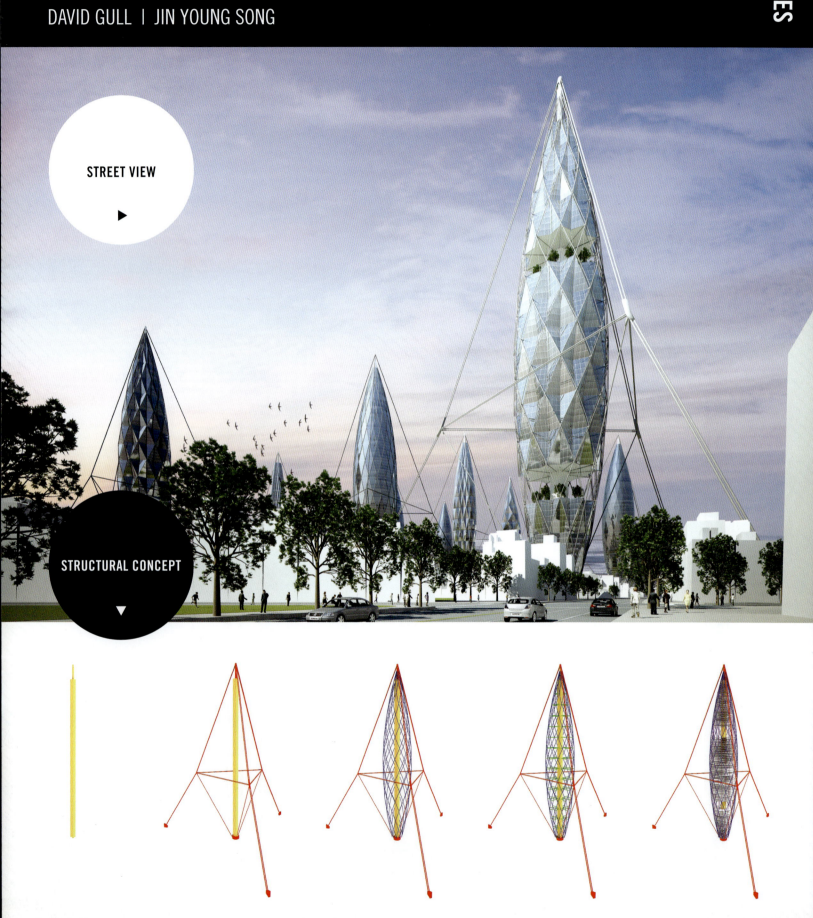

STREET VIEW

▶

STRUCTURAL CONCEPT

▼

The "Tensile Tower" looks to redefine the traditional design of skyscrapers in favor of futuristic "bowed and cocoon-like" forms.

Skyscrapers traditionally have been defined, say the designers of the Tensile Tower, by a rigid core with heavy perimeter columns. It is possible to structure skyscrapers to be more efficient and unburdened by large vertical compression members at the perimeter. Its design gives the Tensile Tower uninterrupted views, open space planning, efficient day lighting and space planning that allows for minimal material use.

The building utilizes one primary mega compression member, which also houses the vertical circulation mechanisms, much like a traditional core of a skyscraper. Tensile cables that are suspended from the top of the mega column support the perimeter edges of the floor slabs. These cables spiral the tower at an angle in both directions, creating a diagonal configuration that provides resistance to torsion and aids overall stability. Further, this gives the structure a lightness and openness to the exterior wall of each floor space. The resulting bow shape acts like an oversized herring truss.

Because the mega column is narrow, a tri-pod cable configuration is needed to provide stability for the building. In redefining the urban grid, the designers imagine many Tensile Towers dotting the urban landscape and also shared cable anchor sites that connect the structures. This creates an overlay on the existing fabric of a grid of polygonal shapes connected at key points with Tensile Towers.

The towers will have retail space on the lower levels, followed by offices, residential units and an observation deck on the very top.

PLANS
▶

INTERIOR VIEW
▼

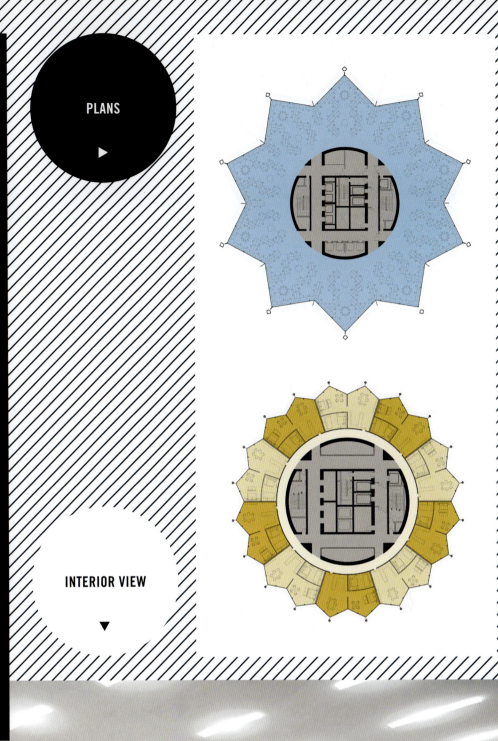

eVolo | Issue 4 | 2012

BARBED WIRE SKYSCRAPER

SOUTH KOREA

HYUNBEOM CHO | JINKYU PAK | HONGSUP KIM | JIWON KIM

VIEW FROM DEMILITARIZED ZONE ◄

ENTRANCE VIEW ◄

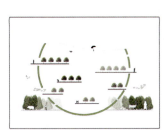

Northern Limit Line
Military Demarcation Line
South Limit Line

▼ CONCEPTUAL SECTIONS

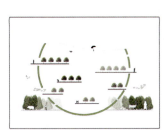
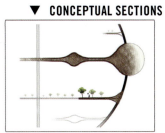

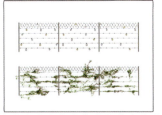

▼ AERIAL VIEW

The "Barbed Wire Skyscraper" hopes to bring peaceful communication between people on both sides of the Demilitarized Zone (DMZ) that separates North and South Korea, through the implementation of several spherical skyscrapers.

The structures, which act as small cities, lie in the lush ecological zone that has developed in the past 50 years within the DMZ, thanks to the lack of human activity in the four-kilometer wide strip. In the center of the DMZ is the actual Military Demarcation Line that separates the two countries; there is a three-strand barbed wire fence that provides literal separation along 250 kilometers of that stretch. To pierce the foreboding divider and foster nonviolent interaction between the two sides, the skyscraper spheres are formed by using a spike to hoist a section of the wire high and reconfiguring its shape to form a hollow circle.

An inner sphere within the structure as a whole provides green and built space for social interaction. This area will have roads for transportation as well as rail and subway facilities. The inner circle is connected to the large structure and other parts within it through bridges. The spike used to reform the wire initially serves as the large structural support for the skyscraper, keeping the sphere wide.

Light bulbs placed all along the wire make the structure glow at night, which increases safety but also warmly invites people from both sides of the DMZ. Strategic placement of these structures along the Military Demarcation Line will help foster peace and further communication between the polarized countries.

▼ INTERIOR VIEW

▼ CROSS SECTION

COASTSCRAPER

GARY KELLETT

EXTERIOR VIEW

The ocean is the most fertile of ecosystems on Earth, but in order to maintain the health of the living organisms within, its waters must stay within a specific pH level. With greenhouse gases filling the atmosphere at an unprecedented rate, the ocean is absorbing higher levels of carbon dioxide than ever. As the water absorbs CO_2, its pH levels fall, creating an acid imbalance – a condition known as "ocean acidification." Simple science dictates that to balance an acidic environment, an alkali must be added. The CoastalScraper structure brings alkalis to the world's oceans on a massive scale.

CoastalScrapers are huge mobile chalk excavators and refineries. The first one is imagined to operate from the White Cliff's of Dover, coastal cliffs composed of chalk in southeast England that span the length of the country. At a depth of five meters per year, the CoastalScraper excavates chalk deposits from the Cliffs. Once the chalk has been taken, the structure refines it and stores it in large silos.

Connected to the CoastalScrapers are Deep Sea Plume Jets that lie on the ocean floor that read the water's pH levels. When the jets detect acidity, they alert the CoastalScrapers which immediately dispense from their silos, via underwater pipes, large amounts of chalk. The jets then spread the chalk along miles-long swaths to help balance the water's pH levels.

The CoastalScrapers refine the chalk into particles no bigger than 500 microns, giving the substance the consistency of flour. This ensures that the chalk can remain suspended in the upper layers of the water for long periods of time and be carried great distances with currents.

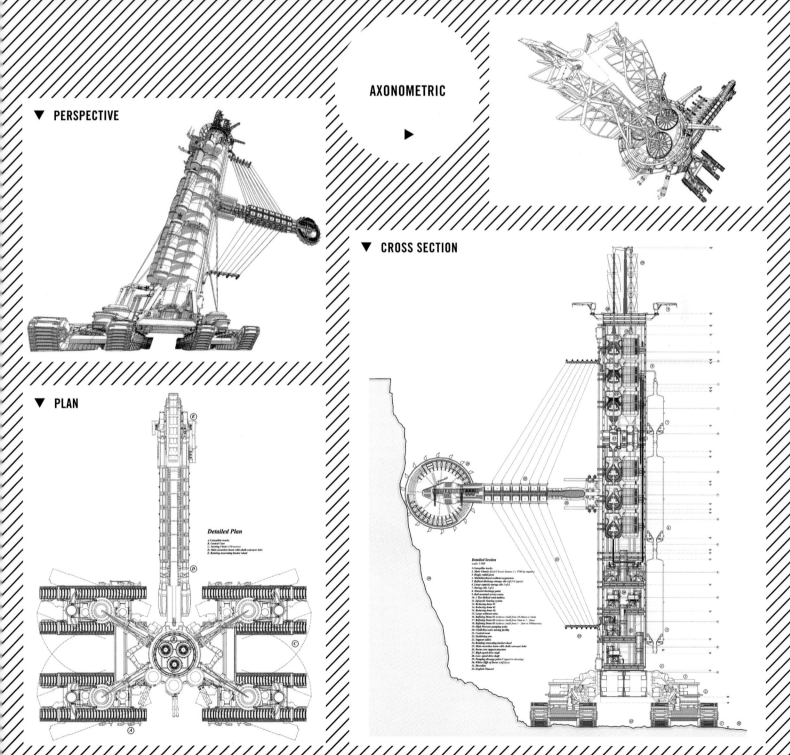

▼ PERSPECTIVE

AXONOMETRIC

▶

▼ CROSS SECTION

▼ PLAN

Detailed Plan

A. Caterpillar tracks.
B. Central Core.
C. Turning Circle (190 meters).
D. Main excavation boom with chalk conveyor belts.
E. Rotating excavating bucket wheel

Detailed Section
scale 1:300

eVolo | Issue 4 | 2012

ICEBERG AUTONOMY SKYSCRAPER

AKRAM FAHMI

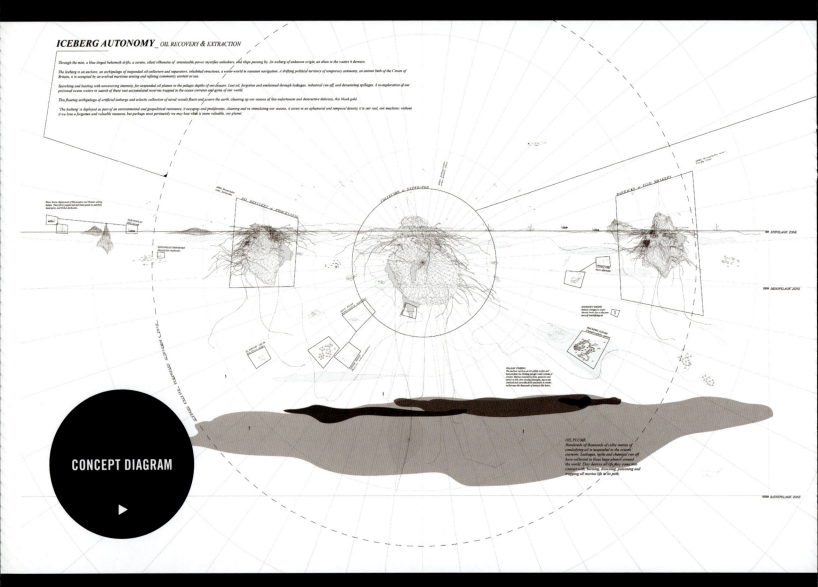

ICEBERG AUTONOMY _ OIL RECOVERY & EXTRACTION

Through the mist, a blue tinged behemoth drifts, a serene, silent silhouette of unteneable power mystifies onlookers, and ships passing by. An iceberg of unknown origin, an alien to the waters it devours.

The Iceberg is an enclave, an archipelago of suspended oil collectors and separators, inhabited structures, a water-world in constant navigation. A drifting political territory of temporary autonomy, an antient limb of the Crown of Britain, it is occupied by an evolved maritime mining and refining community existent at sea.

Searching and hunting with unwavering intensity, for suspended oil plumes in the pelagic depths of our oceans. Lost oil, forgotten and unclaimed through leakages, industrial run off, and devastating spillages. A re-exploration of our poisoned ocean waters in search of these vast accumulated reserves trapped in the ocean currents and gyros of our world.

This floating archipelago of artificial icebergs and eclectic collection of naval vessels floats and scours the earth, cleaning up our oceans of this unfortunate and destructive delicacy, this black gold.

'The Iceberg' is deployed as part of an environmental and geopolitical resistance, it occupies and proliferates, cleaning and re-stimulating our oceans, it exists in an ephemeral and temporal density, it is our tool, our machine; without it we lose a forgotten and valuable resource, but perhaps most pertinently we may lose what is more valuable, our planet.

CONCEPT DIAGRAM ▶

OIL PLUME.
Hundreds of thousands of cubic metres of emulsifying oil is suspended in the ocean's current. Leakages, spills and chemical run off have collected in these huge plumes around the world. They destroy all life they come into contact with, burning, drowning, poisoning and trapping all marine life in its path.

▼ INTERIOR VIEW

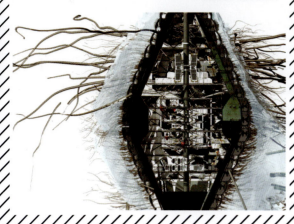

▼ CROSS SECTION

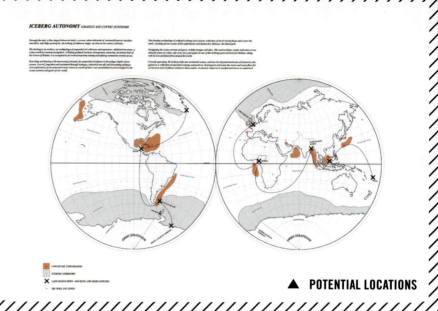

▲ POTENTIAL LOCATIONS

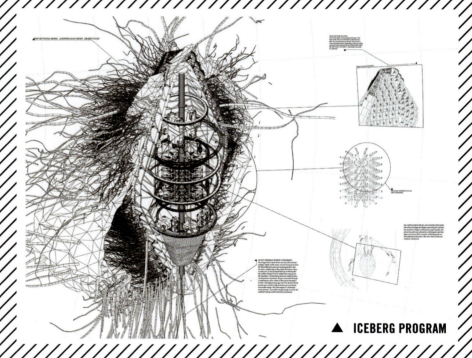

▲ ICEBERG PROGRAM

The massive, slow-moving artificial iceberg behind the "Iceberg Autonomy" project is a floating archipelago that cleans the world's oil-filled oceans, fosters marine life and reclaims oil for reuse through innovative design and processes.

With our world's waters full of lost oil as a result of massive spills and industrial runoff, the artificial iceberg floats the waters like a hunter, zeroing in on highly polluted zones. Once oil plumes are located, extraction pilots and seep torpedoes within the iceberg draw the black gold in and store it in pods.

As it cleans oceans, the iceberg also stimulates the suffering marine life. Marine ecosystems can cling to the underside; phytoplankton repopulates and blooms as it grows underneath the iceberg, and this enacts a chain reaction that stimulates the ecology. More important for the regeneration of the marine environment, however, are the iceberg's long, raking, tentacle-like hairs. The hairs serve as a habitat for marine life and nutrients; they are affixed to the "tectonic plates" that comprise the iceberg via steel neck braces that are watertight. Each is individually removable for maintenance, and they vary significantly in length to best capture a breadth of organisms.

The longest of these hairs are used to help power the structure as a whole. They reach into the coldest regions of the ocean, a process involving pumping natural waste gasses down the hair and capturing the pressure that is created when the heated hair interacts with the freezing water temperatures. The iceberg is an oil prospector, but it needs none of that fuel for itself.

Adaptable living quarters exist on board for the crew. The structure is comprised of an external hull shell, inner bulkhead shell plating, steel lattice rings, a central circulation column with the pilot extractor carousel, and emulsion centrifuges and oil ship containers.

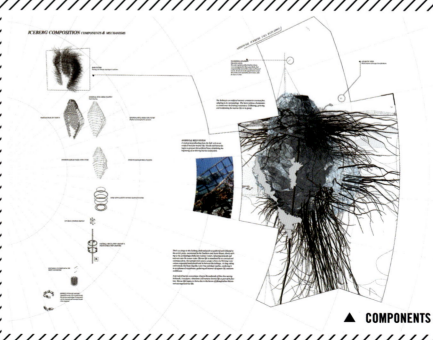

▲ COMPONENTS

LADY LANDFILL SKYSCRAPER

MILORAD VIDOJEVIĆ | JELENA PUCAREVIĆ | MILICA PIHLER

EXTERIOR VIEW
▶

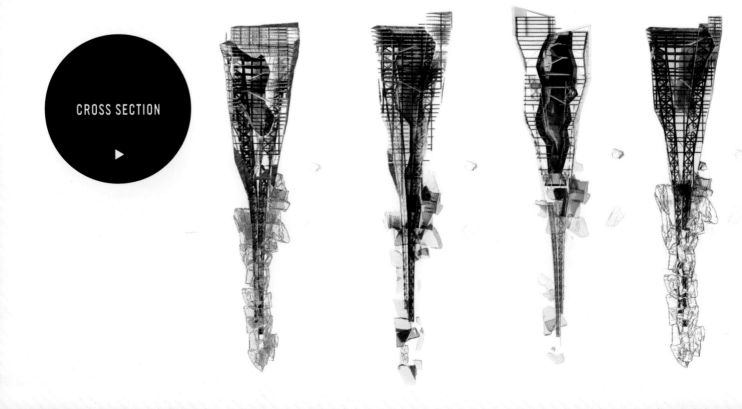

CROSS SECTION
▶

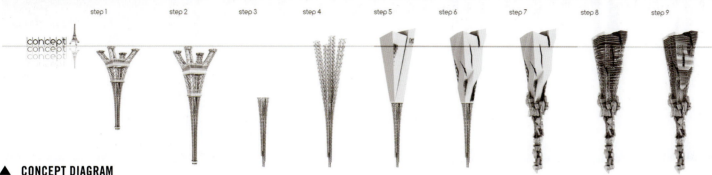

step 1   step 2   step 3   step 4   step 5   step 6   step 7   step 8   step 9

concept
concept
concept

▲ CONCEPT DIAGRAM

The Great Pacific Garbage Patch is made of 3.5 million tons of trash collected in the middle of the Pacific Ocean. The trash is largely non-biodegradable – 80 percent is plastic waste – and the patch reaches 30 meters in depth. The water-based landfill is killing the habitats of the area's sea wildlife, and also the creatures themselves, who succumb after eating trash that is mistaken for food. The designers of the "Lady Landfill Skyscraper" have imagined a floating island that exists to remove the non-biodegradable materials from the water. The building functions to accumulate and recycle the ocean's waste, or use it as an energy source.

The cone-shaped structure reaches deep into the water with only a small platform reaching above sea level. At the very bottom is the building's interior landfill, which vacuums trash in. Garbage is shredded in this lower region of the structure so that recyclable metals can be removed. Recyclable waste then moves to the recycling plant in the middle of the structure. All other waste heads to the garbage conversion system, where it is heated into a gas. Molecules without high-energy volumes stay solid through the process and are later melted with plasma to create a glass-like substance that is used in construction as an aggregate with concrete or asphalt. But the high-energy molecules turn into gas when the garbage is heated and these molecules are sent to a conversion chamber where they are processed into clean fuel.

Ocean Thermal Energy Conversion processes harness the water's thermal energy and wave power. The process does double duty: with every megawatt of energy produced by the OTEC process, 2.36 million tons of desalinated water is produced. The top of the structure holds housing and recreation facilities.

Garbage collecting units
Garbage collecting units
Garbage collecting units

ocean surface
under water

There are units for collecting garbage within the skyscraper. They are made of membrane structures that allow them to shrink and expand. Garbage transportation involves several stages:

Step 1: Collection - on sea or land
Step 2: Transport - floating on the surface of the ocean (which enables the appropriate volume to weight ratio)
Step 3: Dipping - shrinking of the membranes leads to compression of trash(vacuuming), which enables faster shrinking
Step 4: Fixing

▲ UNDERWATER VIEW

▲ PACIFIC GARBAGE PATCH

INTERIOR VIEW ▽

eVolo | Issue 4 | 2012

KINETIC SKYSCRAPER

VICTOR KOPIEIKIN | PAVLO ZABOTIN

It is proposed to implement the modular frame in the building structure, which could "wrap" the building and create the integral, "live" area, filled with water nutrient solution. The system of modular frame should have cell grating, filled with special water solution, where the colonial cyanobacteriae are placed and later reproduce. The operation of such system is simple: a human, when breathing out, produces CO_2, the conditioning system during its operation enriches the water solution and cyanobacteriae with CO_2, and as the result, with the help of perimeter artificial light, the photosynthetic reaction with oxygen separation and natural air ionization happens. In this case, the system of air circulation is close and completely autonomous. The building obtains fresh, rich with oxygen and ionized air being at the same time completely isolated from outer aggressive air medium.

| O2 | Container whith cianobakteria | CO$_2$ |

STRUCTURAL CONCEPT ◄

PROGRAM SECTION ▼

Dwelling unit

But with the deterioration of living standards and the growth of environmental problems of energy-saving functions are becoming scarce. Need to introduce technologies that can protect a person from outside negative influences, whether it be noise, heat or electromagnetic pollution.

| geothermal energy |
| irragation system |
| ventilation system |
| stairs |
| electrical networks |
| hydroponics system |

Hydroponics – a method of growing plants without soil. Depletion and contamination of land in areas adjacent to Mexico City, lead to lower quality food, and water shortages are already acute in some areas of Mexico. Another significant problem is the problem of pesticides that fall in the underground water as well as depletion and irrigation - land. For example, approximately 80% of all fruits and vegetables in Israel are grown hydroponic method.

Structural scheme

| Protective shell of carbon fiber |
| Supporting frame |
| Hydraulic system |

Geothermal energy - the direction of energy, based on the production of electricity and heat by the thermal energy contained in the bowels of the earth. In volcanic areas of circulating water is overheated above the boiling point at relatively shallow depths. Access to the underground thermal waters is possible through deep drilling.
The idea is in the gradual implementation of the alternative energy sources into a building's structure; and with this creating the autonomous energy unit in the system of megapolis.
A building may produce the necessary quantity of energy, not depending on general transmission system of a city. At the same time, such "energy units" should be united into single energy frame, which will allow to redistribute the produced energy the most rationally.
The capacity of such autonomous geothermal station may be about 200-300 MW, which in future will allow to create the wide communication network between similar buildings in the city structure.
One such multi-storey house will be able to supply 2-4 neighbouring areas with energy. Thus, the more buildings of this type, the more the "energy covering" of the city.

Electrical power system

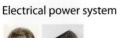

Light Source

Reflected light can also be used afficiently

Solar energy (battery)

Geothermal energy (battery)

The ventilation system (cyanobacteria)

▼ INTERIOR VIEW

The "Kinetic Skyscraper" is a skyscraper located in Mexico City that seeks to preserve the ecological safety of the urban environment and improve the quality of life of its residents. In 40 years, say the designers, Mexico City will be uninhabitable due to suffocating pollution levels. This tower is meant to be replicated across the city, bringing environmental solutions on a grand scale to the region.

The towers will feature systems to support hydroponic growth processes that span several levels. This will allow for vertical growth of fruits and vegetables within the structure without a need for soil. The tower's modules are covered in anti-noise and heat insulating panels that are made of carbon fiber to be light but also dense. Cyanobacteria create closed and completely autonomous systems of air circulation within the building, protecting the interior of the structure from outdoor pollution by providing fresh, ionized oxygen.

The tower's exterior is covered in modules that open and close, blooming like flowers, depending on the position of the Sun and their location's access to solar energy. It is within these modules that the cyanobacteria grow; the modules are filled with a "special water solution" that reacts with carbon dioxide to create an oxygen-producing photosynthesis process that feeds fresh air to the building.

Geothermal wells are drilled throughout the region and then connect to all of the skyscrapers via an underground pipe system. The geothermal system as a whole will generate between 200 and 300 megawatts. As the implementation of this process throughout the metropolis will be gradual, buildings are equipped with spherical solar cells to capture energy for its own use.

▲ AERIAL VIEW

▼ HOUSING UNIT

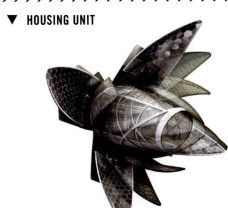

KINETIC MODULES
▶

eVolo | Issue 4 | 2012

RHIZOME TOWER

ITALY

ENRICO TOGNONI | FEDERICO TINTI | DAVIDE MARIANI

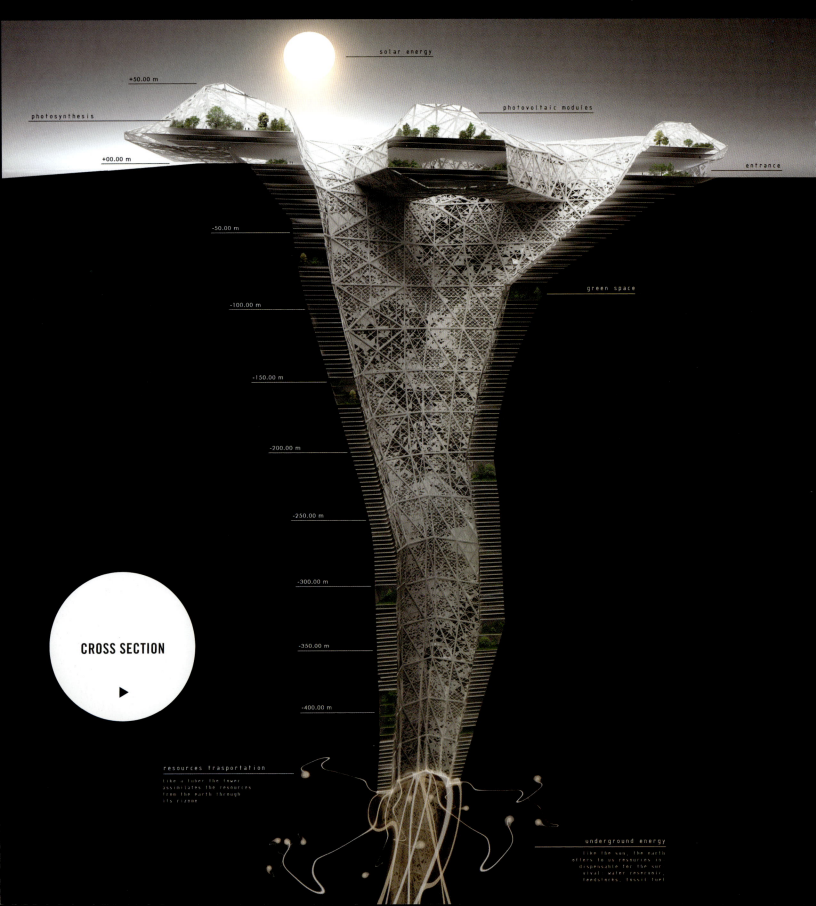

solar energy

+50.00 m

photosynthesis

photovoltaic modules

+00.00 m

entrance

-50.00 m

green space

-100.00 m

-150.00 m

-200.00 m

-250.00 m

CROSS SECTION ▶

-300.00 m

-350.00 m

-400.00 m

resources trasportation

like a tuber the tower assimilates the resources from the earth through its rhizome

underground energy

like the sun, the earth offers to us resources indispensable for the survival: water reservoir, feedstocks, fossil fuel

AERIAL VIEW

▶

▼ INTERIOR VIEW

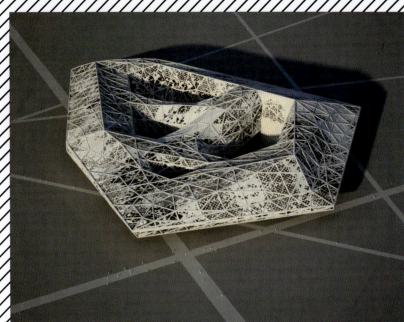

The "Rhizome Tower" is an ever-evolving, indefinable structure prototype of "a thousand plateaus" that expresses its verticality underground, burrowing to a depth of 400 meters or more. Extreme climate change conditions on Earth have caused the designers to envision a plan to "develop elsewhere", and that "elsewhere" is underground.

But it's not entirely accurate to call this plan a "development," because the designers of the Rhizome Tower want to express the antithesis of development: their idea is to remove from the grid instead of adding, to displace instead of place people, to move down instead of up, in terms of verticality. The plan is one comprised of a continually evolving combination of elements, structure and substructure, functions and relationships.

All of the components in the tower prototype have "auto similarity" properties that allow them to reproduce themselves on every scale.

The underground provides much of the building's life source, from fuel to water supplies. The structure supports green spaces interspersed throughout the tower to grow vegetable species dying above ground due to global warming.

Large green space areas provide room for recreation, and interior spaces are designed with maximum flexibility and light. The top of the structure rests on the ground level, and includes the building's entrance and photovoltaic modules to harness solar energy.

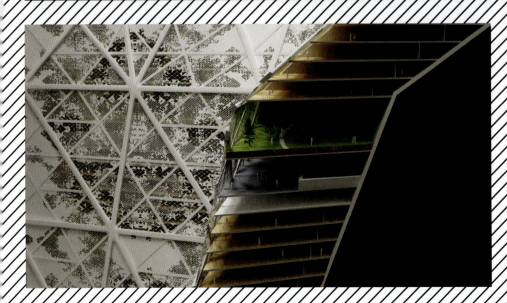

PROGRAN SECTION

◀

▼ SITE

eVolo | Issue 4 | 2012

WHITE CLOUD

NEW ZEALAND

ADRIAN VINCENT KUMAR | YUN KONG SUNG

INTERIOR VIEW

▶

▼ **PROGRAM DIAGRAM**

gaseous
filtration

grey
rain
collected

particulate
absorbed

artificial
rain

induced
condensation

natural
wind
channelled

particulate
filtration

particulate
filtration

particulate
seperator

dust
bricks

water
recycled

air
cleaned

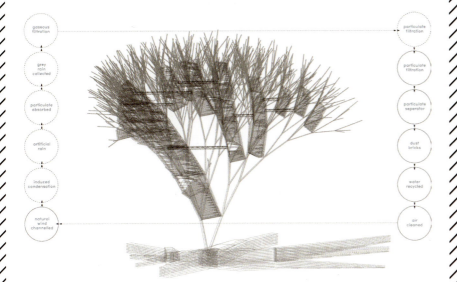

▼ **INTERIOR VIEW**

The "White Cloud Project" examines air pollution as a dangerous and pervasive problem in areas of Asia and around the world due to exhaust from industrial manufacturing, power plants, transportation, and other sources. Skyscrapers should be built as giant air purification machines, say the designers of the White Cloud buildings, utilizing the wind to purify air.

The structures grow and branch out like giant steel trees, with the placement of the branches dictated by local wind patterns. Their arrangement seeks to best capture air movement, as the building's skeleton holds up a cloth-like skin that directs air blown into the branches to a "sky atrium." Once it reaches that point, the air is absorbed by a "fabricated mist."

Once the pollution meets the mist it turns into gray water. The water is directed through a series of filters via structural tubes to a central filtration area. The water is purified in the central filtration chamber. The process results in a distribution for reuse of the clean water throughout the building. The pollutants extracted from the water take the form of dust and are used to create bricks. These bricks are then used as building materials for local infrastructure.

Because the exterior layout of the White Cloud is created individually, according to airflow in each location, the interior cannot be planned until the exterior design is dictated. Once the shape is decided, the interior is laid out with large floor spans being used for communal areas and gardens, and smaller spaces being utilized as residential units. Also housed within the building are healthcare services to address the negative respiratory problems caused by long-term exposure to the pollution that spurred the need for this skyscraper.

NYC BOROUGH NO. 6

JOHN HOUSER

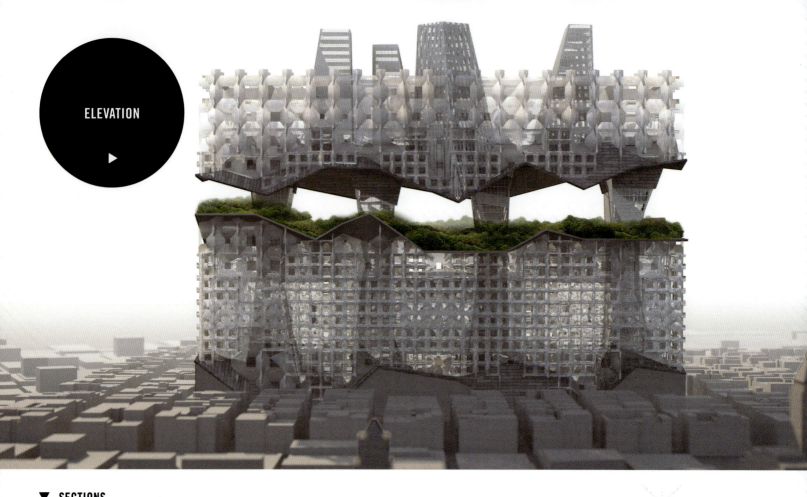

ELEVATION ▶

▼ **SECTIONS**

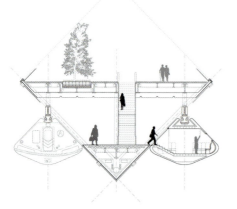
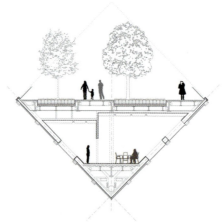
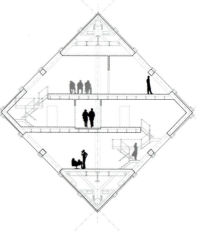

▼ **SITE SECTION**

The "Borough No. 6" project imagines creating a new, autonomous community above Manhattan's Flat Iron District that will serve as New York's newest borough, holding living units, office towers and a grand "high park" from a platform above the blocks between 22nd and 14th Streets and 6th and 7th Avenue.

The structure is a giant grid. Its bottom half, which is developed as residential units, houses a variation of unit types and configurations based off what the grid will allow. Above the residential units there is a giant park, which is the most important part of the structure, the designer says. The public park maintains access to nature for those living in the borough, which is both a necessity and a unique opportunity to escape the city's fast pace while maintaining stunning views of its expanse.

Towering above the park are several large, glass office buildings that serve as offices for residents of the borough.

The building is connected to Manhattan's subway system via a massive expansion in the system's services. The additions allow the trains that service the new borough to travel in all directions, providing access to all of the building's levels. Within the structure itself, pedestrian bridges serve as the main traffic arteries.

By locating the platform above the existing urban fabric of Manhattan, the Borough No. 6 project allows for a maximization of density in an already-crowded landscape.

INTERIOR VIEWS
▶

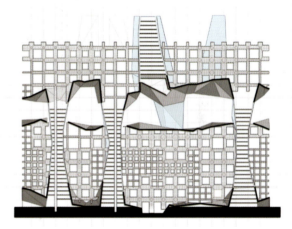

AERIAL VIEW
▼

▼ SECTION

▼ CIRCULATION NODES

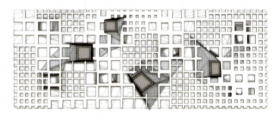

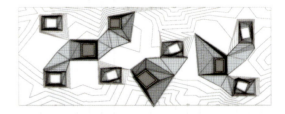

POROUS SKYSCRAPER

GIORGI KHMALADZE

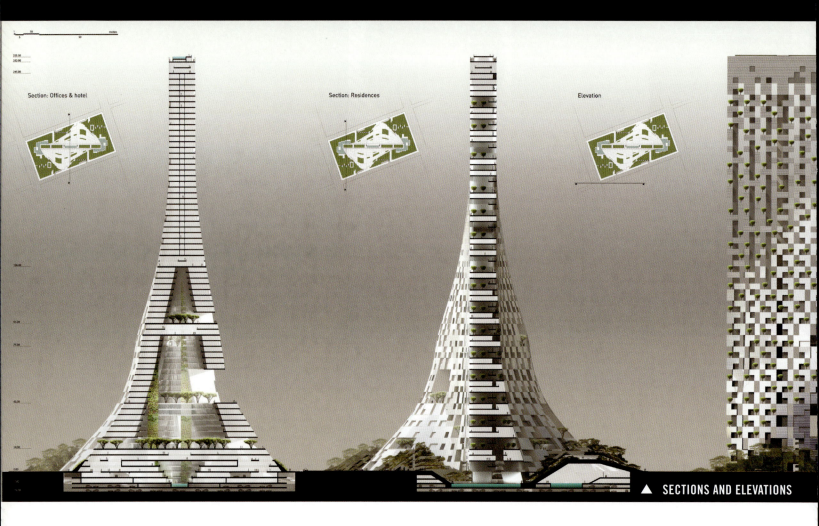

Section: Offices & hotel

Section: Residences

Elevation

▲ **SECTIONS AND ELEVATIONS**

▼ **HOUSING UNITS AGGREGATION**

Unit schemes

Each apartment unit has two floors and occupies space of 10.5 x 16 x 7 meters

STUDIO   1 BEDROOM   2 BEDROOM   3 BEDROOM / LIVE-WORK   LOFT

Building porosity

The tower is porous, which allows the wind to pass through and is expanded towards the base to achieve additional structural stability.

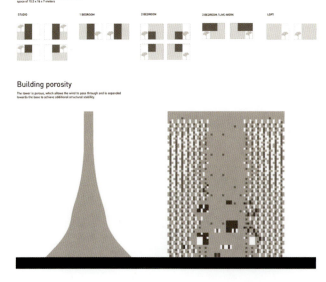

▼ **CONCEPT DIAGRAM**

1 Unit
Each unit consists of living area and private terraced. The shape of each module is determined by the unit type and terrace space. Each unit is equiped with wind turbine to utilize wind power.

2 Unit aggregation
Various unit types aggregate using simple grid. This way, each unit has its own private terace. Both are open towards opposite facades of the building, which makes them perfect for natural ventilation.

3 Building
Free-standing slab, 310 x 160 x 16 m

4 Structural stability
Pull out slab to achieve stability of the structure. This move allows big void for generous atrium.

5 circulation
Corridors and vertical circulation cores.

6 programs
Programs with shared functions connect all distinct programs to one another within entire structure.

7 public & semi-public green spaces
All shared programs house public or semi-public green spaces.

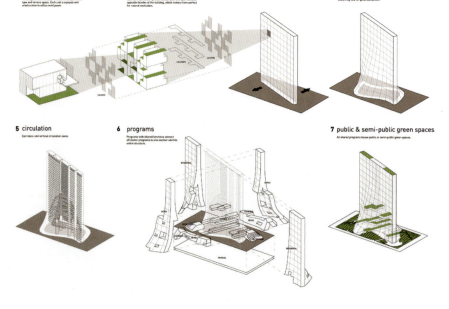

▼ INTERIOR VIEW

▼ INTERIOR VIEW

▼ AERIAL VIEW

New construction is needed on Singapore's water-front, an area that acts as an extension of the existing bustling financial district. However, all new construction should integrate green space because of the city's lack of open land. A special emphasis is placed on the need for buildings that can utilize natural ventilation, collect rainwater and provide shaded, outdoor spaces.

A porous tower that allows wind to pass through for cooling reasons can meet all these demands. The tower, a "free standing slab" structure that is 210 meters wide by 260 meters tall by 16 meters thick, is pulled out on the bottom to provide for extra structural stability. In the void that is created by this bulge, the building's base features a grand atrium. The structure's internal bridges are located in this atrium and provide extra structural support. The atrium also features multiple levels of terraces that are filled with vegetation and provide lush walkways between various shops, restaurants and cafes.

The residential tower also features a rooftop terrace and an outdoor pool and athletic facilities on the ground floor.

Each residential unit, or "villa," has two stories, an open living area, a private terrace, a garden and its own wind turbine for energy generation. Units are amassed using a simple grid layout.

The designer envisions several towers being built using this model type, but each having their own programmatic use. Hotel and office buildings have less pore openings in the middle so that natural ventilation and lighting doesn't interfere with the building's uses. All of the buildings, which will connect to one another, will feature several public and semi-public green spaces.

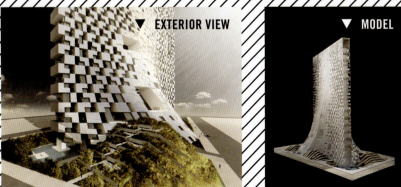
▼ EXTERIOR VIEW   ▼ MODEL

▼ RESIDENTIAL UNIT

Typical 1 bedroom unit

eVolo | Issue 4 | 2012

LUNAR OUTPOST

LUIS QUINONES

UNITED STATES

EXTERIOR VIEW ◀

▼ CONCEPTUAL SECTION

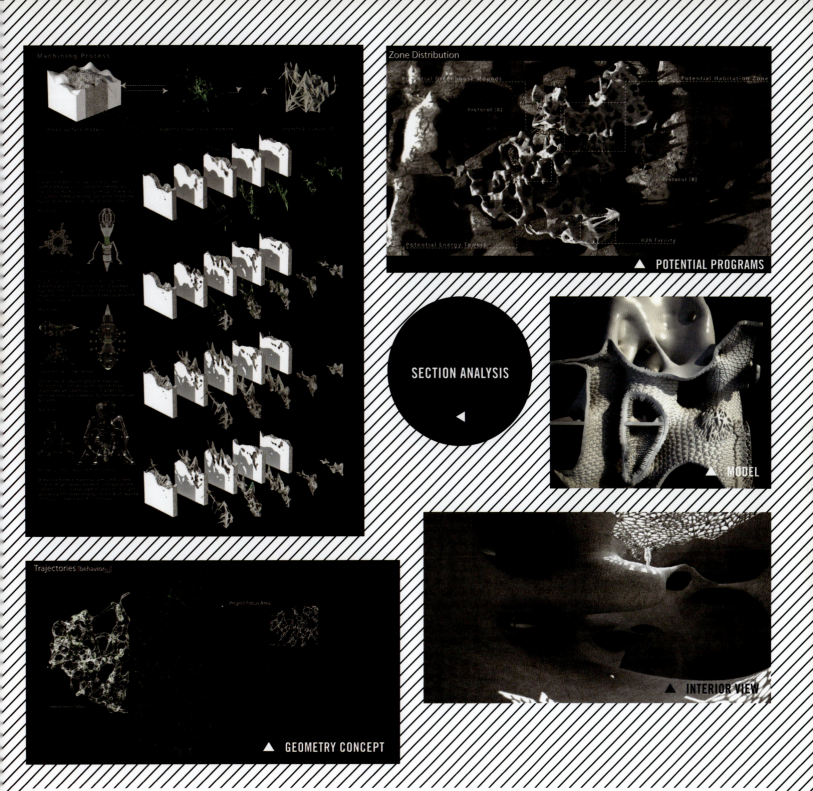

Zone Distribution

Potential Greenhouse Mounds

Potential Habitation Zone

Protocol [B]

Protocol [B]

Potential Energy Towers

H2O Facility

▲ POTENTIAL PROGRAMS

SECTION ANALYSIS ◄

▲ MODEL

▲ INTERIOR VIEW

Trajectories [behavior]

Project Focus Area

▲ GEOMETRY CONCEPT

The "Lunar Outpost" project is a response to fears of overpopulation and resource depletion on planet Earth. Our planet may soon be uninhabitable, the designer poses, and so this project is situated on the Shackleton Crater Rim on the South Pole of the Earth's Moon. While the time span of this project is 60 years, the Lunar Outpost proposal focuses specifically on the first 20 years, when the deployment of robots to the Cabeus Crater facilitates the construction of the structure before humans even arrive.

They are working to construct a colony outpost and research facility. Because of its atmosphere, gravity and other factors, the moon provides an interesting study for architectural creation. It is more conducive to vertical construction because there are not the same limitations that we have on Earth, such as denser gravity, extreme weather conditions, and limited natural resources.

The large traces of frozen water and hydroxyl group (oxygen plus hydrogen) found on the moon by the Chandrayaan Deep Impact Probe in 2008 present interesting possibilities for the use of regenerative fuel cells. Life could be sustained and energy generated by extracting oxygen and hydrogen from the water.

Because of the angle of the Sun, any building on the moon would have to be a skyscraper in order to maximize solar gain. Verticality can also reach underground, in order to protect the buildings from radiation, meteor impacts and temperature differentials.

To construct these structures, robots employ the simple mound building techniques we see in ant or termite colonies. It is through this sort of bottom-up development that a city of contemporary size will one day come to be constructed on this site.

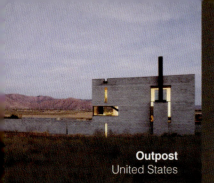
Outpost
United States

De Nieuwe Liefde
Amsterdam, Netherlands

Calabar International Center
Calabar, Nigeria

The Factory
Rives de Seine, France

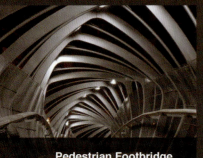
Pedestrian Footbridge
Evry, France

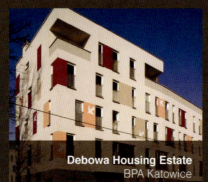
Debowa Housing Estate
BPA Katowice

Bene Flagship Store
Vienna, Austria

House in Vandans
Vandans, Austria

Heathdale House
Toronto, Canada

Bamboo Forest House
Taiwan, China

Tokyo French Embassy
Tokyo, Japan

Boa Nova Church
Estoril, Portugal

Lucke Orozco House
Guadalajara, Mexico

Das Aigner
Ybbsitz, Austria

Zeidler House
Aptos, United States

Fukoku Tower
Osaka, Japan

Marché Lier
Lier, Norway

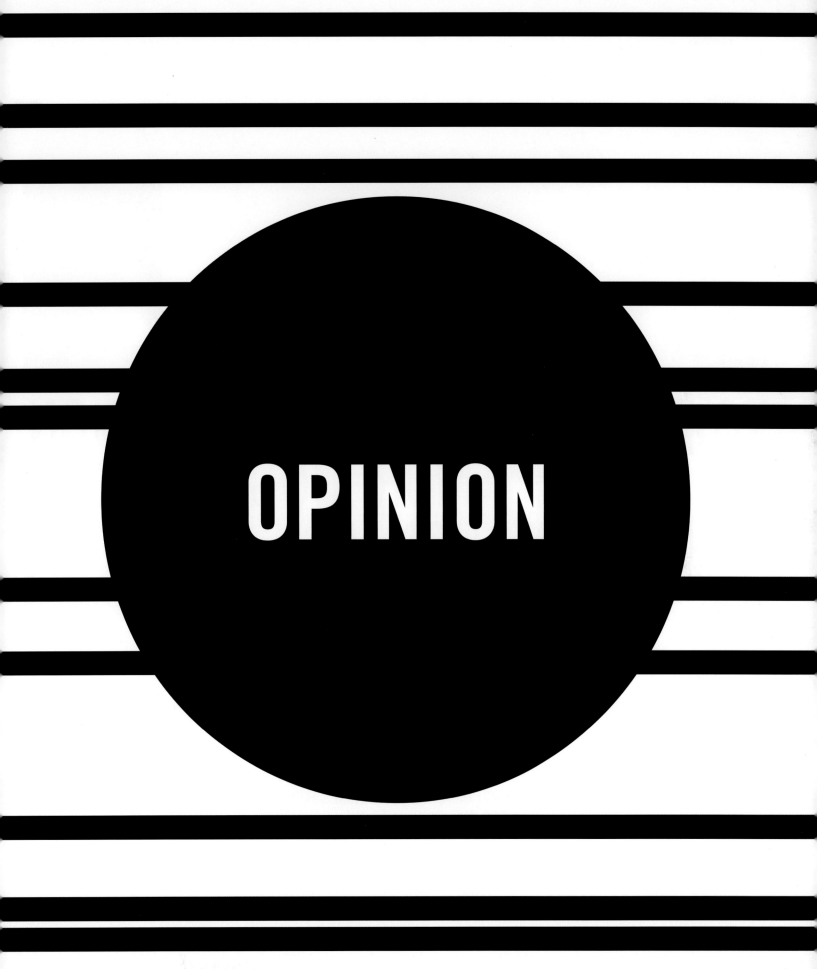

OPINION

eVolo | Issue 4 | 2012

TOWARDS THE EVOLUTION OF MORPHOGENETIC COMPUTATIONAL DESIGN

TEXT AND IMAGES: EMMANUEL RUFFO

THE PRESENT ARTICLE DISCUSSES A POSSIBLE APPROACH FOR THE EVOLUTION OF MORPHOGENETIC COMPUTATIONAL DESIGN. IT PRESENTS A NOVEL UNDERSTANDING OF EMBEDDED STRUCTURAL PATTERN FORMATION. THE FIRST PART OF THE ARTICLE IS FOCUSED ON EXPLAINING DIFFERENT STRATEGIES FOR UNDERSTANDING DIGITAL FORMATION OF PATTERN GENERATIONS, WHILST THE SECOND ONE, DISCUSSES THE PRACTICE OF THE PATTERN FORMATION THROUGH CASE STUDIES THAT EXPLORE DIGITAL EVOLUTION AND ITS PHYSICAL MATTER. THE ONGOING RESEARCH PROJECTS DEAL WITH BOTH THE DIGITAL AND THE PHYSICAL CONSTRUCTION OF NONSTANDARD GEOMETRIES THROUGH THE USE OF SELF-ORGANIZATION PROCESSES AND THE LOGICS OF MORPHOGENESIS. THIS LATTER BECOMES SIGNIFICANT WHEN IT TURNS AND SIMPLIFIES THE LOGICS EMBEDDED IN NATURAL SYSTEMS INTO SINGLE MULTI-PERFORMATIVE MACHINES THAT MIGHT INTEGRATE A SERIES OF POSSIBLE 'BEHAVIOURS' IN RELATION TO THE UNCERTAINTIES OF THE PHYSICAL ENVIRONMENT. THE LOGICS OF THE PRESENT RESEARCH IS TO PROVIDE AN ATTITUDE TOWARDS THE INTEGRATION OF CURRENT AND NOVEL FABRICATION TECHNOLOGIES, BUILDING SHAPE, GEOMETRICAL, PHYSICAL AND COMPUTATIONAL CONSTRAINTS INTO A MAJOR MULTIDISCIPLINARY COLLABORATION FOR THE DESIGN OUTSET IN ORDER TO FORMULATE A CORE BASIS FOR THE EDUCATION OF DESIGN AND THE PRACTICE OF COMPUTATIONAL MORPHOGENESIS.

NATURAL SYSTEMS AND OPTIMISATION

Natural Systems inherently build a relationship between structure, form and performance, which consequently produces evolutionary adaptive and topological forms. These forms are fundamentally governed by material logics that are ultimately shaped by the evolutionary transformations and conditions of the environment. The hierarchical division and organization between material, geometry and structural conditions is a human concern, whilst in natural systems these conditions are integrated in order to emerge 'new permutations' determined by the behaviour of a system. Natural systems automatically negotiate among the boundaries of these conditions in order to self-organize its components and find out the most appropriate permutation for environmental requirements i.e. the principles of optimization. For instance, a natural system might select to self-organize its material properties on top of the other conditions in order to increase the thickness of a determined animal' skin for embracing weather conditions. In another stage of the life cycle of the same animal, for instance, the geometrical and structural properties of its body might be developed further in order for that animal to reach other animals for feeding himself or help to track in faster speed long distances.

These examples highlight that the interplay between material, geometry and structure has the capacity to be organized differently i.e. into a 'new pattern', and also, this 'new permutation or pattern,' has the fundamental task to preserve the integration of the logics that govern the overall system. Over and over again, a natural system may search for the most appropriate pattern in order to adapt to new phenomena: changes in colour, shape, geometry, material and structure, will keep morphing into new permutations and forms in order to generate self-adaptation and self-evolutionary systems, giving rise to diversity and to a series of beautiful patterns.

PATTERN FORMATION, SELF-ORGANIZATION AND MORPHOGENESIS

Patterns describe a particular state in the evolution of a system. Even though sometimes we might need advanced technology for visualizing and studying patterns, these are always there. Patterns, as seen by Andrea Sella (2010), are everywhere; they are just waiting to happen. Everything, any process, any material, any object, any system, any circumstance rationally or incidentally developed, conceived or formed by any means describe the evolution of pattern formation.

The science of pattern formation deals with the visible orderly outcomes of self-organization and the common principles behind similar patterns and deals with the generation of complex organizations of cell outcome in space and time. The understanding of a shape, more precisely its morphology, almost always requires us to understand the process of its formation, namely its *morphogenesis*. Pattern formation often implies a selection mechanism, whose criteria must be determined. In other words, self-assembling refers to processes leading to equilibrium structures, while self-organization processes refers to far from equilibrium pattern formation [1].

Self-organization is one of the most well known examples of pattern formation and overall it is a central process that unfolds the basis for morphogenesis. In an essay published in 1790, Johann Wolfgang von Goethe coined the word 'morphology'. In that paper he proposed a bold unifying hypothesis, according to which most of the main plant forms had evolved from one archetypal plant (Urpflanze). Goethe foreshadowed the work of the founder of morphogenesis, D'Arcy Thompson [2]. Morphogenesis is defined as a biological process that deals with the development of a shape and controls the organized spatial distribution of cells during the embryonic process. It is one of the three fundamental aspects of developmental biology along with the control of cell growth and cellular differentiation [i].

In 1952 with the release of the paper 'The Chemical Basis of *Morphogenesis*' [3], the English mathematician Alan Turing not only discussed the possible behaviour of morphogens - chemical particles phenomena- but also he described a series of phenomena that eventually originated, among these, the basis for *self-organization, emergence and pattern-recognizing* behaviours. The mechanism described on that astonishing paper focused on explaining the behaviour of those morphogens through periods of time. Aside from being one of the earliest examples in cross-multidisciplinary analysis, biology through mathematics, the core interest of Turing's experiments was based on the importance of pattern differentiation [ii, 4].

INTELLIGENCE IN COMPUTATIONAL MORPHOGENESIS

In architectural design, on the other hand, there are a few strategies on how to use natural systems into design buildings. According to Julian Vincent [2009], in architecture there are mainly three forms for applying patterns into buildings design: by copying a form from nature, by searching for a form, namely form finding, and by extracting the logics of natural forms —mainly used for processes of engineering optimization [5].

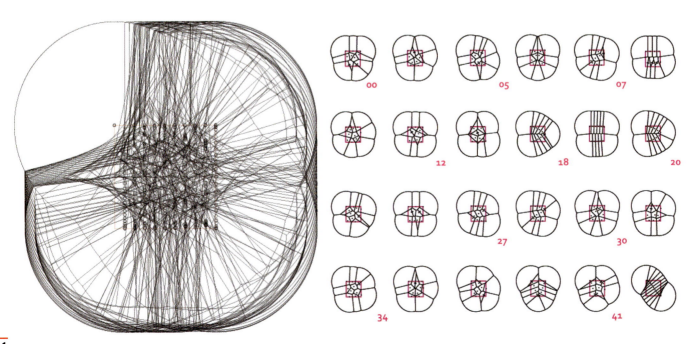

Fig. 1

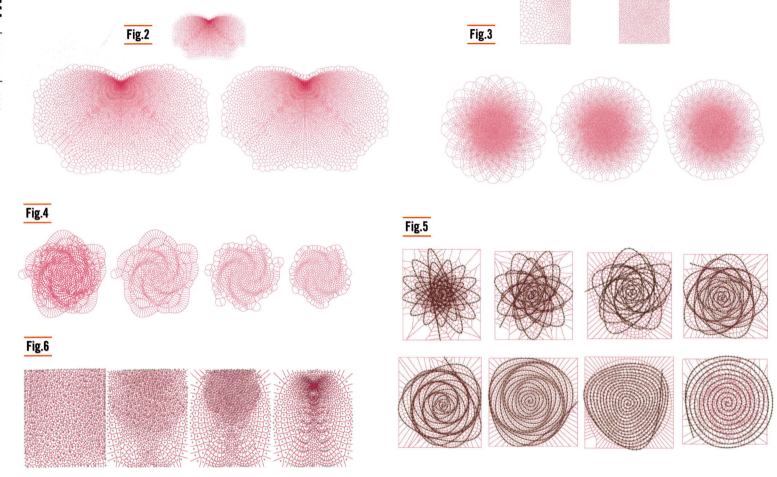

Fig.2

Fig.3

Fig.4

Fig.5

Fig.6

Fig.7

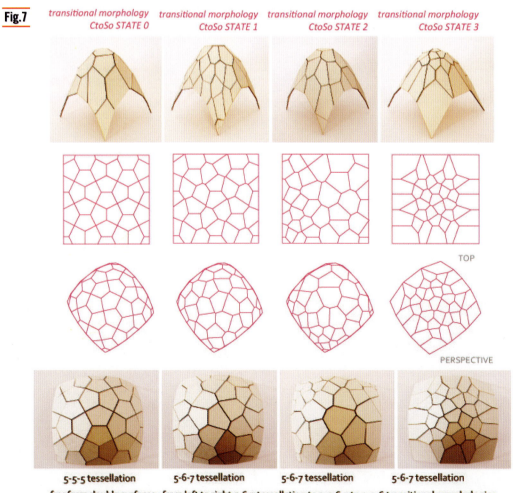

transitional morphology CtoSo STATE 0   *transitional morphology CtoSo STATE 1*   *transitional morphology CtoSo STATE 2*   *transitional morphology CtoSo STATE 3*

TOP

PERSPECTIVE

5-5-5 tessellation   5-6-7 tessellation   5-6-7 tessellation   5-6-7 tessellation

freeform double surfaces : from left to right 5-6-7 tessellation to 3-5-6-7 to 4-5-6 transitional morphologies

Our interests are central to processes of form finding and on those understanding the logics behind a natural system in the first place. As explained and featured by different architectural researchers and theoreticians [6, 7, 8] a morphogenetic process must be one that integrates different parameters as correlated functions and in relation to the physical environment. However, as discussed before, natural systems behave as a continuous process of adaptation and of regulation of negotiations [iii]. In other words, there is an enclosed condition that helps to evolve a system in response to the environmental conditions and thus allow creating evolution. This latter process must be seen as 'natural intelligence'.

Intelligence, in the investigations presented here, is not only understood as a feedback loop or a series of processes that identify and regulate different states for equilibrium, which is the central process for any parametric and associative design. Our investigations go beyond this latter approach, since intelligence here is seen as a series of logical processes that ultimately will form specific behaviours for self-recognizing and self-controlling an overall system in relation to the uncertainties of the environment. This process is called machine learning, a branch of the artificial intelligence field.

Similar to the *Machine Learning* [iv] paradigm, our interest lies on generating systems that allow us to evolve behaviours through learning processes. If a system is capable of 'learning' then it can take advantage of the generated information [v] in order to preserve certain features of interest of their unknown underlying probability distribution. A fundamental focus of machine learning research is to automatically learn to recognize complex patterns and make intelligent decisions based on information. Complex patterns are those arranged out of components that are different to one another.

In the following we will illustrate a few projects that surface on the fundamental basis of morphogenetic computational design and moreover they propose a synthesis in which *Machine Learning Systems* might be of particular interest.

LOGICS GOVERNING PATTERN FORMATION IN PRACTICE

In this project we are coupling different logics of 'pattern formation' in order to integrate advanced structural formations, building conditions and aesthetical design permutations. Figure 1 demonstrates very basic but substantial Voronoi dia-

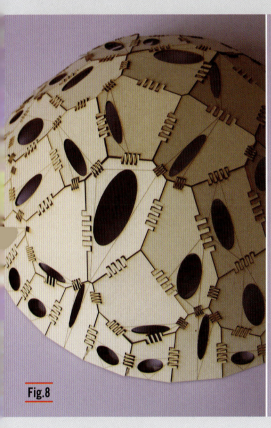  

Fig.8

grams' relationships for pattern formation based on U-V elements —system 'vd-csA'. These individual formations could be extended indefinitely in order, for example, to envelope a standard or nonstandard surface. This particular diagram has been generated using mathematical algorithms but if the control of the system needs to go beyond the basic surface of particular diagrams, we need to employ distinct but integrative logical rules. Figure 2, 3 and 4 were organized and consequently designed using self-organizing components —system 'so-cpB'.

There are two core differences between the logics behind the system 'vd-csA' and system 'so-cpB'. The first lies in the logics governing the spatial relationships, whilst in the vd-csA system all is organized following UV rules (horizontal and vertical organizations), the second system employs a series of Fibonacci numbers for the formation of the pattern. According to Leach (2009) 'formation', here, must be recognized as being linked to the terms 'information' and 'performance' over time. In figure 4, we organize the 'logics of the system' in a different way producing a completely new behaviour ending up in indefinite permutations [vi]. The second difference is that we employ 4D self-organizing techniques for understanding the topological behaviour. In this particular case, our interest is to avoid topological formations based on triangular or quadrilateral polygons since the system need to form vertices where only three polygonal elements meet. This is a major issue that might be useful for different engineering rationalizations [see 'intelligent flat entities'

project].

If we go back to the formation of the logics in the first place we, then, can interpret the rules and needs that a system might be able to embed. Figure 5 demonstrates eight steps from a series of an individual system that by negotiating between digital geometries and digital tectonics [8] is capable to generate a spectacular example of what we mean by learning systems. Thus, similar to 'convergent evolution phenomena' [vii], figure 6, unfolds and reverts on one single system the logics governing both UV conditions and Fibonacci numbers.

Whilst in the previous project our intention was to clarify, enhance and demonstrate the importance of the organization and construction of the logics governing morphogenesis, pattern

Fig.9

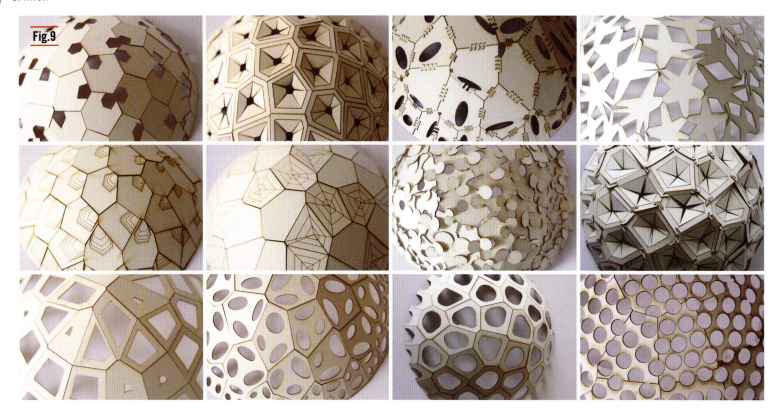

formation and self-organizing systems, in the following project ´Intelligent Flat Entities´ our intention is to provide novel information about how a simple and complex mathematical issue might raise the opportunity to explore computational entities in order to develop one unique behaviour: flatness.

TOWARDS INTELLIGENT FLAT ENTITIES [viii]

Most of the projects governing the digital era in architectural design focus on writing or assembling rules that generate a whole system capable of performing single or multiple tasks, which are, in the best scenario, related to the environment. However, these algorithms or systems whilst being able to self-recognition are not able to learn. Learning is a process that develops over time and in this way 'experience' emerges. Machine learning is an algorithmic process that computers use in order to automate and optimize certain skills over time. In other words, the features that result from the interaction of the logics of a system with the environment during time is the evolution of its behaviour, which is no longer controlled by the initial set of data but by the data they collect throughout time.

Since the beginning of the 90's and moreover since the beginning of this decade, different research groups have been trying to solve a major mathematical and geometrical issue [9,10,11]. While some of these proposals are based on tangent plane elements, some others apply advanced algorithms

Fig.11

Fig.10

eVolo | Issue 4 | 2012

to optimize sequentially a 'possible solution'. Both cases search for a final static solution that approximates, in the first place, the desired building shape i.e. a top-down process. The project discussed here goes beyond these possibilities. On the one hand we know that the geometrical, material and building constraints play a fundamental role that might be solved mathematically while on the other one, the logics governing all of them are no longer materializing mathematical [ix] possibilities, but the physical entities that govern the environment [x].

Figure 7 enhance two possibilities that could be solved by employing learning systems. The first one is that the so-called 'Cairo tessellation' is difficult to aim in arbitrary 3D surfaces enveloped out of flat panels. A series of empirical data was transformed over time in order to perform this optimization. The second possibility, which is inherently part of the tilling issues, is that when four panels in a 3D environment meet might cause building construction and assembling issues. For solving this latter issue we 'educate' our system to recognize when four or more panels meet in one point and solve these situations with a different permutation, which eventually meet aesthetical and structural conditions.

A similar example is the one shown in images 8, 9, 10 and 11 [xi]. These images are part of a series of projects of a workshop entitled *Morphogenetic Computational Geometry* led by the author and developed at the Institute for Architecture and Media in Graz Austria. These projects try to answer a very simple question: how to design and control differentiation?

The *Morphogenetic Computational Geometry* workshop focused on three different but integrated conditions. The first condition was to design a pattern that could envelope and control the flat ornaments on a double curved surface [Fig. 8]. The second condition was that the resultant pattern should keep a close relationship with both the self-supporting structure and the geometrical rules governing the surface [Fig. 8-9]. A third condition was to design a joint and assembling system based on the two preliminary conditions [Fig.10]. Eventually, during the four days workshop, the participants went back and forth with the negotiations between the boundaries of design, pattern formation, geometry, shape building, fabrication and assembling techniques [Fig. 10-11]. For us, it was of particular interest to deal with ancient assembling techniques and mixed them with the advanced computational and fabrication technologies [Fig. 10-11]. The rules governing the design strategies have a logic that could be employed on different situations and indefinitely. The logics behind the structural formations of the output forms are of particular interest since they could be replicated for both standard and nonstandard constructions. This latter feature enclose a complex logic that needs to be thought over and over again in order to find out a simple rather elegant formula that governs complexity commonly similar to that hidden in 'natural systems'.

SEARCHING FOR THE LOGICS GOVERNING A SYSTEM

Previously, we discussed how simple rules might be able to output complex formations. We discussed and exemplified the importance of the relationship between behaviour and environment. Moreover, based on machine learning systems, we propose a way on how the computational morphogenesis paradigm might evolve.

Our interest to look at natural systems emerges from the understanding that different systems could 'naturally' couple to replicate evolution. Computing systems might be able to multi-perform advanced skills in response to the physical environment. For doing so, we have to understand the logics that design and spatial relationships involve, and the mathematical logics governing these relationships in order to behave accordingly to the environment.

Computation has moved from being a mere representative tool to means where ideas could be further and indefinite explored. New knowledge produces new configurations of patterns in our brains, but also enhances cognition for designing and generating creativity. At the end of this proposal a question emerges: how and when are we seeing this 'learning systems' evolving as chemical entities of material permutations responding to the changing environment?

----

[i] See http://www.sciencedaily.com/articles/m/morphogenesis.htm

[ii] Eventually it was proved that the underlying organization of the morphogens was not only the intelligence of the particles themselves but also the climatic circumstances that eventually originated a change of form, position and overall beautiful patterns that were produced through temperature variations.

[iii] These adaptations and negotiations are and must be developed in relation to the environment. Environment is the one that originates the formation of the physical features of a system whether is physical or digital, but these adaptations as well, at least in natural systems, must be seen as intelligent systems.

[iv] Machine Learning is a branch of Artificial Intelligence, is a scientific discipline concerned with the design and development of algorithms that allow computers to evolve behaviours based on empirical data.

[v] Information, in this scenario, is understood as as 'prototypes of data' that demonstrate the underlying relationships among observed variables.

[vi] This particular diagram has been organised and design-using Grasshopper developed by David Rutten and Kangaroo developed by Daniel Piker. Both software-tools are functional under the Rhinoceros environment.

[vii] See http://www.biology-online.org/dictionary/Convergent_evolution or http://bioweb.cs.earlham.edu/9-12/evolution/HTML/converge.html

[viii] This is an ongoing research develop at the Institute of Architecture and Media of the Graz University of Technology.

[ix] Mathematics here is understood as a language for communication but also logics might be understood similarly.

[x] This is already leading some of the most astonishing fields such as, among others, knowledge discovery.

[xii] These projects were designed by Markus Bartaky, Marco Baumgartner, Michael Deutsch,

Maria Fellinger, Melanie Glatz, Mario Harin, Claudia M. Hoehenberger, Martina Karner, Olivia Killian, Stefan Kropsch, Christopher Leitner, George Nikolov, Thomas Ochensberger, Helmut Pessl, Stephanie Posch, Matthias Prosekar, Johanna Regger, Johannes M. Ruderer, Christina Tammerl and Judith Willnauer at the Morphogenetic Computational Geometry workshop led by Emmanuel Ruffo and assisted by Georg Fassl during the summer semester 2011 at the Graz University of Technology in Austria.

----

1. Lesne A. and Bourgine P. (2011). 'Morphogenesis: Origins of Patterns and Shapes'. Springer, Berlin pp. 1-6.

2. Idem, pp. 295.

3. Turing A.M. (1952). 'The Chemical Basis of Morphogenesis'. Phil. Trans. R. Soc. London B237.

4. Ruffo Calderon E. (2011). 'Towards Differentiation for Enhancing Architectural Design'. Design Principles and Practices. Conference Proceedings, Rome.

5. Vincent J. (2009). 'Biomimetic Patterns in Architectural Design'. AD Wiley Academy London, pp.74-81.

6. Hensel M., Menges A. and Weinstock M. (2006). Emergence: Techniques and Technologies in Morphogenetic Design. AD Wiley Academy, London.

7. Leach N. (2009). 'Digital Morphogenesis'in Theoretical Meltdown. AD Wiley Academy, London, pp. 32-37.

8. Oxman R. (2009). 'Digital Tectonic as a Morphogenetic Process'. Proceedings of the International Association for Shell and Spatial Structures (IAAS), Valencia.

9. Hansen K. F. (1993). A method for faceting double curved surfaces. International, Journal of Space Structures, 34(3).

10. Pottmann H., Asperl A., Hofer M., and Killian A. (2007). Architectural Geometry, Bentley Institute Press, Exton, Pennsylvania.

11. Bagger A. (2010). Plate Shell Structures of Glass. Studies leading to guidelines for structural design. PhD Thesis. Department of Civil Engineering. Technical University of Denmark.

Emmanuel Ruffo (Mexico City, 1978) is the founder of Rethinking Architecture and Rethinking Academic Series. He is an educator and a scientific researcher focused on 'morphogenetic computational design', 'pattern formation and mathematical form finding', 'design strategies and innovation in fabrication techniques and technologies' and in 'theory of self-organization, evolutionary and machine learning systems'.

Currently he is a researcher based at the Graz University of Technology supported by the FWF Austrian Science Fund. He is a lecturer on "Digital Processes and Embodied Design" and on "Morphogenetic Computational Design" at the Institute for Architecture and Media. He is a scientific advisor at the International CAAD Futures, CAADRIA, SiGraDi and Design Principles and Practices conferences.

Formerly he was Professor of Digital Technologies and Environmental Design at the School of Architecture Anahuac, in Mexico City, where he co-founded the Laboratory for Digital Fabrication. He has collaborated with Mangera Yvars LLP Architects in London UK; M Fuksas D in Rome, Italy; Cloud 9 and Hybrid_A Studio in Barcelona and with MAD Design in Beijing China. He has received awards in different scenarios. His research, projects and articles have been published in scientific proceedings, newspapers, books and magazines and on international exhibitions. He has delivered lectures and public presentations in Asia, America and Europe. research@emmanuelruffo.com

O' MIGHTY GREEN

BY BEATRIZ RAMO – STAR STRATEGIES + ARCHITECTURE

0. INTRODUCTION

Sustainability currently shares many qualities with God; *supreme concept, omnipotent, omnipresent, and omniscient; creator and judge, protector, and (...) saviour of the universe and the humanity*. And, like God, it has millions of believers. Since we humans are relatively simpleminded and suspicious and need evidence before belief can become conviction, *Green* has come to represent sustainability; has become its incarnation in the human world. But sustainability, like God, might not have a form, nor a colour…

1. EMANCIPATION

1.1 The word *Sustainability* has been raped, abused, and insulted by architects, politicians, advertisers …in essence, by everybody. The musical harmony in the perfect trio - the social, the environmental, and the economic - is eclipsed by a simplistic solo performance of the environmental, entitled *the Green*.

1.2 In a desperate attempt to give shape to an all-encompassing ideology the *Green* proves to work as the quickest and easiest representation of sustainability. The *Green* is the only symbol able to keep pace with today's lack of patience and hunger for images; a Lady Gaga-Sustainability: effective, noticeable, creative, sensationalist. In a persistent effort to become the allegory of Sustainability, *Green* has been emancipated as its caricature.

1.3 The simplification of the initial idea is so extreme that *Green* does not even need to be nature, or natural, it may just as well be plastic and painted. Look around… you'll see a *green* facade, *green* embellishments, walls painted *green*, a *green* McDonald's sign, a *green* website, a *green* papier-mâché shop window; the *Green* City is here.

2. FUNCTION

2.1 If the Iconic buildings simply needed to be iconic, the *Green* buildings simply need to be *green*. The situation could not get more superficial: *Green* as a function. *Green* allows sustainability to be bought per m2, or to be painted on, or glued on. Sustainability is a Photoshop filter in CS6: Ctrl+*Green*.
Similar to the Icons, the *Green* is also providing identity, *generic* identity.

2.2 Although the thought initially came with the best of intentions, as every good idea these days, it needed to be simplified by a factor of a hundred to be stripped of any meaning in order to be successfully commercialized. Only then could it

eVolo

Issue 4

2012

Eco-Pantheon, Rome 126AD / © STAR 2011

be digested by *the masses*. Somehow it looks very democratic… Just as a fake Prada bag allows every woman to feel the sensation of *Prada* and carry its status.

2.3 The repeated-until-it-hurts pretext that *at least people are aware of sustainability* had an effect; but the attention was diverted from the main concern. People are more likely to buy *Green* products, juries in competitions are delighted by *Green* epic stories, and politicians know that playing the *Green* card is always safe; impeccable demagogy.

2.4 If all the visions for city design and all the architecture competitions won with the powers of *Green* were realized the city would be turned into

a sophisticated version of the current Chernobyl Alienation Zone (See Pripyat in spring).

2.5 *Green* walls are being commercialized as interior space dividers too. They are made of Norwegian reindeer moss (the stuff for the trees in model train sets) as a huge cemetery of nature, *with excellent natural acoustics*. These dust collectors can be produced in 20 different colours; a white *Green* Wall, a red *Green* Wall, a violet *Green* Wall, to match with the other decorations.

3. STYLE

3.1   Modernism,   Postmodernism,

Eco-friendly Villa La Rotonda, Vicenza – Palladio, 1566 / © STAR 2011

Deconstructivism… We have now definitely entered Sustainabilism. Unlike in previous movements every architect can be a Sustainabilist: whether avant-garde, commercial, young, established… It can be even combined with other styles: Eco-Deconstructivism, *Green* Postmodernism… It is *the* democratic style. Architectural magazines and commercial brochures found a common language: the *Green*. *Green* is also the point on which the architect, the client, the developer, the politician, and the user agree. It is fantastic. *Green* flattens out the differences; it is the saviour of the Tower of Babel; we will finally reach the Heavens. For the first time ever we have a genuine International Style; from Madrid to Copenhagen, to Dallas, to Istanbul. The *Green* is so superior that it works everywhere; it is the wining style, the global victor - though this could make it terribly unsustainable. Unlike other styles - imagine an entire city planned on Deconstructivism - it is possible to have an entire city built on *Green*. It can be implemented everywhere and on every scale; a skyscraper or a small private house, even an interior space - all is possible. It can accommodate any taste: *Green* can be applied and treated as a hairstyle: long and fluffy, thick and compact, partly shaved creating ornaments.

3.2 *Green* buildings can be *Ducks* or *Decorated sheds*, and there are some interesting cases of being both at the same time: the *Decorated Ducks*.

3.3 *Green* should be added as the sixth principle to Le Corbusier's five points, and as the fourth quality to Vitruvius' triad: Venustas, Utilitas, Firmitas and *Sustinebilitas*

3.4 *The built … product of* Sustainability *is not* sustainable *architecture but Green. Green is what remains after* Sustainability *has run its course or, more precisely, what coagulates while* Sustainability *is in progress, its fallout…* [1]

3.5 *Green* is the new Black.

4. RELIGION

4.1 *Green* works as faith. The Catholic Church will need to add Saint *Green* to its Roman Calendar. Saint *Green* will watch over the sustainable architects, and will guide them in the *green* direction. If we pray to him every day Saint *Green* will compensate our veneration: politicians obtain more votes, architects win more competitions, and companies sell more products…

4.2 *Green* works in mysterious ways…Architects who are not really sustainable call themselves *Green*, while the architects that seriously care don't like to be called *Green*.

4.3 *Oh Lord, blessed be the Daltonics who will see more green than others… and help those who see Red where there is Green.*

4.4 *Green* works as confession. The guiltier we feel, the *greener* we try. The *green*-looking is usually indirectly proportional to its sustainability achievements. *Green* has the capacity of reducing

Eco-friendly Villa Savoya, Poissy – Le Corbusier, 1929 / © STAR 2011

all that matters to one single problem, and one single solution: *Green*. *Green* is able to absolve all our sins.

4.5 *Green* is double-miraculous. As if trying to heal cancer with aspirins, *Green* is the phenomenal formula that turns sustainable everything that it touches. It can also hide graceless designs. 'When all candles be out, all cats be gray'. Ugly *Green* buildings are more readily accepted than ugly buildings.

4.6 *Green* is able to enlighten us retroactively. We architects rewrite our full history according to sustainability; what we did once with *common sense*, we now brand as sustainable; back then, we were already unconsciously under the influence of *Green*…as real visionaries.

5. AMBIGUITY

5.1 But the *Green* also hides a perverse dimension… As in a David Lynch movie; everything appears to be calm and harmonious but there is something disturbing… rotting… The *Green* is the common lie, the secret consensus, the perfect crime; everybody knows that it cannot be that good, that it cannot be that easy, but why bother? It sells, and there is enough *Green* for everybody. A new kind of (friendly) intimidation: *Green* terrorism.

5.2 *Green* suffers from split personalities; *Green* gurus, *Green* followers, *Green* saviours…. preaching contradictory statements. But this seems not to be

Il Monumento Continuo e Sostenibile, NewYork / © Original Superstudio, courtesy of Adolfo Natalini

Berlin Eco-Wall, 1989 / © STAR 2011

Sustainable Catholicism.
Green Crucifixion (Corpus Hypercubus,
Dali 1954 / © STAR 2011

a problem, as long as it is *Green*, because everybody likes - *has to like* - *Green*. If not, he is considered a horrible human being. The exponential need for public approval makes *Green* the instrument par excellence. Green: *I Like*.

5.3 The Microsoft dictionary for Word in Spanish offers the following synonyms for *Green*: Obscene, indecent, improper, dishonest, free, and gross. In English, apart from those referring to the colour, it offers: immature and inexpert.

5.4 Here we are now, entertainers.

---

6. APPENDIX

The relation between some architects and *Green* reminds us of the "discovery" of the Americas, not only was the "New World" always there; but these architects will remain as happily mistaken as Christopher Columbus was… convinced that he had landed in the East Indies.

(1) Taken from Rem Koolhaas text: *Junkspace,* and substituting: *Modernity* for *Sustainability* and *Junkspace* for *Green*

PARABLE

A long time ago in a not so faraway land, a deep economic crisis and a need for identity accelerated the creation of the *Green City*. In the *Green City* all companies changed their logos to *Green* or to vegetable motives. They only provided *green* products and eco-friendly services. Its inhabitants lived in healthy competition with one another to be the *green*est of them all. In the *Green* City,

Nuclear Power Plants were eco-friendly. Black and white movies were *green* too. In the *Green City* the powers of *Green* were so strong that they could alleviate the shame of the past: concentration camps, Berlin walls…, any moment of history could become sustainable retroactively. *Green* acquired confessional status and could absolve any sins. In the *Green City* military uniforms were the ultimate fashion, the Hulk was a superhero, and Chernobyl's Zone the most booked *green* holiday destination. Architects were overexcited in their use of the *Green*. Facades, roofs, partition walls… everything that could be clad, was clad by *Green*. But behind the scenes the *Green* Bubble was growing out of control… Nobody dared to mention it and in an attack of greed, fearing the end of this cash cow, they started using *Green* psychotically. The *Green City* turned into a seemingly boundless golf course. The confusion was colossal and in a Saturnial act the *Green City* started devouring its inhabitants. But then, and only at that point, a second Age of Enlightenment began to flourish… The surviving inhabitants slowly awakened and did no longer need to see the *Green* to believe in Sustainability - as they did not need to see the pillars to believe in structural stability - and the *Green City* began to fade away slowly…The *Green* mucus was cleaned away, the *Green* parties were obsolete and McDonald's became red again.

The Sleep of Reason Produces Monsters, very *Green* Hairy Monsters.

Beatriz Ramo (1979, Spain) graduated from the Technical School of Architecture in Valencia – ETSAV, in Spain. In 2002 she received a scholarship to study at the Technische Universiteit in Eindhoven, moving to the Netherlands, where she has lived ever since. During 2003 and 2004 Beatriz Ramo worked at the Office for Metropolitan Architecture (OMA) in Rotterdam. In 2006 she founded STAR strategies + architecture in Rotterdam. STAR is a practice dealing with architecture in all its forms. STAR is interested in all topics directly or indirectly related to architecture, working on projects and doing research in the fields of architecture, urbanism, and landscape design. Since 2007 Beatriz Ramo is teaching at the Academy of Architecture in Tilburg where she ran a research/design studio in the framework of Architecture and Market, and a research/criticism studio called God Save Architecture

FIRST TRUE ZERO-ENERGY BUILDING – GLOBAL HEALTH COMMUNITY

DR. EUGENE TSSUI

Just as the United States was the first country to set a man on the moon by the end of the 1960's, so it is that China, in 2012, may be the first country to research, design, and construct the first true zero electricity for heating, ventilation, and air conditioning (HVAC systems), housing complex in the world. The feat may not seem as colossal as placing a man on the moon but, in ecological terms, it is nearly as unbelievable. We've heard of "zero energy" before, but, in truth, that only meant offsetting electricity use by "alternative" technologies such as windmills, PV solar panels, and geo-thermal systems to name a few. But, in this case, zero energy really means, no energy consumption at all for internal heating, cooling and ventilation. The project designed for 3500 inhabitants is called, the Global Health Community, encompasses five million square feet and it is 100 feet below ground.

Taking up one square kilometer of land, this radically innovative habitat was first conceived in 2009 and went through nearly 40 scenarios of laboratory testing and analysis at the State Key Laboratory for Sub-Tropical Building Science (a national laboratory) at South China University of Science and Technology in Guangzhou, China. Their goal was to create a comfortable habitat for living that uses completely passive HVAC systems for environmental control. Instead the building uses a 6-foot thick ceiling of safety glass and vacuum-sealed space for natural lighting and insulation.

Up to now, "zero energy" has denoted offsetting mechanical/electricity use by photovoltaic solar panels, windmills, geo-thermal, water currents or some other electricity producing "green" method[1]. "Zero-energy " isn't really zero energy. It is a euphemism promoted by "green" move-

ment zealots. Electricity is still required. But China is preparing to construct the real thing: A multi family, health oriented apartment complex for 3500 inhabitants that will be built in one of the most challenging of climates; hot, muggy, mosquito laden, Guangzhou, China [2].

Globally, up to 40% of all environmental pollution is caused by buildings [3] due to the manufacturing of construction materials and the coal burning-to-electricity needed to push cold or hot air through them. A building is a constant source of energy consumption just to create a comfortable habitat in an otherwise bothersome natural environment.

At current rates of air pollution and resultant sea water pollution (acidification of the oceans through polluted air), the oceans will cease to sustain life within 40 years and respiratory disease and deaths will continue to accelerate annually

Aerial View

African Termite Mound

(UN Global Warming Report, January 25, 2010). We must find ways to stop this progressive increase of environmental pollution.

How could we design a zero-energy environment? When achieving the impossible, nature seems to be a good source of reference. Recall the "impossibility" of bumblebee flight [4]; the impossibility of organisms surviving in boiling temperature sea-water (Thermophile Bacteria) or the impossibility of organisms surviving in outer space (the Tardigrade) [5]. The guiding model, for this project in China, is the Termite's nest of central Africa; located in a hot, humid climate with an easily reachable underground water table, very similar to the climate and geology of southern China and the city of Guangzhou.

The African Termite's nest stands some 7 to 8 meters tall, with a 3 meter wide base. If the 1.5 million termites that inhabit this fortress were enlarged to the size of human beings, the nest structure would proportionately rise one mile high. Their main building material is water, dirt, saliva, and mud [6]. Inside, the temperature is between 18 to 31 degrees Celsius, depending on outdoor temperatures. Termites are blind so the interior environment is totally sealed and dark [7].

How do termites then breathe in such an enclosed structure? The simplest way to describe it is to understand the termite's nest and mound structures as a living, breathing organism. It works similarly to the human lungs. The entire nest is an intersecting network of hollow channels, like the Trachea, bronchi, bronchioles, alveolar ducts and alveoli of our human lungs. The termites themselves are the final gas exchanging mechanism in this finely tuned breathing apparatus. The upper part of the nest "inhales" air to mix internally with the underground, cooler air, to create a sloshing layer of motion that has been described as the "Pendeluft" effect. This gas exchange process causes an actual expansion and contraction of the nest [8]. There is a measurable resonant motion in the nest at 10-20 hertz/second creating a pulsing effect that also promotes gas exchange. The high frequency air is at the nest's upper portion and the lower frequency is at the lower portion. The mound surface is porous and produces a kind of oscillating current leading to a behavior of impedance where the air and water molecules combine creating an oscillation process. Termites themselves account for about 15% of the oxygen exchange of the nest. The other 85% comes from the fungi grown internally [9]. The fungi is termite feces and molding, regurgitated wood pulp which eventually becomes the humidity absorbing mechanism for keeping cool the nest. Humidity is also controlled by the active transport of wet soil at the bottom of the nest to the top of the nest. High frequency wind at the top dries the water. The humidity sponges regulate humidity at 80%.

The physical appearance of the termite nest is a working partnership between the termites and the natural forces of the exterior. Termites are constantly bringing to the interior, new building material through vertical channels making the nest taller every year. However, there are a wide variety of nest shapes, completely created by the external weather conditions. For example, in a very rainy climate the nests are umbrella-shaped with multiple layers. This is created from the force of frequent rains beating down the termite nest tops to form a convex helmet-like top. As the termites pile interior materials out to the nest tops the rain immediately beats the dirt into a rounded bowl to form a distinctive mushroom appearance.

This project is an investigation to create a tall habitat based on the analysis of the termites' mound. We have changed the overall volumetric size of the interior to see how it affects temperature, humidity, and wind flow. Test models mimic the original proportional characteristics of the African termite's nest to create a base source of data. From there, we can see what happens when various aspects of the original proportions are altered [10].

The building is 33 meters underground to use the natural cooling of ground temperatures—between 22 degrees Celsius and 26 degrees Celsius, as the mean interior temperature of the community without using any mechanical systems or power; additional power for utilities is generated by several roof-mounted windmills and non-silicon based photovoltaic cells. The convex, domical roof design also catches rain and morning dew to be collected into an underground cistern that runs through a labyrinth of constructed wetlands, for cleaning, which is eventually used for grey water in each apartment. The windmill and solar panel systems are seamlessly integrated into a series of vertical glass skylight towers which give the building its distinctive "glass mountain" character.

A 3-meter thick soil roof with grass, flowers,

and vegetables produces a huge insular roof structure that filters rain through the soil into catch basins for reuse as grey water. The community is surrounded by apple, plum, mango, dragon eye, leeche, peach, orange, coconut and pear trees and the entire community shares in the collection of ripe fruits during the fruit-picking season. The roof can also be used for vegetable gardens if necessary.

Only non-gasoline vehicles are allowed on the community site and walking, running, horseback riding and bicycling are the main forms of transportation in and around the community. Outside parking is primarily for guests. Residents use a carpool and taxi service to come and go. Long distance travel is organized by pre-arrangement.

The research team at the national laboratory in southern China, The State Key Laboratory of Sub-tropical Building Science, performed nearly forty tests on selected aspects of the design. The goal was to collect enough verifiable information to give us confidence to design a working human model. The additional challenge was the creation of natural light throughout the habitable space. Termites are blind. They have no light inside their nest-- a completely sealed, absolutely dark environment that accommodates their necessity for a controlled habitat. The challenge was to achieve similar interior control with added natural light. This pointed to the design development of high levels of glass insulation.

What was developed was a glass insulation system similar to the wasp nest layering design. Three-quarters of an inch thick of wasp nest wall is equivalent in R value to a solid 18 inch thick masonry wall. The secret is in the air spacing in-between the paper layers. The research and design team expanded on this design and created a 1.75-meter thick skylight ceiling of 5 layers of safety glass and air vacuum equivalent to an R-value of 50-100. In addition, being largely underground, natural dirt is the cheapest and most effective material for insulation. For waterproofing, the styrene-concrete block system was employed at three layers with a back-up water drainage cavity between each layer. So natural light and insulation, on the whole, is functionally designed to create the effective envelope and structure of the building in its roof areas.

We are testing the use of a mushroom and rice husk-based waterproof insulation material originated in the eastern USA. This material is rigid and waterproof and creates a lightweight, organic, non-toxic variety of building insulation. In addition, to eliminate the use of plumbing and water for toilets and to encourage the understanding and use of composting, one-third of the toilets in the community are saw-dust toilets; that is, saw dust is used to mix with human manure, urine and toilet paper which is daily collected and placed in a one to two year composting area to eventually return to dirt for growing vegetables and fruit.

One of the biggest challenges is how to mini-

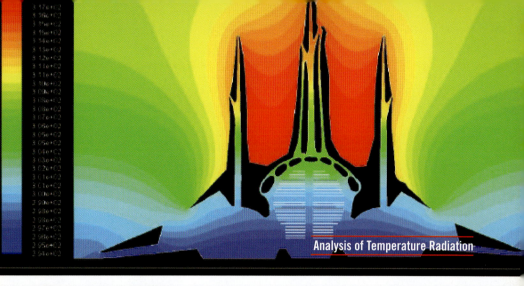

Analysis of Temperature Radiation

Ground Level

Apartments

Issue 4 2012

Interior View

for testing the idea of private communities as public venues for arts, education, sports and social programs. The model proposes that outstanding activities of community benefit be held in your own backyard and such activities be developed and tested by members of the community. The results can then be assessed at a community level and future directives established. In effect, the 3500-person community becomes pro-active initiators and participants in directing and developing their future and the future's of the next generation of inhabitants.

- -

1. Zero Energy Buildings: A Critical Look at the Definition, Torcellini, June 2006, National Energy Renewable Laboratory).
2. World Architecture Review, October issue, 2010.
3. US Environmental Protection Agency, General Building Basic Information, October 28, 2009
4. Bumblebees Finally Cleared for Takeoff, Cornell Chronicle, March 20, 2000
5. The Tardigrade Newsletter, John Blatchford, March 11, 2009
6. Evolution Biology of Termites, FM Weesner, 1960, Annual Review of Entomology
7. Piper, Ross, 2007, Extraordinary Animals: An Encyclopedia of Curious and Unusual Animals, Greenwood Press
8. Beyond biomimicry: What termites can tell us about realizing the living building, J Scott Turner and Rupert C. Soar, 2009
9. Extended physiology of an insect built structure, American Entomologist, J. Scott Turner, 2005.
10. JS Turner, Architecture and Morphogenisis in the mound of Macrotermes in northern Namibia, 2000.
11. Sir R. Attenborough, Nature's Architects, BBC, National Geographic.
12. Leo Buscaglia, Living, Loving and Learning, 1982.

mize the presence of exterior hot, humid air and maximize the interior cool air. We made some careful studies of the African termite nest entrance system, finding that air is suctioned through the entrance holes to accelerate into the nest—the Venturi Effect. Using this as a clue, we placed 12 entrance stacks, with solar powered elevators and broad stairways, leading down to a sub 28 meter depth, exiting to a gently sloped, broad ramp which leads to the underground housing complex. These 12 "nostrils" supply outside accelerated air to the interior spaces. The hot, upper level air, falls downward and cools, and accelerates to enter the main living areas. Humidity is significantly lowered during this 290 meter journey.

Inside, additional humidity is taken out of the air with another "secret" of the Termite nest design—suspended, vertical plates on the ceiling forming concentric circles of undulating surfaces that collect moisture in the air and let it evaporate from the upper ceiling heat. The evaporation creates a cooling effect that further aids in temperature control. In addition to their remarkable purpose, the aesthetic characteristics of these plates, reminds one of nature's magnificent artistic abilities to surprise and inspire curiosity, and look like something centuries ahead of our times [11].

An important aspect of living in China, is the sense of neighborhood—of community, and the friendships that can be built within the community. The social environment is as important as the physical environment. That is why there was great consideration for many programs that allow the 3500 inhabitants to learn and engage many new things and to transcend old stigmas and behaviors. Traditions should be reinforced if they are healthy and promote one's humanity, one's benefit to others and the capacity to question and create [12].

Apartment units are configured in a hexagonal plan, 12 to 24 stories high, linked by multiple bridge-ways at multiple levels, for centralized access to athletic facilities, residential vegetable and fruit tree gardens, retail, recreation and education facilities, auditorium, exhibition center, restaurants and open green space. The social program encourages daily athletic activities, residential food production, educational and mentorship programs, ecology, garbage minimization and behavioral studies and a shared child-rearing program among residents. An in-house school tutors children, teenagers and adults in a wide variety of subjects and classes geared towards enhancing personal subject interests, university entrance exams and adult, post university education.

The design incorporates an Olympic quality, running stadium track with a grassy center for soccer, rugby, lacrosse and a variety of other sports. Ten running lanes leave plenty of room for the casual runner as well as national competitions. This includes areas for Javelin, shot put and discus throwing, pole vault, high jump, long jump and triple jump. Inhabitants visually relate to the areas and feel like they are a part of something here-- part of a larger conscience. Other areas of the Global Health Community have areas for tennis, badminton, volleyball, table tennis, boxing, martial arts, wrestling, gymnastics, archery, rifle/pistol shoot, racquet ball and hand ball and these areas can be added to and modified.

There is a large, open grass park area for strolling and picnics another area for growing one's own family vegetables and fruits. The entire complex is surrounded by fruit trees and additional garden plots on the outside. The shopping areas are surrounded by lakes and streams. Families can buy and trade fruits and vegetables with other families. Other areas include a large exhibition hall, performance auditorium, retail and offices, restaurants, classrooms and conference rooms, wood shop/machine shop and materials construction workshops and music performance facilities.

The Global Health Community is a model

eDesign and Research Team - State Key Laboratory of Sub-Tropical Building Science, South China University of Science and Technology, Guangzhou, China: Dr. Eugene Tssui, Principal architect and concept development. Dr. Xiao Da Wei, Associate Architect and Supervisor, Vice-Dean, School of Architecture. Mr. Ni Yang and Dr. Xiao Yi Chiang, Consulting Architects. Dr. Jeffrey Scott Turner, Biologist-USA. Dr. Rupert Soar, Scientist-England. Mr. Mick Pearce, architect-Africa. Science consultants: Dr. Zhao Li Hua, Environment and Energy Consultant. Mr. Shen Jie, Chief of Research Systems and Software. Mr. Wang Wei Nan, Assistant to the Principal architect.

Dr. Eugene Tssui, architect, author, and international professor engaged in research and teaching at the University of California, Berkeley, South China University of Science and Technology in Guangzhou, China, and Harbin Graduate School of Technology in Shenzhen, China. He is the author of six books and additional portfolios on ecological thinking and design and the winner of multiple grants and awards. He has architecture offices in the USA and China and is annually featured in global publications and documentary television programs such as National Geographic, Discovery Channel, MTV, The History Channel, PBS, CNN, the BBC, CCTV China Television, Euro TV and others. He attended Columbia University Graduate School of Design, the University of Oregon and the University of California, Berkeley, where he obtained an Interdisciplinary Ph.D. in Architecture and Education.
He can be reached at: eugenetssui@gmail.com

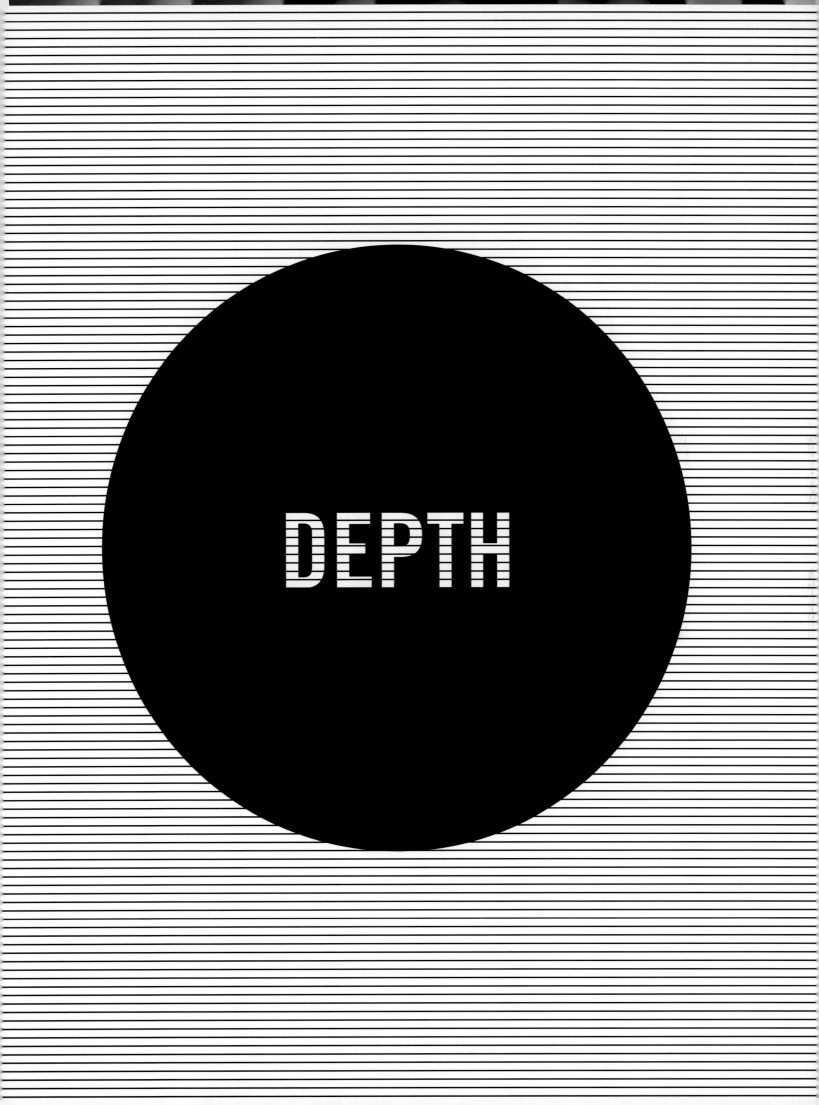

eVolo | issue 4 | 2012

CHINA
COMIC
AND
ANIMATION
MUSEUM

MVRDV

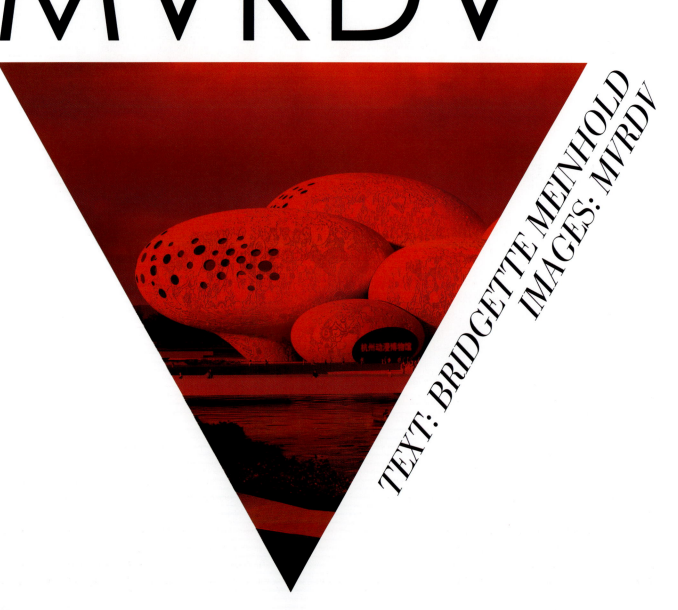

TEXT: BRIDGETTE MEINHOLD
IMAGES: MVRDV

Comics and anime are a big deal in China. Just ask any one of the 235 million children in the country under the age of 14. With the largest target audience for comics and animation in the world and a major influx of work from foreign countries, China certainly has reason to believe their industry could top all the rest, even those of the United States and Japan. On top of that, comics and animation are becoming more respected as art forms rather than just entertainment, so it's no wonder that the People's Republic has set aside a whole section of a Hangzhou for a new expo center and museum dedicated to cartoons, comics, anime, and film. For seven years running now, Hangzhou has held the China International Cartoon and Animation Festival (CICAF), an annual fixture of the city's cultural activities, and now the festival will have a permanent home at the new China Comic and Animation Museum (CCAM).

During the spring of 2011, the Hangzhou Urban Planning Bureau held an international design competition seeking an innovative and exciting new center dedicated to comics and animation. At the end of the CICAF festival in May, the planning bureau announced The Netherlands firm, MVRDV, as the winner for their design inspired by a classic fixture in all comics – the speech balloon. Composed of six intersecting thought bubble-like volumes, the China Comic and Animation Museum is decidedly cartoonish and out of the ordinary, but then again, when you're dedicating an entire museum to cartoons, it should be a bit comical.

The 32,000 square-meter facilities will house an IMAX theater, exhibition rooms, a permanent collection, interactive exhibits as well as a café and administration and collaborative office spaces. Perched over White Horse Lake in Binjiang District of Hangzhou on the south side of the Qiantang River and surrounded by plazas, parks and water, the CCAM is part of a much larger development, which also includes an office complex, a hotel and 15,000 m2 expo center. If all goes as planned the CCAM will be the epicenter of comics and animation in China and will draw millions of people from around the world for festivals, conferences, jobs, research and even tourism. A large international complex wholly dedicated to the niche industry is more than any other country has and if they can pull it off, the CCAM will propel China to the head of the pack and maybe even become the animation capital of the world.

MVRDV based their design on the recognizable speech balloon, one of comics' prime attributes. Expanded from a flat 2D shape into a 3D volume, the balloons serve as the building block for the entire museum. Intersecting to create large cavernous spaces, each balloons serves as independent areas dedicated to different program. The 'legs' of the balloon act as the pillars on which the museum rests, some of which are in the water, while others sit on dry land. Each leg holds utilities, lifts, fire escapes and access points into the museum.

The façade is monochromatic white concrete and allows the building to look like real speech bubbles with texts are projected onto the surface. A cartoon relief, inspired by Chinese vases and designed in collaboration with Amsterdam-based graphic designers, JongeMeesters, covers the façade. Both large and small circular windows create a visual connection between the interior and exterior and continue the theme of the thought bubble while pulling daylight into the specific spaces.

Visitors to the museum enter through one of the large legs and up through an escalator to reach the spherical lobby, a grand open space.

evolo | Issue 4 | 2012

BAY VIEW

Immediately, visitors are greeted with statues and images of their favorite comic heroes and can choose a variety of paths to explore. Adjacent to the lobby is the museum's permanent collection, housed in a large cavernous space. To explore the collection in depth, visitors will travel along a spiraling walkway chronologically following the history of comics and animation. This circulation configuration, designed by Amsterdam-based exhibition architects, Kossman.deJong, allows visitors to travel at the own pace depending on their interests and their available time. Exhibited in the permanent collection are small objects, like toys and memorabilia as well as original drawings, books, posters and videos. Visitors without much time can fast track their way through the permanent exhibition via a bridge that cuts across the space on to the next room.

After the permanent collection is the Interaction Zone, a room where visitors can actively participate in the world of animation. Here, visitors can step up to consoles on terraced platforms and play a variety of games projected onto large screens. Visitors can also try their hand at experimenting with different animation techniques like blue screen, stop motion, drawing, and creating character emotions. The highlight of this space is a giant 3D

PLAZA VIEW

zoetrope. Behind the screens of the Interaction Zone are several floors where museum staff holds their offices and work on cartoons, gaming and animations. While this area is not open to the public, it is a vital section to the museum and is utilized for research, collaborative work and advancement of the art and industry.

Past the Interaction Zone is the museum's Library Zone, housing the museum's expansive collection of comic books. Stacks upon stacks of books, posters and other comic and animation related literature fill the void in concentric rings. A temporary exhibition space located at the bottom of the void is accessed via terraced steps. Next to the library void is a reading room and storage area, while above in the dome, are several rings of workspaces extending upwards. A large circular window looks out over the lake like a giant eye and fills the space with lots of natural daylight.

If the library is a bit too slow paced, round the bend and enter the Cinema Zone, an entire bubble dedicated to animated films. This dome contains an IMAX theater plus two smaller theaters with a total of 1,111 seats. Each theater occupies its own closed volume and the roofs of the theaters act as lounges, while the spaces between the theaters act as a lobby and cafe. The Cinema Zone's theaters, lounges and lobby will serve as the main facilities for the annual China International Cartoon and Animation Festival. Otherwise all three theaters will regularly hold showings of various cartoons, anime and films for the museum's visitors. Up on top of the Cinema Zone bubble is a restaurant and bar plus a large outdoor deck with views out over the lake and the city.

After the Cinema Zone is the final area of the museum – the Education Zone, which provides space for a variety of educational programs. This area includes conference and flex-rooms for classes, meetings and other programs. This last bubble completes the circuit and reconnects with the entrance lobby. Various circulations paths exist within the museum allowing visitors to quickly access the cinemas, education area and rooftop terrace restaurant without having to circumnavigate the entire museum.

The museum is just one part of the entire complex though, and visitors have easy access to a number of other activities. From the museum, ramps through the legs of the bubbles exit down to a series of islands surrounding White Horse Lake with special boat tours around the lake and paths into the theme park. The boat tours wind around the museum's legs and enjoy the cool shade underneath. Reed beds planted in and around the lake work to increase the amount of urban green space and also improve the water quality by filtering and processing toxins.

MVRDV worked closely with ARUP on the structural engineering, sustainable strategies and climate design in order to reduce energy use

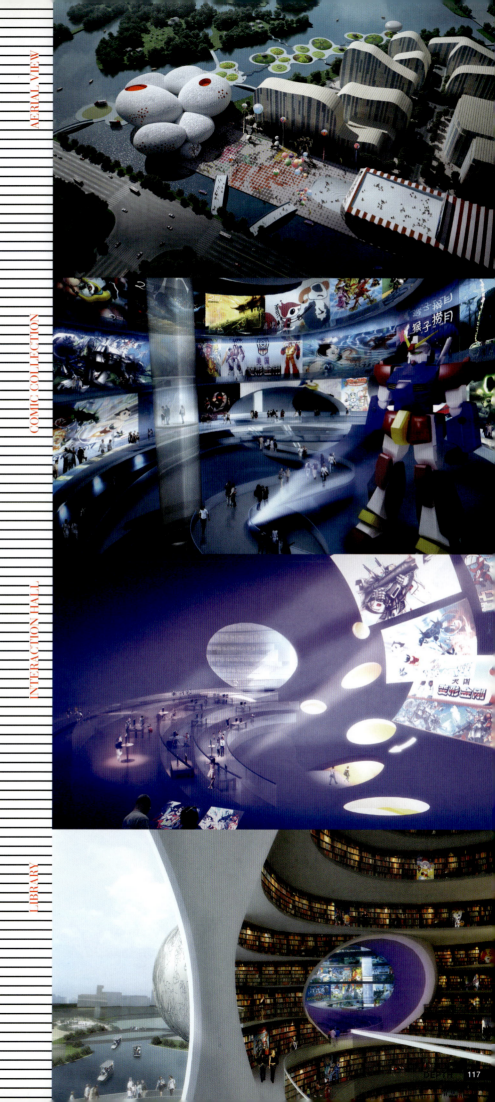

AERIAL VIEW

COMIC COLLECTION

INTERACTION HALL

LIBRARY

PLAN - LEVEL +18M [left]

PLAN - LEVEL +27M [right]

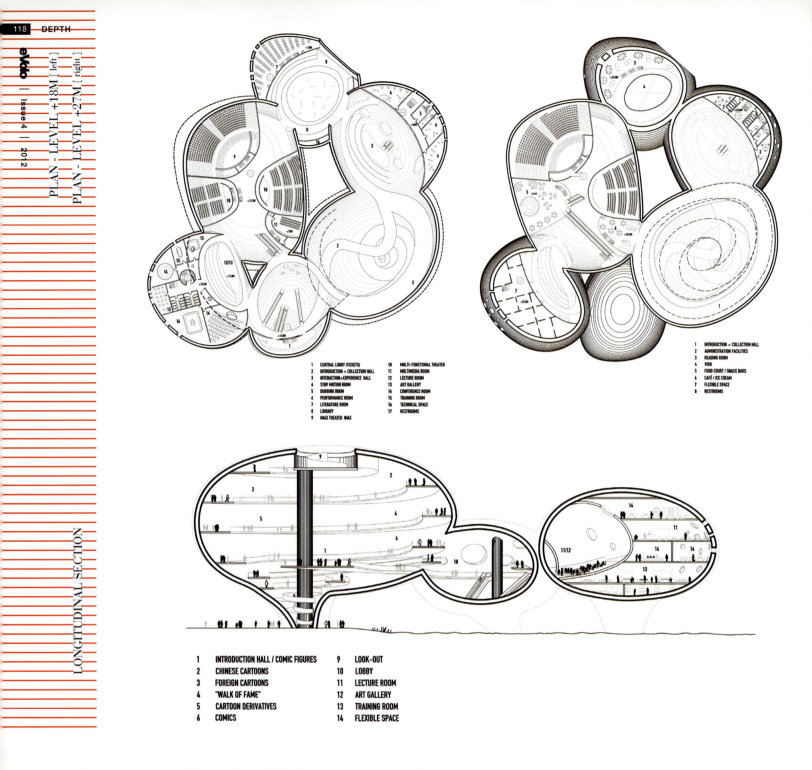

1 CENTRAL LOBBY (TICKETS)
2 INTRODUCTION + COLLECTION HALL
3 INTERACTION + EXPERIENCE HALL
4 STOP MOTION ROOM
5 DUBBING ROOM
6 PERFORMANCE ROOM
7 LITERATURE ROOM
8 LIBRARY
9 IMAX THEATER IMAX
10 MULTI-FUNCTIONAL THEATER
11 MULTIMEDIA ROOM
12 LECTURE ROOM
13 ART GALLERY
14 CONFERENCE ROOM
15 TRAINING ROOM
16 TECHNICAL SPACE
17 RESTROOMS

1 INTRODUCTION + COLLECTION HALL
2 ADMINISTRATION FACILITIES
3 READING ROOM
4 VOID
5 FOOD COURT / SNACK BARS
6 CAFÉ / ICE CREAM
7 FLEXIBLE SPACE
8 RESTROOMS

LONGITUDINAL SECTION

1 INTRODUCTION HALL / COMIC FIGURES
2 CHINESE CARTOONS
3 FOREIGN CARTOONS
4 "WALK OF FAME"
5 CARTOON DERIVATIVES
6 COMICS
9 LOOK-OUT
10 LOBBY
11 LECTURE ROOM
12 ART GALLERY
13 TRAINING ROOM
14 FLEXIBLE SPACE

and minimize environmental impact. The bubble shell structure of the museum will be constructed with a hybrid system of lightweight structural steel and sandwich of concrete-steel-concrete, which will allow the entire weight of the building to be supported by just the six legs. Interestingly, the museum is not elevated only for looks. The legs also minimize effects from flooding during the rainy season and water levels can rise or fall without causing damage to the building. The building's aerodynamic shape distributes wind pressure evenly over the façade and encourages natural ventilation, lowering the need for forced air conditioning. As the building is located right over a body of water, evaporative cooling will naturally reduce temperatures.

Inside, the bubbles are constructed as a "box-in-box", which allows each area's climate to be individually controlled, thus reducing unnecessary energy consumption. Heating and cooling systems, like ground water heating and cooling and combined heat and power (CHP) will be employed along with adjustable micro-climates to balance comfort and energy use efficiently. ARUP is also designing waste purification and

waste separation systems into the scheme to further reduce the building's environmental impact.

Hangzhou, which is located about 180 km southwest of Shanghai, is actively working to promote itself as the new mecca for animation and comics. The first phase of the complex, containing offices, a hotel and a conference centre is nearing completion. Work on the museum is expected to begin sometime in 2012 and cost approximately 92 million Euro. When the China Comic and Animation Museum is complete as early as 2013, it will become the star of the show and an icon for industry at large. It seems then that cheap goods and electronics won't be China's only export to the world now.

Bridgette Meinhold is a freelance writer and artist based in Park City, UT, living in a small A-frame cabin in an aspen grove with her husband and dog. She has a Master's degree in Civil & Environmental Engineering from Stanford and is an online contributor for eVolo as well as the Architecture Editor for Inhabitat.com. Bridgette also maintains her own blog devoted to sustainable DIY and art at www.ettestudios.com. When she's not writing about sustainable architecture and green design, she's either hiking in the woods or in her recycled shipping container studio painting flowers and bees.

DILLER SCOFIDIO +RENFRO RETHINKS

HOW TO DESIGN "ART FOR THE PUBLIC" IN PLANS FOR L.A.'S

THE BROAD MUSEUM

TEXT: DANIELLE DEL SOL
IMAGES AND DRAWINGS:
DILLER SCOFIDIO + RENFRO

EXTERIOR VIEW AND MAIN ENTRANCE

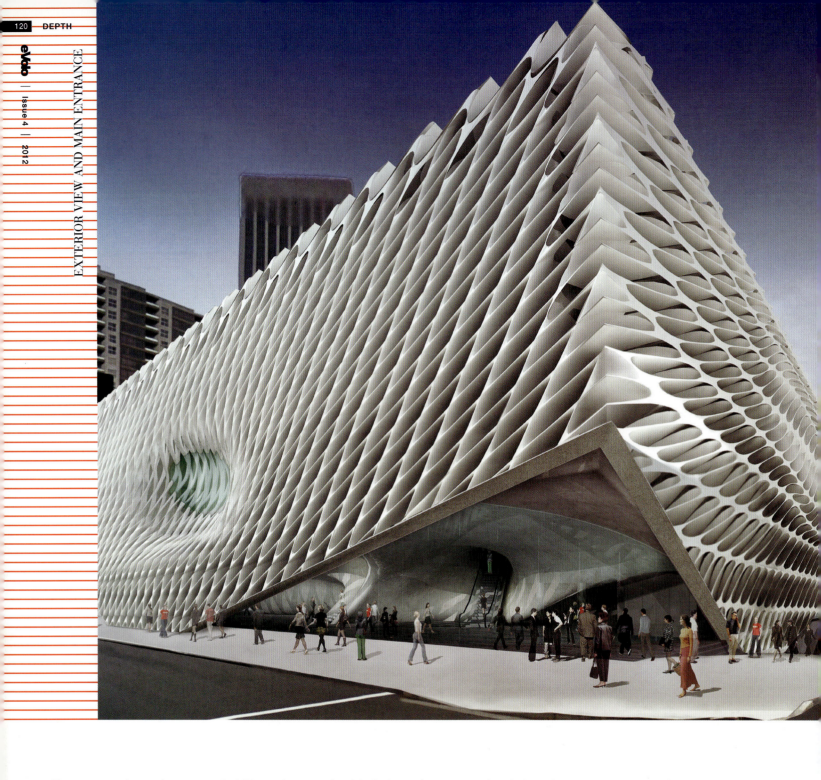

The newest modern and monumental addition to downtown Los Angeles' Grand Avenue, which in recent years has been evolving as one of the country's premiere boulevards for innovative architecture and planning, was unveiled in 2011 by philanthropists Eli and Edythe Broad. 'The Broad," a contemporary art museum that will be built and endowed by the couple, has been designed by world-renowned New York architecture firm Diller Scofidio + Renfro.

The firm's renderings for The Broad, which will be built next to the Frank Gehry-designed Walt Disney Concert Hall, reveal the 120,000 square foot structure to have a clean, techie look, with the majority of the three-story building covered in a white honeycomb "veil" of hollow, rectangular shapes. Its progressive design matches the art inside—Eli and Edythe Broad are well-known patrons of modern art, and The Broad's galleries will be filled with works from the couple's 2,000-piece private collection, which includes original pieces by Salvador Dali, Henri Mattise, Joan Miró, Pablo Picasso, and others.

Much like Gehry's concert hall design, The Broad's goal as a public structure is to invite and engage travelers along Grand Avenue, and yet is designed as an overpowering, and perhaps overwhelming, mass of geometric forms. The exterior's porous veil sheath, which resembles a plastic protector, covers the majority of the museum, with the exception of the entrance, where an invisible string seems to pull a lip of the veil up to expose a glass entryway.

Diller Scofidio + Renfro's design for The Broad has been dubbed "the veil and the vault:" The veil refers of the white honeycomb exterior, while the vault is the building's interior core, which grows as an organic concrete form from the ground floor into a fully encasing solid mass that cups and holds the entire second floor. The solid gray vault stands in direct contrast to the exterior glass walls of the lobby and third floors, and the third floor ceiling (whose transparency allow the veil's visual prominence to dominate).

While the lobby features both the veil and the vault prominently, with the exterior walls made of glass and the center of the space defined by the curvaceous, cave-like walls created by the vault, the second and third stories are defined by those elements separated out. The second floor, as mentioned before, is defined entirely by the vault; the entire story is a concrete encasement for the museum's precious papers and research areas. The third floor, then, is seemingly all veil, with the honeycomb pattern serving as a ceiling. Skylights are installed in the pattern's openings to provide soft, natural light for the galleries.

While the lobby and second floor have significant space restrictions because of the vault, the third floor is almost totally open, with moveable walls creating the ability for galleries to be created and rearranged at a curator's whim. The designers boast that The Broad will have "almost an acre of column-free gallery space;" the exact figure is 40,000 square feet of gallery space on the third floor.

The lobby is open to the public and features display space, a multi-media gallery, a bookshop and an espresso bar. Diller Scofidio + Renfro's design of the lobby as a directed, curving, and half tunnel-like space stands in stark contrast to the layouts of lobbies of other prominent national art museums, including ones the firm itself has designed. Rather than offering an open, multi-story gathering space for visitors, The Broad's lobby offers a short open space to those entering from the street. From there, visitors can either ascend directly to the third floor galleries from a front-and-center escalator, or walk along the exterior edges of the lobby, following the paths created by the protruding cement base of the vault. The base's cave-like slopes extend further into the lobby at the top of the walls' heights than their bases, segregating the lobby into separate and distinct sections.

The designers' stated purpose in making the vault such a prominent element in the lobby's layout was to avoid making the museum's archives a "secondary" part of the museum's perceivable mission (as in, the message it sends through its design). The vault's physical prominence is meant to signal to visitors that The Broad offers more than visual richness—it has an academic, research-oriented wealth as well within its archives.

While the contents of the archives are generously extended for research and even for loan to interested researchers and curators, the items are not accessible to the public. In emphasizing the archive's importance through the building's design, but failing to make it a space that's accessible to the public, The Broad's design makes a strong distinction in its separate private and public uses. The general public can ascend from the lobby through the second floor (without stopping) to the third floor galleries on an escalator, and later can glimpse from behind glass the goings-on of workers in the archives as they descend back to the lobby via staircase. But only approved guests are actually allowed entry onto the second floor archives.

Diller Scofidio + Renfro have emerged as an international design leader in the category of museums and art institutions in the 21st century, with a portfolio including the redesign of Alice Tully

CONCEPT DIAGRAM – FROM BOTTOM TO TOP: LOBBY, ARCHIVE, GALLERY, VEIL

LOBBY

GALLERY

Hall and the renovation and expansion of The Juilliard School, both part of the Lincoln Center for the Performing Arts redevelopment project, the design for the Berkeley Art Museum and Pacific Film Archive in Berkeley, CA, the Museum of Image & Sound in Rio de Janeiro, and the Institute of Contemporary Art in Boston, among others. The latter provides an interesting case study for which to contrast the design of The Broad. The Institute of Contemporary Art, which opened to much critical architectural acclaim in 2006, was designed to be an extension of, and contributing element in, a 43 mile-long network of boardwalks along Boston's Back Bay. The ground-floor lobby is clad largely with tall glass windows and steel beams that offer expansive views of the waterfront, and the interior also embraces expanse as an aesthetic, with open floor space interrupted only by a grand staircase. New York Times architecture critic Nicolai Ourousoff called the design, which is transparent from the exterior and glows at night, a "startling expression of public-spiritedness." The building's expert ability, through Diller Scofidio + Renfro's design, to weave artful architecture with civic life made it, Ourousoff said, the "most important building to rise [on that waterfront] in a generation."

Though Grand Avenue is meant, in its recent years of redesign, to be a promenade that attracts public use, The Broad lacks the message of accessibility that radiates from the Institute of Contemporary Art. Its benefactors have certainly not intended to make the impressively endowed collection inaccessible; in fact, Eli Broad emphasized, at the design's unveiling, that The Broad would serve as an important cultural resource for Los Angeles' 15 million residents. However, the architects' design of the entry—The Broad's visitors are asked to duck into an opening in the overpowering veil, and then read the cave-like core of the lobby as inviting and accessible—uses an opposite ethos than was employed in Boston.

Visitors are also expected to arrive by car; the structure has three levels of parking below the ground floor. Other building features include a 200-seat theater, study and art storage spaces within the archive, and 24 foot tall ceilings in the block-long expanse of gallery space on the third floor.

Principal Elizabeth Diller explained the veil's prominence as the exterior design feature as a direct aesthetic response to Gehry's design next door. "Our goal for the museum is to hold its ground next to Gehry's much larger and very exuberant Walt Disney Concert Hall through contrast," she stated at a press conference in January. "As opposed to Disney Hall's smooth and shiny exterior that reflects light, The Broad will be porous and absorptive, channeling light into its public spaces and galleries. The veil will play a role in the urbanization of Grand Avenue by activating two-way views that connect the museum and the street."

Its impact is meant to be much greater than visual: economists estimate that a museum that costs $100 million to build and endow yields at least $65 million in returns, including contributions to local employment. With no estimate yet on the cost to build The Broad, but a guaranteed endowment of $200 million from Eli and Edythe, it stands to reason that the museum's lasting impact on downtown Los Angeles could be as prominent as its design.

Danielle Del Sol is a New Orleans-based writer and deputy editor of Preservation in Print, the monthly magazine of the Preservation Resource Center, one of the nation's leading historic preservation nonprofits. She hails from both Miami, Florida and Fayetteville, Arkansas — two very different, but equally inspiring worlds — and holds a master's degree in preservation studies from the Tulane University School of Architecture. She writes for national and local publications on architecture, urban planning, policy and culture, and is passionate about reporting on the impact that land use decisions have on our everyday lives.

GEMINI: AMERICA'S CUP PAVILION

SAN DIEGO, CA
DANIEL CARPER

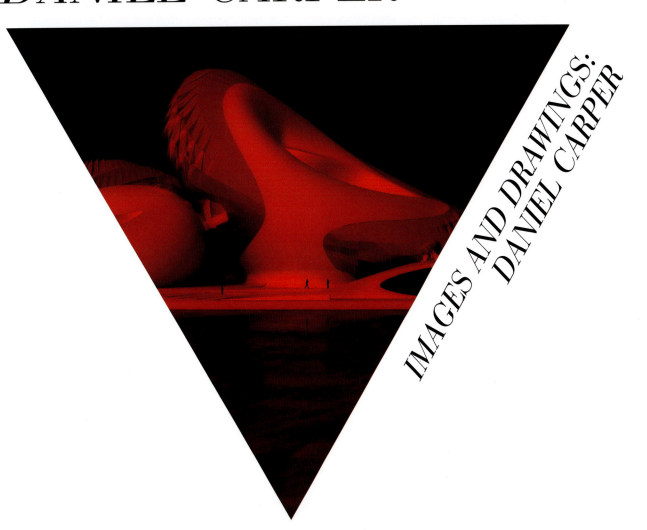

IMAGES AND DRAWINGS:
DANIEL CARPER

The America's Cup is the most prestigious regatta in the sport of sailing. With such prominence, this international competition draws throngs of hundred-member crews and fans wanting to partake in the spectacle of the race. The America's Cup Pavilion functions as an epicenter for varied activities. Its function, being temporal and specific, conforms to two separate agendas: that of a landmark building with expansive and outwardly-focused race observation decks, and that of an entertainment center with internally-focused post and pre-race programs.

This project seeks to address the multifarious behavior of the America's Cup Pavilion through building disfigurement and uninterrupted entertainment. Unlike the landmark qualities of a shore-lining lighthouse, the project's interests lie in designing a building that disfigures its distinguishable form through a mechanized skin. This skin utilizes mobile enclosure panels that shift space from conditioned to unconditioned, interior to exterior, dim to luminous, smooth to armored, in an effort to present various and unexpected spatial experiences to the user. Despite formal and spatial variation,

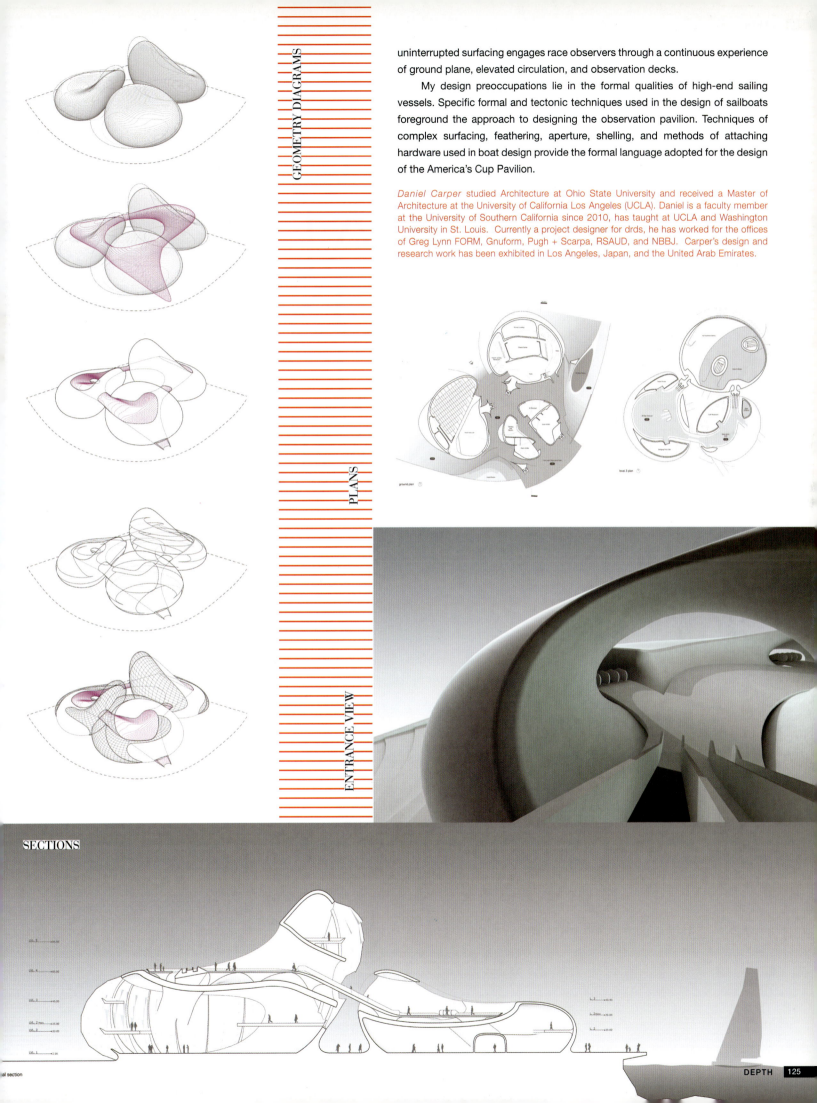

uninterrupted surfacing engages race observers through a continuous experience of ground plane, elevated circulation, and observation decks.

My design preoccupations lie in the formal qualities of high-end sailing vessels. Specific formal and tectonic techniques used in the design of sailboats foreground the approach to designing the observation pavilion. Techniques of complex surfacing, feathering, aperture, shelling, and methods of attaching hardware used in boat design provide the formal language adopted for the design of the America's Cup Pavilion.

Daniel Carper studied Architecture at Ohio State University and received a Master of Architecture at the University of California Los Angeles (UCLA). Daniel is a faculty member at the University of Southern California since 2010, has taught at UCLA and Washington University in St. Louis. Currently a project designer for drds, he has worked for the offices of Greg Lynn FORM, Gnuform, Pugh + Scarpa, RSAUD, and NBBJ. Carper's design and research work has been exhibited in Los Angeles, Japan, and the United Arab Emirates.

GEOMETRY DIAGRAMS

PLANS

ENTRANCE VIEW

SECTIONS

eVolo

| Issue 4 | 2012

ATLANTIC CITY BOARDWALK HOLOCAUST MEMORIAL

ATLANTIC CITY, NEW JERSEY

CHRISTOPHER WARREN [WORD]

IMAGES AND DRAWINGS: WORD

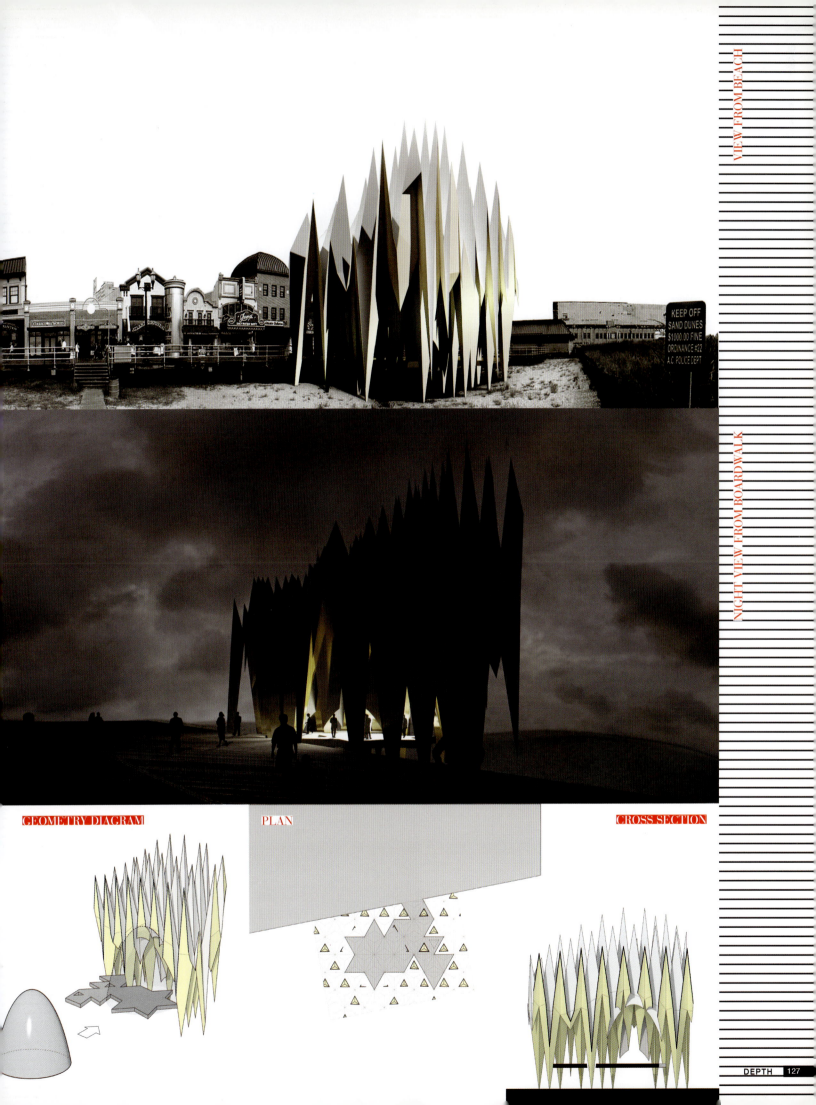

NIGHT VIEW FROM BOARDWALK

GEOMETRY DIAGRAM

PLAN

CROSS SECTION

eVolo | Issue 4 | 2012

Similar to Kafka's "harrow", rising from the dunes as a jagged form, the Atlantic City Boardwalk Holocaust Memorial acts as an inscriptive apparatus which etches the history of the Holocaust in our memory. Although from the exterior it appears frenetic and chaotic, once entered, the memorial becomes a calm, ordered and luminous space for peaceful reflection.

The memorial seemingly stands as a series of undulating triangular peaks and valleys, but is actually composed of a continuous surface that has undergone drastic topological manipulation. It has been pushed and pulled, and folded in on itself in order to create a three dimensional construct from what began as a single plane – at once gesturing toward the sky while embedding itself in the sand. Any sectional cut through its plate construction reveals only a single undulating line; that line being utilized to create shelter, structure and a variety of spaces. The apex of the peaks follows the same triangular logic of the plan, while its rhythmic form is reminiscent of the passage of time and the ever changing swell of emotions that great tragedies impart upon civilization. Conceived as an endless construct, the pavilion's edges are simply sheared off at the site's boundary, reinforcing its conceptual continuity. The platform detaches from the boardwalk and weaves amongst the structure, and within it the space of a dome is subtracted from the whole, further revealing the order of the memorial and its ceremonial potential.

WORD (Warren Office for Research and Design)
Project Team: Chris Hyun, Hana Ogita, Ryan Ramirez, Christopher Warren

Christopher Warren founded the Warren Office for Research and Design in 2009. Prior to its formation, he served a six year tenure at Morphosis, working as project designer on over twenty commissions. He later also co-founded Studio Shift in 2004, where he served as partner for five years. Christopher received his Master of Architecture degree from the University of Pennsylvania. In search of a more progressive and pioneering environment in which to practice, he moved to Los Angeles and immediately began working with Pritzker Prize winner Thom Mayne at Morphosis.

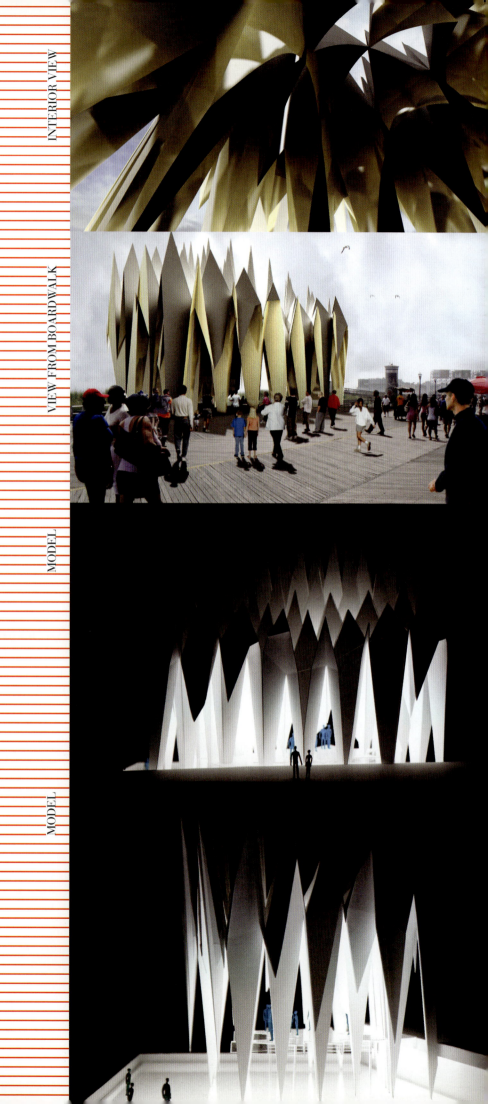

INTERIOR VIEW

VIEW FROM BOARDWALK

MODEL

MODEL

HOPE TREE

TOKYO, JAPAN
24° STUDIO

IMAGES AND DRAWINGS:
24° STUDIO

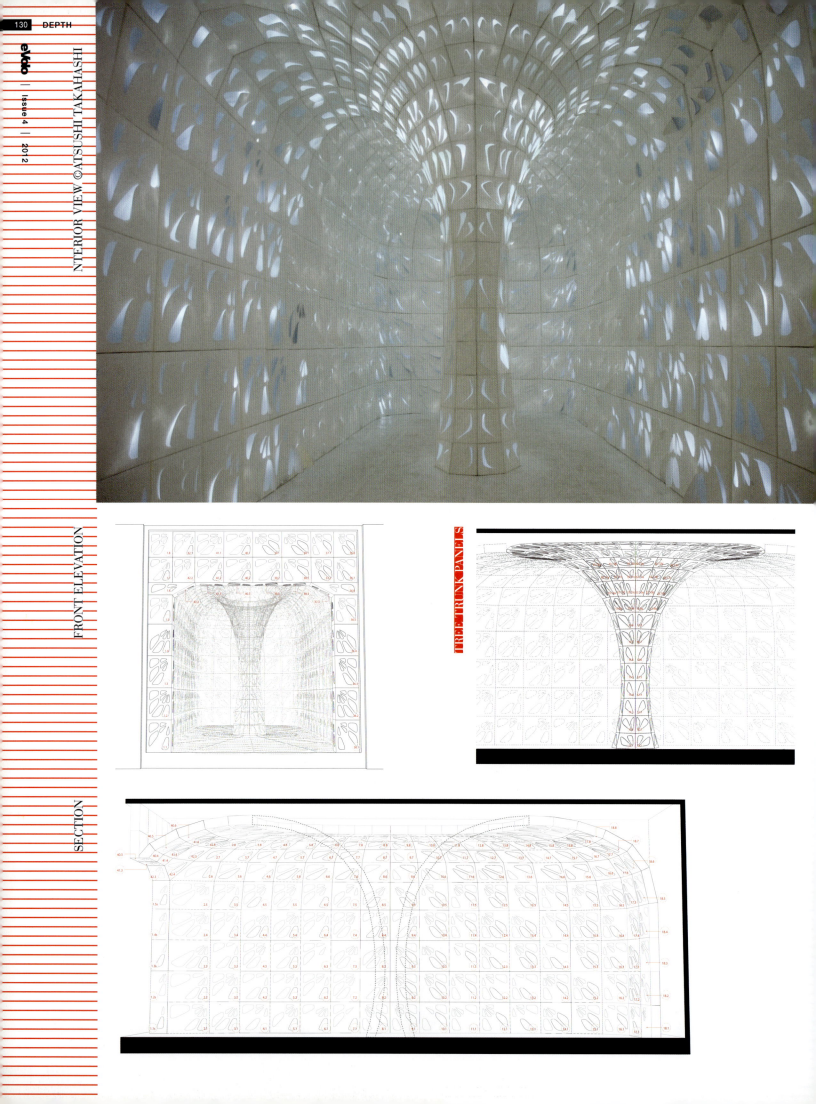

eVolo || Issue 4 || 2012

INTERIOR VIEW ©ATSUSHI TAKAHASHI

FRONT ELEVATION

SECTION

TREE TRUNK PANELS

The Hope Tree installation in Tokyo, Japan was envisioned as a space to question our relationship with the environment. It hopes to create a discussion about the way we live and transform the natural landscape. Nowadays, we are bombarded with "sustainable" products that try to deal with the consequences of environmental changes around the world, but we overlook the causes of these problems and do not fully understand its potential catasptrophic consequences.

The form of a tree was chosen as departing point for the design as we, universally identify with it. Throughout millennia, trees have been our most primitive form of shelter and loyal companions. Human innovation and technological advances have transformed trees into an array of products from a single sheet of paper to entire buildings. This installation reminds us of the beauty and necessity of trees by creating a toroidal surface composed of 670 self-supporting watercolor paper panels. Each panel was reinforced with cardboard edges to create stiff boxes. The symmetry of the form allowed for minimized typological variation and also eased the manufacturing process.

The box panels were assembled in a spatial arch, inspired by the traditional masonry arch construction. This allowed the elliptical ceiling arch load to be equally distributed between the central column and the perimeter wall.

Leaf-like cutouts were strategically sized and deformed accordingly to the geometry of the box panels. The openings were backed with tracing paper, which performed as a diffusing surface for the LED string lighting. The application of string LED lighting attached behind the box panels allowed a beautiful illumination of the entire space with minimal electricity consumption of under 500 watts.

Furthermore, the property of watercolor paper provided a dynamic response to the environment. The constant changes in humidity warped the paper in different directions creating a new lighting experience each day.

24° Studio (Fumio Hirakawa + Marina Topunova) is a multidisciplinary practice established in 2008 in New York City and Tokyo. The Studio works at the intersection of architecture, technology, and the environment. 24° Studio believes that the process of integrating multiple perspectives will lead to innovative result, thus redefining the connection between our body and the environment.

WATERCOLOR PAPER PANELS @ATSUSHI TAKAHASHI

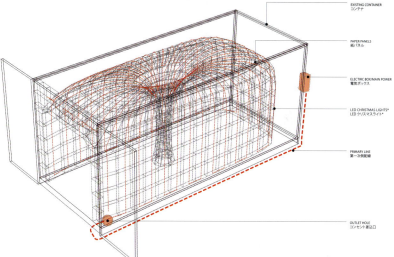

LIGHTING DIAGRAM

EXISTING CONTAINER
コンテナ

PAPER PANELS
紙パネル

ELECTRIC BOX/MAIN POWER
電気ボックス

LED CHRISTMAS LIGHTS*
LED クリスマスライト*

PRIMARY LINE
第一次側配線

OUTLET HOLE
コンセント差込口

INTERIOR VIEW @ LUKE HAYES

ONE OCEAN: THEMATIC PAVILION EXPO 2012

YEOSU, SOUTH KOREA
SOMA / ISOCHROM

DRAWINGS AND IMAGES:
SOMA / ISOCHROM

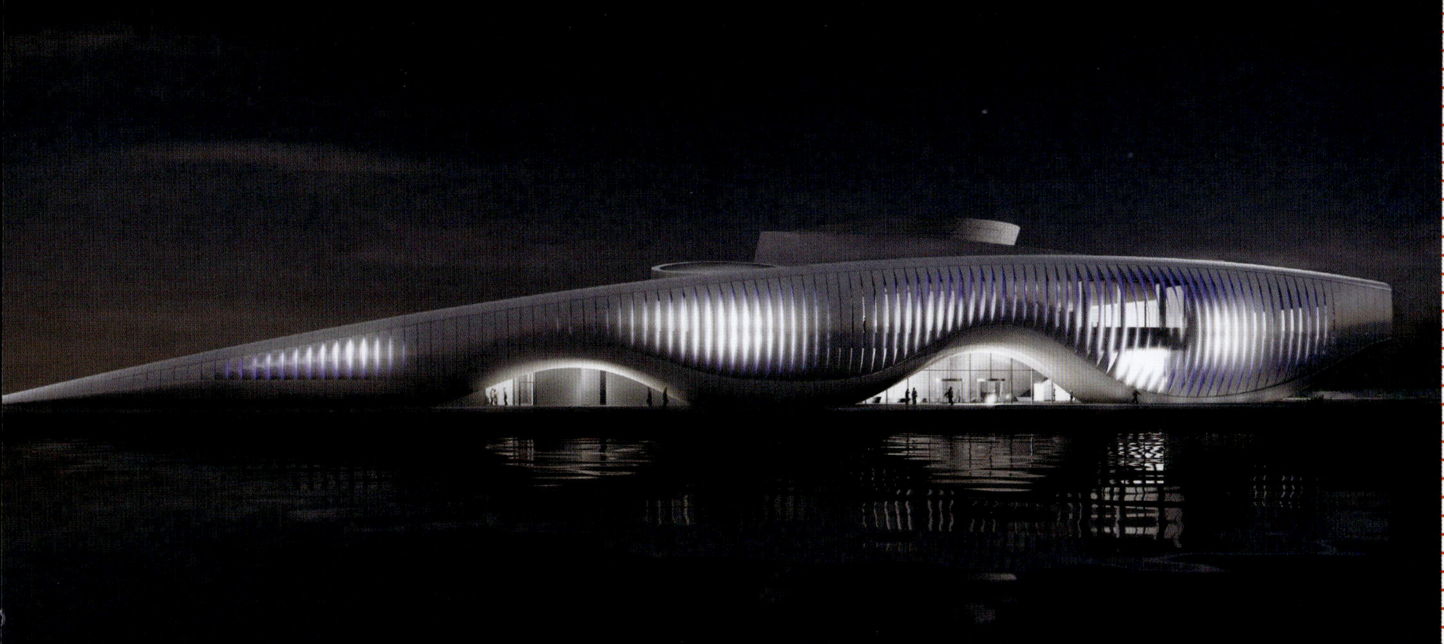

NIGHT VIEW FROM OCEAN

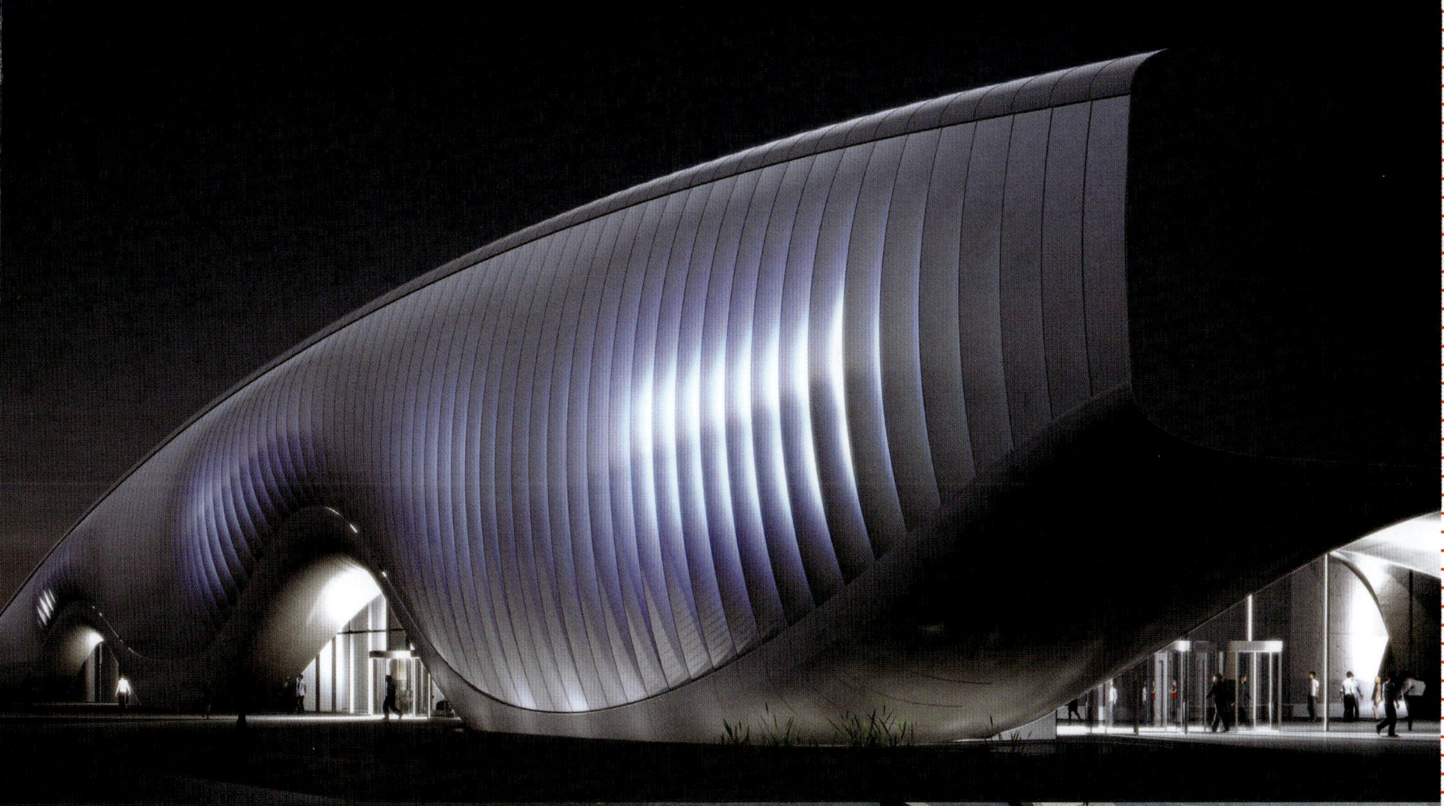

ENTRANCE AT NIGHT

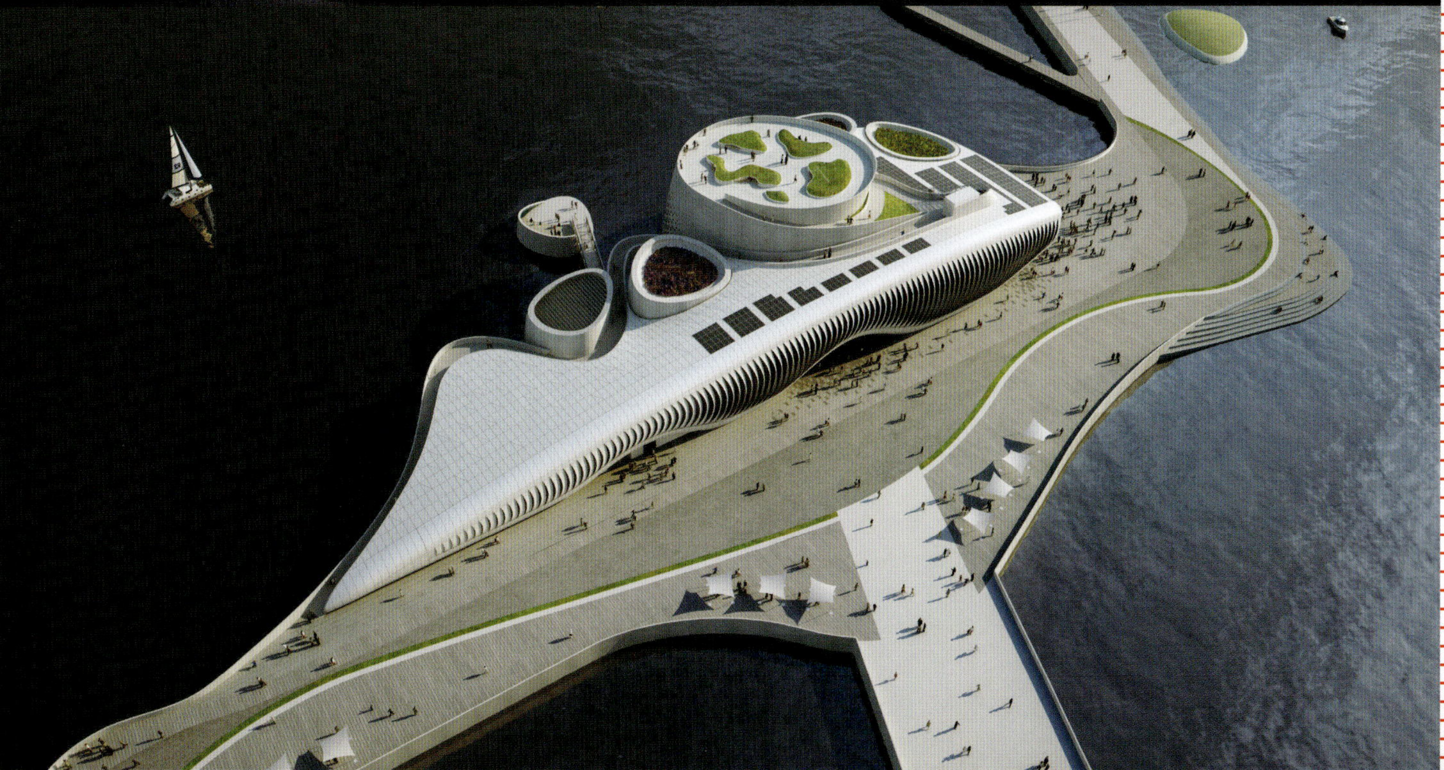

AERIAL VIEW

eVolo | Issue 4 | 2012

VIEW FROM PLAZA

DAY VIEW FROM OCEAN

ENTRANCE WITH LAMELLAS

GEOMETRY AGGREGATION DIAGRAM

The Thematic Pavilion is a major and permanent building for the Expo 2012 in Yeosu, South Korea. Soma's design proposal was selected as the first prize in an open international architecture competition.

As a major and permanent facility the Thematic Pavilion embodies the Expo's theme "The Living Ocean and Coast" through its architecture. We experience the Ocean in two different ways, as an endless surface and as an endless volume of water. This spatial duality creates the building's spatial and organizational concepts. Continuous surfaces twist from vertical to horizontal orientation and define all interior spaces while vertical cones induce the visitor into the exhibition. Continuous transitions between contrasting experiences also form the outer appearance of the Pavilion. Towards the sea the cluster of solid vertical cones define a new meandering coastline, a soft edge that is in constant negotiation between water and land. On the opposite side, the pavilion peels out from the ground into an artificial landscape with gardens and scenic paths.

The aim of the design was to implement the EXPO's agenda through sustainable design.

As a counterpart to the virtual multi-media shows of the thematic exhibition that will take place in the interior spaces, the façade emphasizes the multiple potentials of analogue architectural effects.

The facade covers a total length of about

140 meters, and is between 3 and 13 meters high. It consists of 108 kinetic lamellas, which are supported at the top and the bottom edges of the façade. The lamellas are made of reinforced glass polymers (GFRP), which combine high tensile strength with low bending stiffness, allowing for large reversible elastic deformations. The lamellas are moved by actuators on both the upper and lower edges of the GFRP blades, which induce compression forces to create the complex elastic deformation. Each lamella can be addressed individually within a specific movement to show different choreographies and operation modes. The material performance of the lamellas produces an interrelated effect of geometry, movement, and light: the longer a single lamella is, the wider the angle of it's opening.

The main entrance is situated on the 'Ocean Plaza', which is partly covered by the pavilion to achieve a shaded outdoor waiting area. The space boundaries of the open foyer are defined by the twisting surfaces of the cones. The interstitial spaces between them frame the view onto the Ocean and create niches for the visitors to take a pause during the exhibition. The sequence of people's movement through pre-show, main show, and post show is also spatially modulated: lingering through the first two small cones with a ceiling height of 8 meters people arrive at the main show, a breath-taking 20 meter-high space. After the show the visitors move to the lower and more intimate post-show areas that finally lead to the café and a swimming island in the open water, where they can relax and experience the Ocean. Visitors with a deeper interest can take the escalator to the second level, where institutions will present their research about renewable energies and marine technology. The roof functions as a third exhibition area, which invites people to relax and enjoy a 360-degree view over the Expo site. Roof gardens will be covered with local plants.

The foyer and exhibition areas are naturally ventilated. Therefore the interstitial spaces between the cones were orientated towards the prevailing wind flow to create air nozzles. In the larger vertical exhibitions, air will be infused through the floor. At daytime, the kinetic lamellas are used to control solar exposure.

SOMA is an Austrian practice founded in 2007 by Stefan Rutzinger, Martin Oberascher, Kristina Schinegger, and Günther Weber. The studio engages architecture as an ongoing inquiry and speculative experimentation. The studio's field of activities ranges from the development of contemporary design strategies and innovative realization methods to theoretical research. SOMA understands architecture as thinking in concepts that deploy their potentials in spatial, physical, and sensuous experiences.

Design team: Lukas Galehr, Christoph Treberspurg, Alice Mayer, Victorie Senesova, Alex Matl, Karin Dobbler, Kathrin Dörfler, Raimund Krenmüller

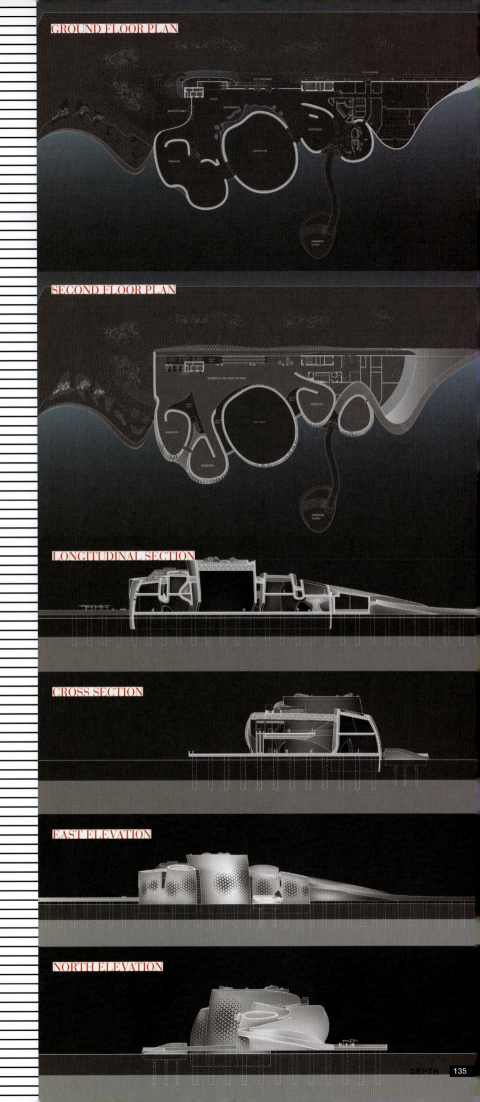

GROUND FLOOR PLAN

SECOND FLOOR PLAN

LONGITUDINAL SECTION

CROSS SECTION

EAST ELEVATION

NORTH ELEVATION

MUSEUM OF OCEAN AND SURF

BIARRITZ, FRANCE
STEVEN HOLL ARCHITECTS

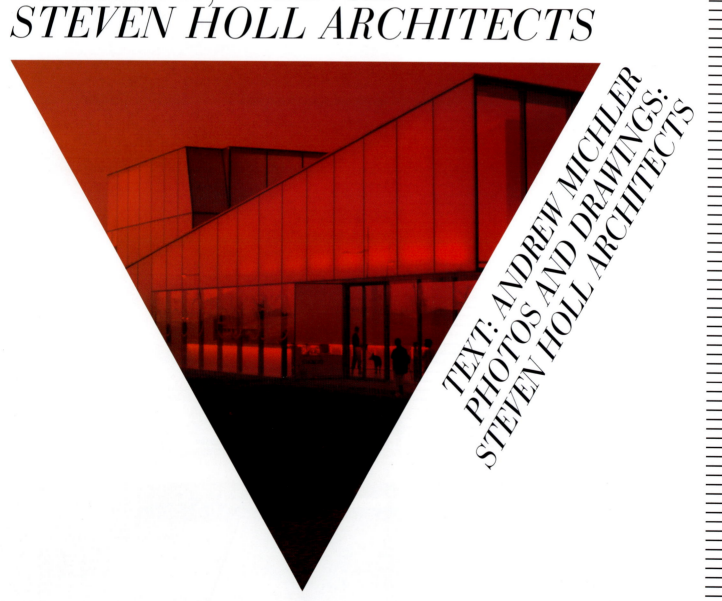

TEXT: ANDREW MICHLER
PHOTOS AND DRAWINGS:
STEVEN HOLL ARCHITECTS

A new breed of museum has been emerging in which the buildings themselves are expressions of the institution's program. The result of a collaboration between Steven Holl Architects and Solange Fabião, using formal elements as metaphor and site specific references, Cité de l'Océan et du Surf Museum's mission of creating awareness of issues pertaining to the ocean is realized by its sculpted contour, intended to immerse visitors as soon as they step on the museum's grounds. Set near the Atlantic shores of the famed surf spot Biarritz in southern France, the museum rests just 11 miles from the border with Spain overlooking a public park which funnels to the shore. The museum's broad curatorial programming concerns itself with all aspects of the surf and ocean with exhibits on physics, biology, environmental concerns, and human interaction with the water geared towards a younger audience. The interpretive quality of the exhibitions is part of a newer breed of museum programming, concerned as much with entertainment as information, attempting to appeal to an audience accustomed to multimedia as expression.

As gesture the building's design succeeds in emulating the kinetic sensibility of the ocean. The immersive quality of the sweeping walls, evoking waves in which the trough is broken by glazed "rocks", is intended to create disorientation from one's typical terrestrial perspective. The horizon is cut off to the south and north, creating the claustrophobic condition of being placed between

VIEW FROM PARK

COBBLESTONE DETAIL

ROOF PLAN

PLAN AT + 28.70 M

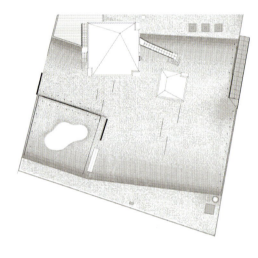

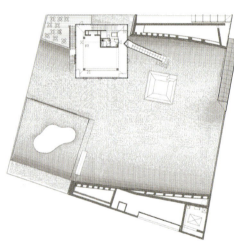

PLAN AT + 17.50 M M

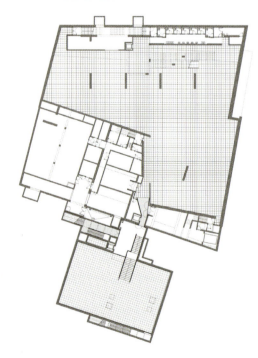

PLAN AT + 25.10 M

PLAN AT + 20.70 M

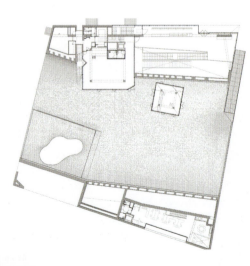

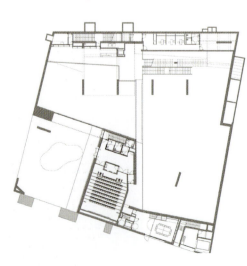

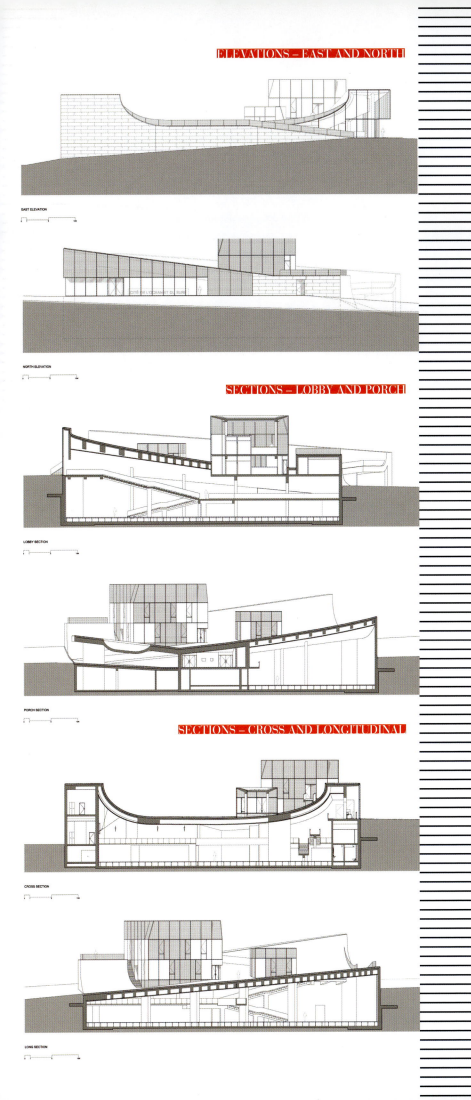

ELEVATIONS – EAST AND NORTH

EAST ELEVATION

NORTH ELEVATION

SECTIONS – LOBBY AND PORCH

LOBBY SECTION

PORCH SECTION

SECTIONS – CROSS AND LONGITUDINAL

CROSS SECTION

LONG SECTION

two enormous swells which is then relieved by the long horizontal lines intersecting with the ocean's horizon. In an early watercolor concept sketch Steven Holl created for submission to the closed design competition, the scale, mass, and form of the building is clearly resolved. Two main perspectives are noted on the sheet: "Sous le Ciel / Sous l'Ocean", under the sky / under the sea, driving the design sensibility of space and elements. The intention of that first sketch is largely maintained by the final design with one important omission in the watercolor. Two large, beacon-like masses are added to provide a kind of shelter in the swept space. The milky glazed boxes, made from high performance Okalux glass, emerge from the swell of pavestones and act as islands by breaking the monotony of the plaza. They are scaled and positioned to echo the two sea-borne rocks at the nearby shore line, pegging the building to its site. Fabião inserted a skateboard pool, turning the plaza into a full scale public park. Departing from the original sketch egress tends to chop the plaza into a less fluid shape, like a song with added notes that jump out of sequence.

The chalky white finish of the rooftop plaza is the result of the diligent use of Portuguese Calçada cobblestones, a historical building method that is losing favor for its labor intensity. Where the pitch of the plaza becomes suitably reduced the pavers are framed in grass, further softening the space and enhancing the transition to the green park stretching to the coast. The cobblestones anchor the contemporary design to tradition, encouraging nostalgic reflections of a southern European plaza. The concrete walls, made from local white quarried aggregate, lighten the bulkiness of the building's facade. The plaza's combination of high albedo and porous properties, allowing rainwater to transition back to vapor, will have a positive effect on internal cooling loads. The pervious surface's capacity to absorb storm water may be a moot point as the building is not in a densely developed area with significant surrounding hardscape.

While Holl references[1] how the plaza ends skyward, cleaving a connection to building and atmosphere, his allegory of "under the sea" is more successful by tucking the program not only below the plaza but into the earth itself. The main exhibition area stretches mostly below the surface as the program steps down with the site. The overall scale is difficult to determine from the street, with the full height evident at the main entrance but tapering down to where the building's boundaries diffuse. The underlying message is about the true mystery of the ocean, an environment whose complexities and diversity are well hidden below human habitat. In practical terms the effort to place the bulk of the museum's mass below ground reduces the visual impact, making the development a good citizen in the established neighborhood.

The museum's approach of providing a

MAIN ENTRANCE

GLASS VOLUMES DETAIL

public space on its roof and tucking program below the terrain seems to be a hot commodity in the course of recent museum design with LA Holocaust Museum coming immediately to mind. Opened in October 2010, the subterranean space rests directly adjacent to the Pan Pacific Park in Los Angeles. Belzburg Architects' aesthetic has a relationship closer with bone and catacombs than movement and sky. Paths cross over its green roof, which is open to the public and has quickly become a part of the neighborhood. The complexities of opening an outdoor program to the public, allowing ordinary life to spill into privileged sites is not a new phenomenon, but designing for it is. The skateboard pool at Cité has a magnetic quality for the city's teenagers, adding the grinding of trucks, squeak of wheels and sometimes boisterous voices to what would be otherwise a place of contemplation. The restaurant in one of the "rocks" and a surf station in the other further the effort in resolving the space for layers of utilization. Adding a large covered plaza below the pool creates a natural gathering space for events. The exterior morphs from a place of contemplation into one of play.

Another underground museum is under construction in Monterrey, Mexico, with a mission that is similar to Cité. Architect Iñaki Echeverria's Interactive Childrens Museum Papalote Verdewill also caters to a younger audience about the natural world. The building will push the limits of subterranean program, only revealing itself with a glazed roof and a deeply sunken courtyard to connect visitors with the outdoors and uses the grounds as an interpretive garden. Perhaps the statement of land (or sea) as museum adds a contemporary logic to sustainable structure, making the building become landscape, and landscape serving as public trust.

The museum entrance provides an opportunity to create interesting relationships with its occupants. The entry could be likened to going through ocean breakers as the visitor is immediately met with a pitched roofline mimicking the perspective of a swell from beneath. Illuminated by projected stills and video scenes on the ceiling, visitors are granted a birds-eye-view of the exhibition halls. The bowed roof provides an elegant interior volume for the auditorium and theater, and the overall sweep of the roof adds appealing drama and funnels daylight. Visitors are then introduced to a great stairway descending into the main exhibit area with balconies providing multiple orientations to the spaces below. Further inside, a second lower floor contains temporary exhibitions with the auditorium to the side. Having the majority of the volume below ground buffers the building from

weather conditions and naturally maintains temperature. Raised floor heating and displacement cooling are not only efficient, but the system frees the ceiling of mechanicals, greatly aiding in the design of the roof curvature.

The open floor space of the main gallery is designed to easily accommodate changing exhibitions over time. The current form of interpretive multi-media displays sits somewhat awkwardly in the space as a result. Originally planned as a surf themed museum the programming morphed into the exploration of the sciences. Perhaps it is asking too much for museums, under constant pressure to compete with all forms of new media, to settle with a long term installation, but the rooms feel stuffed with oversized kiosks rather than integrated programming. In this respect the design falls flat. Rather than immersive in a multi-dimensional and engaging exploration of the natural world, the exhibition hall becomes a big room filled with simulations of nature. Integrating the building's interior with the exhibitions on a more intimate level would have done much to serve the museum's mission. This is in contrast to Holl's successful program with the Nelson Atkins Art Museum in Kansas City which uses light, negative space and form to frame the artwork, highlighting perhaps his comfort in designing for fine art.

The overall context of the museum is palpable however. By using site appropriate materials and design evoking the quality surf, Holl and Fabião will make a mark on the region, where the relationship of the ocean and humans is highly integrated. The Cité de l'Océan et du Surf is not just a place of entertainment, knowledge, or esthetic release but of meditation on the vast yet precarious quality of ocean. The expressive experience of the space itself is intended to be recalled as attentiveness to the environment is cultivated. If visitors leave with a greater emotional awareness of the planet's oceans then the design can rightly be measured as a success.

Cite de l'Ocean et du Surf, Biarritz: Interview With Steven Holl & Solange Fabião. www.huffingtonpost.com/carla-leitao/cite-de-locean-et-du-surf_b_894241. html#s329037

Andrew Michler, LEED AP BD+C, is a consultant and writer, and has been living off-grid in Masonville, Colorado since 1995. He is the owner of Baosol LLC Adaptive, a sustainable building consulting company that specializes in design, education and advocacy. His formal education is in the fine arts and focuses primarily on conceptual art installations. He is currently chair of the Northern Colorado Renewable Energy Society. Writing extensively about sustainable building projects, theory and practice, his efforts are directed at helping develop a low entropy society.

MUSEUM OF POLISH HISTORY

WARSAW, POLAND
PAUL PREISSNER ARCHITECTS

IMAGES AND DRAWINGS:
PAUL PREISSNER ARCHITECTS

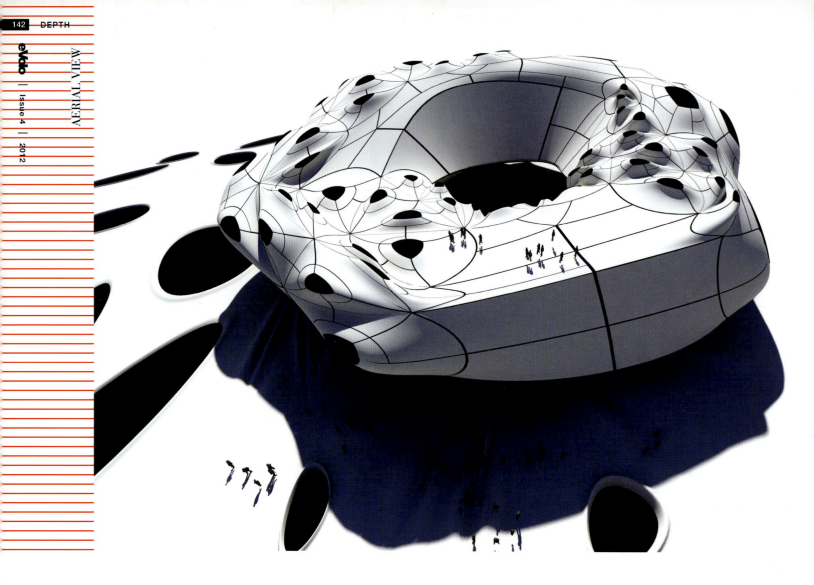

For this project for a country and historic culture of nearly 40 million citizens, Paul Preissner Architects put forth a design solution that understands the significant role of history in the development of a country, but more importantly, recognizes the intricate and directional relationship to its future. The Museum of Polish History and its surrounding development site stands not just to signify and remember the path to the present, but also provides a literal platform for the continued progressive development of Polish culture.

Using a policy to promote cultural and educational activities, this proposal performs as an central character in the play of Polish culture, not only for the users of the facility and its surrounding park, but also for the entire culture of Poland; becoming a new Center for the discovery and empathetic learning of history.

The site is holistically looked at as both a territory to preservations, natural management of resources, contemporary intervention, and radical cultural and commercial development. Conceptually turning the site into both a museum of landscape and artifactual history and a model of progressive cultural and environmental development. The site is divided into sections that range from complete replacement of existing conditions to utmost preservation of its historic shape and allowing the site to exist as both park and narrator.

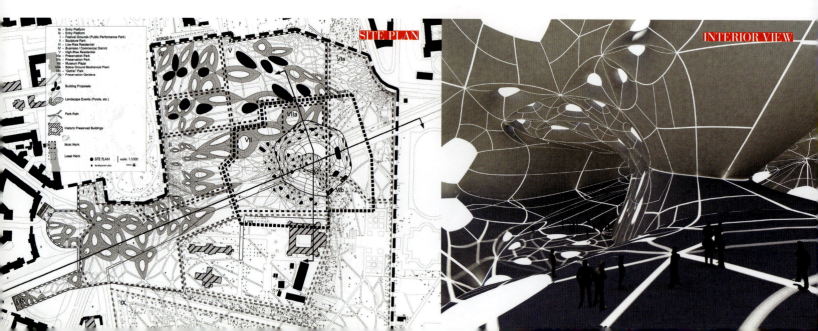

SITE PLAN

INTERIOR VIEW

The park site is specifically developed to maximize the excitement, energy, and functionality of all forms of urban transit, including automobile, bus, truck, bicycle, and pedestrian pathways. The major construction move of separating the infrastructural travel (trucks, cars, and bus) from the human scale methods of movement (pedestrian and bicycle) allows for dense transportation needs in plan to be satisfied through sectional diversity. New commercial, retail, residential, and cultural facilities can be accessed and serviced without prohibiting more personal and human means of circulation. The park deck connects the entire site with a universal and level network of paths that create both pleasure and opportunity in movement.

The museum's sculptural volume is designed along conceptual terms of fluidity, velocity and lightness in order to produce a seductive and progressive artifact within the historic context of the city. The building appears like a mystical object floating above the extensive artificial landscape strip, both spanning the Trasa Lazienkowska right up at the edge of the embankment. This seemingly defying gravity by exposing dramatic undercuts towards the surrounding entrance plazas. The building does not sit as a barrier to the site, but another viewing opportunity to the historic context and surrounding city.

Paul Preissner established his practice in Chicago, IL in 2005. He brings 20 years of experience to the office in architecture and project management, having worked for Peter Eisenman, Philip Johnson and Skidmore Owings and Merill, as well as serving as a Project Architect for Wood-Zapata on the renovation of Chicago' Soldier Field. Paul received a Bachelor of Science in Architecture from the University of Illinois, Urbana-Champaign (1996) and Masters in Architecture from Columbia University (2000). Paul has taught at SCI-Arc, held the endowed Hyde Chair at the University of Nebraska, and been a Visiting Artist the Art Institute of Chicago. He currently is an Assistant Professor at the University of Illinois at Chicago School of Architecture.

COURTYARD

PLANS

PLAN DIAGRAM

SECTION DIAGRAM

ELEVATIONS

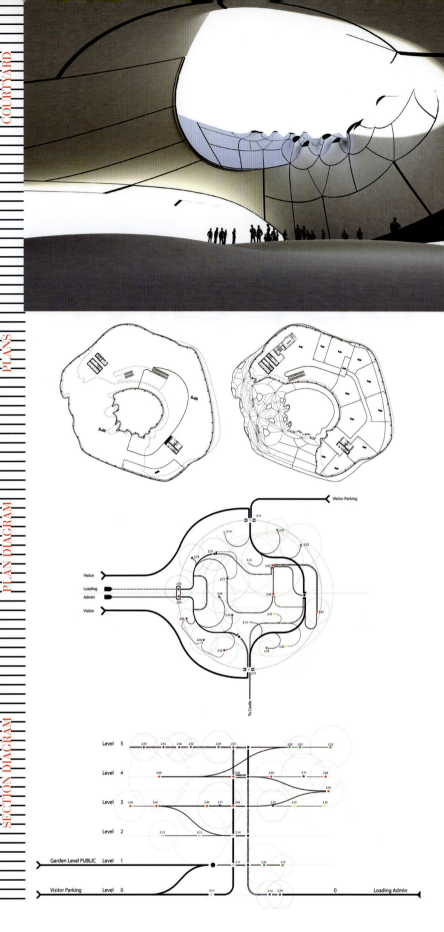

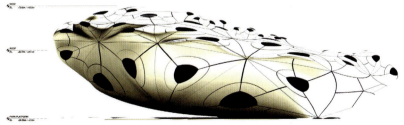

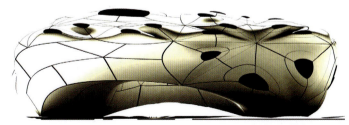

PREHISOTRY MUSEUM

JEONGOK, SOUTH KOREA

TEXT: JASON LEVY

PHOTOS AND DRAWINGS:
X-TU ARCHITECTS

MUSEUM AS A BRIDGE [left]
EXTERIOR VIEW [right]

MAIN PATH

LOBBY / CAFÉ [left]
MAIN STAIRS [right]

Humans often ponder time travel, wishing they could experience the styles and cultures of our past. Or better yet, to jump forward to see what we, as a society, will one day be capable of. This is especially true as architectural trends and theories evolve. As computer software for generating 2D, 3D and even 4D models is improved, the potential for detail within the architectural design increases exponentially.

The French studio X-TU Architects (Anouk Legendre + Nicolas Desmazieres) envision the Prehistory Museum in Jeongok, South Korea as a response to this urge for traveling through time by creating a futuristic "vessel" to take patrons back through the past to learn about South Korea's origins. The sleek museum is located atop two small hills along the Hantan River landscape. This building serves as a continuation of the surrounding terrain that gave birth to the first inhabitants of Korea. The design follows the current design trend of allowing the site to tell its own story, achieved by utilizing innovative technology and architecture to set the stage. The chasm between the two hills is dug out and the reflective surface of the museum's stainless steel panel system showcases the landscape below. The structure was built into the hollowed out hillside, allowing for a smooth-looking iconic finish. More private programs such as the museum's stockrooms are safely hidden away below the ground. The significance of the geological crack is visible when looking at the building's mass in plan. The curved center of the building's mass helps to better unveil the earth below. Even the circulation around the path is a reflection on the paths taken by animals and primitive

humans going to the river for water at the dawn of mankind. Upon parking at the Prehistory Museum, the patrons must travel these same paths and venture into the hill's chasm to gain entrance to the museum's interior.

X-TU Architects describe the Prehistory Museum as an "immaterial-abstract-shaped time vessel." Visitors of the museum get the counterintuitive experience of seeing futuristic design techniques and technologies being used to educate them about the early development of mankind. The building's skin was designed parametrically; the architects use computer-aided technologies to create the rounded stainless steel facade with predetermined perforations that give the building an almost organic feel. The design has complete control of natural light that enters various programmatic spaces within, including a theater, lecture space, a variety of exhibition spaces, a gift shop and a café. From the roof's walkway the visitor gets an unparalleled 360-degree view of the surrounding landscape and river. Each programmatic node was conceived as a separate landscape, similar to the various landscapes primitive man walked across.

The envelope is made of a double metal system of vertical panels. These panels are glazed according to their placement within the site to better reflect the ground plane below. Within this envelope is an exterior circulation path embedded behind the exterior panel. This path is rather similar to the circulation paths of the Docks De Paris by architects Jakob + Macfarlane. In that project, a steel undulating structure is added to a preexisting concrete shipping depot structure with a rigorous column grid layout. Similar to how

HALLWAY / GALLERY

LOBBY / GALLERY [left]
LOBBY / MUSEUM SHOP [right]

the docks' concrete base structure serves as a contrast to the newer steel addition, the contrast between old and new in the Prehistory Museum is made present in the comparison of exterior vs. interior material choices. Unlike its futuristic, loud and shimmering exterior, the interior of the museum is quiet and composed of archaic and primitive materials. The result is a calm interior that appears to be carved out the cliff itself.

In their article "The Museum of the Twenty-first Century," Ben van Berkel and Caroline Bos of UN Studio explain that there are two types of circulation possible for contemporary museums. The first, more popular choice is to have an open floor plan using spaces that offer various circulation paths. The user is given the option to choose his or her own way through the exhibitions and can have a unique experience each time he or she visits the museum. This option is particularly successful in larger museums. However, in smaller museums with a very specific topic, such as the Prehistory Museum, a predetermined circulation path through the space is deployed, giving the designer control of how the user walks through the areas. The Prehistory Museum attempts to merge these two ideas into what they call "The Great Walk of Evolution." Upon entering the museum patrons will see a timeline printed on the floor that will guide them through the museum and thus through the history of mankind in Jeongok. While walking, they are led to a series of exhibition clusters, many of which offer an interactive experience. Projectors and audio features are embedded within the interior walls to give another layer of exhibition possibilities. Within these exhibition clusters is where the patron has the freedom to choose his own experience. While still following the main circulation path, the users are given freedom to explore within the various exhibition clusters. To further the sense of chronologically flowing through time, the entrance and exit of the museum are positioned in different locations of the structure. Inside the museum, artifacts are displayed in a few different ways. The floor raises in some areas to become the display space, the walls have openings for smaller pieces, and there are additional side niches. This variety in display is the architects' response to the endless display case technique of exhibition that can be seen at any typical museum.

The Prehistory Museum can be thought of as a time capsule. Although it features a futuristic façade, its design details are deeply rooted in the history of mankind's development in South Korea. It is the architects' time machine that becomes a new icon of South Korean pride.

Jason Levy is an architecture student at Tulane University; he is interested on urban renewal and volunteer work focused on rebuilding. Jason spent a semester in Rome, Italy studying classical and contemporary architecture which has led to an appreciation and understanding of architecture evolution through history.

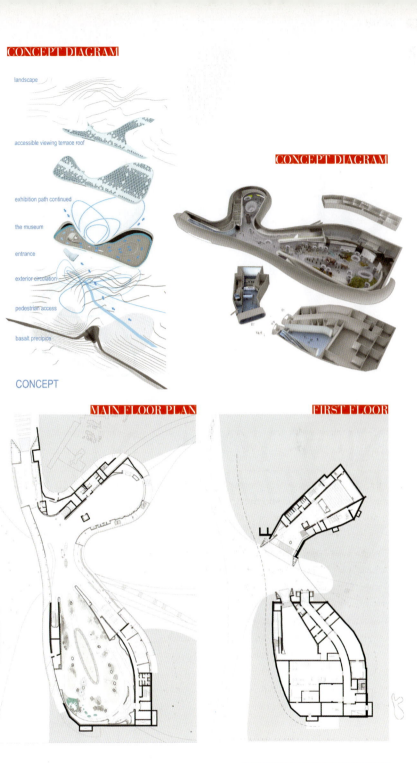

CONCEPT DIAGRAM

landscape

accessible viewing terrace roof

exhibition path continued

the museum

entrance

exterior circulation

pedestrian access

basalt precipice

CONCEPT

CONCEPT DIAGRAM

MAIN FLOOR PLAN

FIRST FLOOR

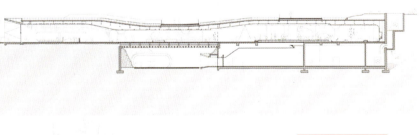

LONGITUDINAL SECTION

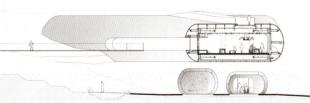

CROSS SECTION

evolo | issue 4 | 2012

SPERONE WESTWATER GALLERY

NEW YORK, NY
FOSTER + PARTNERS

TEXT: HEIDI DRUCKEMILLER

PHOTOS: NIGEL YOUNG / FOSTER + PARTNERS

Sir Norman Foster is an architect renowned as much for his sophisticated, high-tech approach to the design and construction process as he is for his iconic, name-brand projects. With work completed in 150 cities and more than fifty countries he is, in many ways, the epitome of the globe-trotting, "star," architect, called upon to create signature projects that add some sheen to environments in need of uplifting, or simply more stature to many of the world's most desirable locales. His firm, Foster + Partners, is one of an enviable few that is able to straddle the tricky divide of being both a successful, large-scale, corporate-style practice and one whose work is innovative on a level to have captured the highly coveted Pritzker Architecture Prize.

Foster designed the Hongkong and Shanghai Bank Headquarters (1986) and the Chek Lap Kok Airport (1998) in Hong Kong long before the rest of his ilk began designing all of the new celebrated buildings in mainland China. He figures prominently in that mix as well, however, completing the largest and most technologically advanced airport in the world in Beijing in 2008. His latest project in New York City, the Sperone Westwater gallery, is a considerably more modest affair, but the fact that New York and Beijing each has a new Norman Foster building is perhaps an appropriate metaphor for the two cities' current competition for international cultural dominance. That said, a side-by-side comparison of the two projects makes it obvious that the Chinese capital is clearly pulling ahead.

The Sperone Westwater gallery opened in 1975 with a Carl Andre exhibition and presently represents artists such as Susan Rothenberg, William Wegman, and Bruce Nauman. Partners Angela Westwater and Gian Enzo Sperone operated galleries in SoHo and Chelsea before their recent move to the Bowery, one of the oldest and most storied streets in Lower Manhattan, and currently a focal point for those who argue that New York City's artistic nexus has edged its way over to the Lower East Side. Tokyo-based firm Kazuyo Sejima + Ryue Nishizawa/SANAA's New Museum opened its doors on the Bowery in December 2007, and was heralded as the first major art museum to be constructed in downtown Manhattan in the city's modern history. The building's design, comprising a teetering tower of stacked rectilinear boxes, was an immediate hit with both museum-goers and critics alike, many of whom were quick to point out that the structure's seemingly ad hoc form was the architects' intentional nod to the Bowery's colorful, rough-and-tumble history.

On the exterior, the Sperone Westwater gallery also has a somewhat ad hoc appearance, but it lacks the underlying elegance of the New Museum's design, which manages to retain an air of lightness and whimsy despite the fact that it is, essentially, a pile of building blocks. Sperone Westwater is, by comparison, just a single block, but all together the black, corrugated metal cladding; I-beam frame; and large panes of translucent glass that comprise its façade lend the building an oddly makeshift air. The severity of the structure's box-like appearance is accentuated by the constraints of its narrow lot that measures 25'x 100,' small dimensions that also help give the impression that the building stands taller than its eight stories. The structure's single, dramatic setback draws yet further attention to its attenuated form, though it unfortunately also draws a comparison to the setback created by the cheap and unsightly addition that sits atop the roof of the small building to its left—doubtful an outcome the architect intended.

The central design element of the gallery is unquestionably the glass

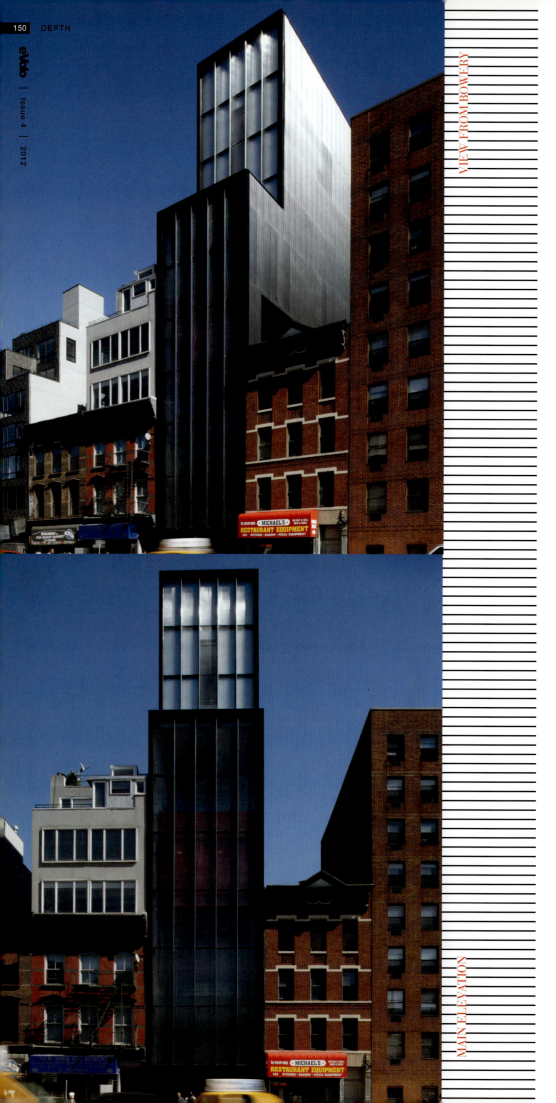

eVolo | Issue 4 | 2012

VIEW FROM BOWERY

MAIN ELEVATION

selected to be the principal building material of the façade. This is not surprising considering that an innovative and prominent use of glass is a common thread throughout Foster's work in general. The rebuilding of the Reichstag as a new German Parliament in Berlin and the Great Court at the British Museum of London are but two of the architect's elegant and high-profile projects whose salient features are variations on prominent glass domes. Swiss Re HQ, 30 St Mary Axe, (Foster's iconic London skyscraper colloquially known as "the Gherkin"), also features a glass dome at the top of the building, and the overall placement of small glass quadrilaterals on the skyscraper's curved structure creates the effect that the entire building has a bulging, rounded form. Keeping those projects in mind, it is all the more disappointing that Foster's use of glass in the design of the Sperone Westwater renders a result that is rather mundane in comparison.

The gallery's most engaging feature is the giant red elevator that is visible from the street behind the building's glass façade as it travels between the second and fifth floors. When it's not moving, it's not clear what it is, but it's still an interesting focal point and splash of color on the otherwise plain exterior. On the inside the elevator feels a bit claustrophobic and does not make an interesting space in which to view art, particularly if it's not in motion, which, apparently, it won't be for every installation. Even though Foster outfitted the elevator with all the finishes of a typical gallery such as sophisticated lighting, environmental controls, fire proofing, and security, etc., it is not comparable to the other quiet and elegant galleries on the Sperone Westwater's surrounding floors, which are similar exhibition spaces in some respects, but benefit from higher ceilings, less constrictive dimensions, and an infusion of natural light. The double-height space on the gallery's ground floor is supremely elegant and by far the building's greatest success as a showcase for exhibiting art. A twenty-seven-foot wall stretches past the second floor's mezzanine perched behind a curvilinear glass balustrade, and overall the space projects a sense of grandeur without being overbearing. Upon entering the room, one is overtaken by the type of distinctive experiential quality usually expected of a project designed by Norman Foster.

When Foster was named the 1999 Pritzker Prize Laureate, a member of the jury commented that the architect's "vision forges the materials of our age into a crystalline, lyrical purity that is highly personal, brilliantly functional, and—shy as we are about using the word—just downright beautiful." Though the Sperone Westwater gallery doesn't embody the architect's usual panache, it's worth considering whether that's partly a problem of context. Like SANAA before him, Foster perhaps decided to veer away from creating a building with too much polish given its location on the Bowery, which has never been an elegant street. Though it dates back to the Dutch Colonial era—when the "Great Bouwerie" was a tract a land extending from what is now 5th Street to 17th Street, along the East River, and westward to present-day Fourth Avenue—the Bowery came of age in the 19th century when it reigned as the city's first and largest entertainment district. Not long afterward the street became vice-ridden and openly tawdry, but its iconic status as the birthplace of Vaudeville, Yiddish Theater, tap dance, and, later, punk rock is undisputed. By the turn of the 21st century, the Bowery had shaken its more dangerous edge, but it retained its longtime down-and-out feel, even as it boasted a fair amount of commercial activity as the center of a shopping district characterized by a curious mix of restaurant suppliers and lighting fixture retailers.

Some have watched with a certain degree of trepidation as widespread gentrification has recently taken hold on the Bowery, largely in the form of bland condominium buildings, and, more tragically, in the loss of legendary venues like CBGB's, which closed its doors in 2006. A John Varvatos store has taken its place. Taking that into consideration, institutions such as the New Museum and Sperone Westwater are a more welcome addition to the Bowery and its ongoing evolution. Though a far cry from the notoriously lowbrow institutions that characterized the Bowery in the past, at least these new high-end art venues lend a more relevant voice to contemporary cultural discourse than does pricey housing or a clothing store. The Bowery deserves better, and Foster should be commended for tackling the difficult task of designing a new addition to an urban context with such an entrenched sense of place. While his respect for the spirit of the Sperone Westwater's surroundings is admirable—and proof of a sensitivity that way too many of his colleagues deliberately dismiss—Foster went too far in his design for the gallery by creating a building that lacks his signature sophistication and swagger, and doesn't do justice to his incredible talent. While successfully paying homage to the Bowery's unpretentious past, the Sperone Westwater's rough-hewn exterior doesn't ring true as the work of Norman Foster, an instance of inauthenticity that runs counter to the best of what the Bowery has always embodied.

Heidi Druckemiller is an architectural historian, writer and preservation consultant living in New York City. She studied the History of Art and Architecture at Brown University and Architectural History and Theory at Columbia University's Graduate School of Architecture, Planning and Preservation where she was an editor of Future Anterior, the school's journal of historic preservation, history, theory and criticism. Heidi also worked for many years promoting several architects and architectural firms in New York City and abroad and writes about both contemporary and historic architecture, with particular interest in how they intersect in an urban context.

ELEVATOR GALLERY   GALLERIES

eVolo | Issue 4 | 2012

EXCURSIONS OF THE FIGURAL IN THE FAR EAST:

THE CIVIC SPORTS CENTER AND 2013 NATIONAL GAMES ARENA

SHENYANG, CHINA
EMERGENT

TEXT: BENJAMIN RICE

IMAGES AND DRAWINGS: EMERGENT

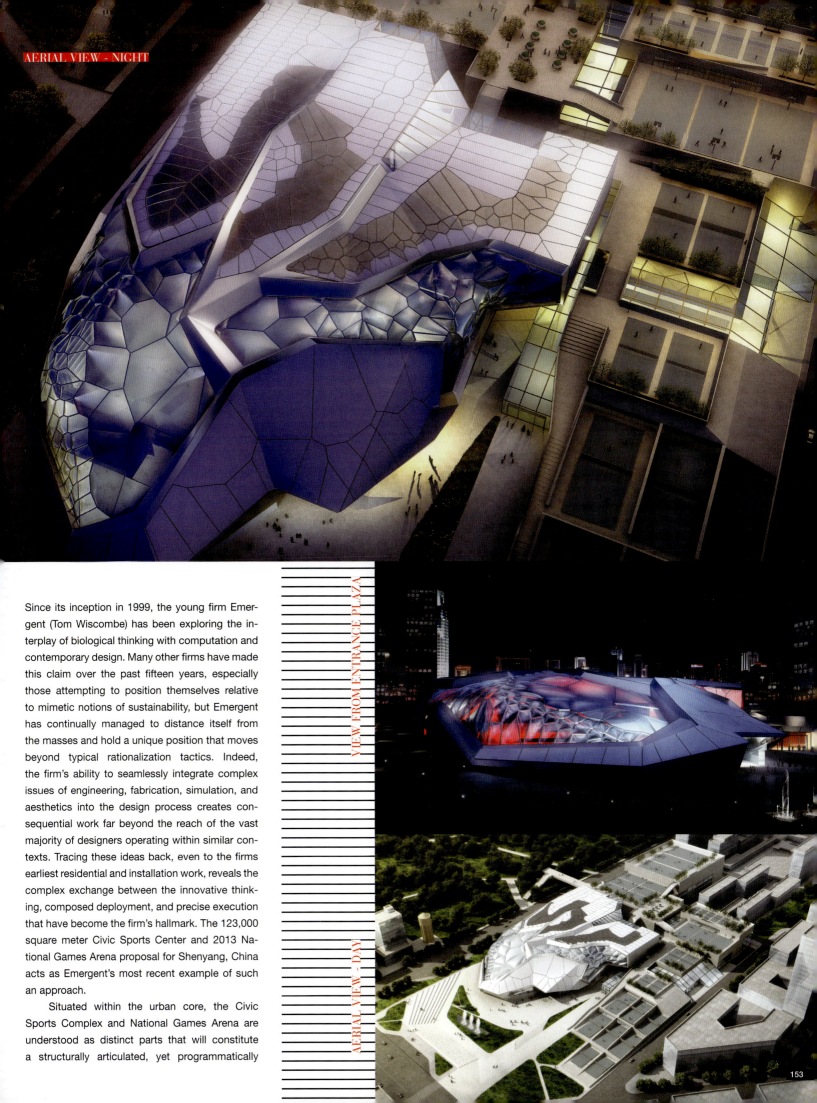

VIEW FROM ENTRANCE PLAZA

AERIAL VIEW - DAY

Since its inception in 1999, the young firm Emergent (Tom Wiscombe) has been exploring the interplay of biological thinking with computation and contemporary design. Many other firms have made this claim over the past fifteen years, especially those attempting to position themselves relative to mimetic notions of sustainability, but Emergent has continually managed to distance itself from the masses and hold a unique position that moves beyond typical rationalization tactics. Indeed, the firm's ability to seamlessly integrate complex issues of engineering, fabrication, simulation, and aesthetics into the design process creates consequential work far beyond the reach of the vast majority of designers operating within similar contexts. Tracing these ideas back, even to the firms earliest residential and installation work, reveals the complex exchange between the innovative thinking, composed deployment, and precise execution that have become the firm's hallmark. The 123,000 square meter Civic Sports Center and 2013 National Games Arena proposal for Shenyang, China acts as Emergent's most recent example of such an approach.

Situated within the urban core, the Civic Sports Complex and National Games Arena are understood as distinct parts that will constitute a structurally articulated, yet programmatically

eVolo || Issue 4 || 2012

PROGRAM

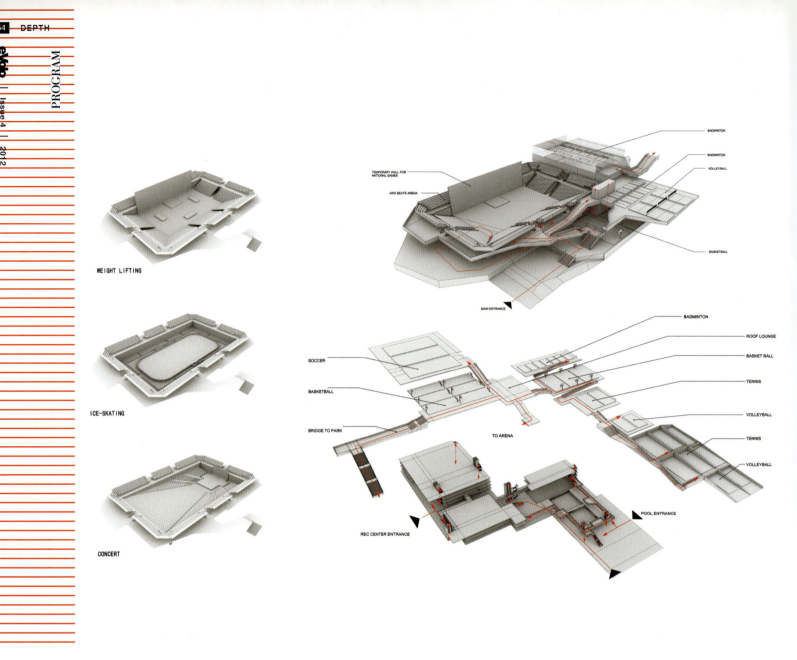

WEIGHT LIFTING

ICE-SKATING

CONCERT

interconnected and continuous whole. The cascading landscape of the Civic Sports Complex moves from the northern edge to the eastern portion of the site, facing the city center, and will house many specific spaces for diverse sporting activities, such as volleyball, tennis, basketball, and badminton courts, as well as soccer fields and a swimming arena. The National Games Arena occupies the western end of the site facing Zhongshan Park, and has the ability to convert into multiple configurations in order to accommodate a variety of activities as disparate as NBA games, Disney events, and concerts of varying kinds. The two buildings will be interconnected at various points on various levels to allow for both the full integration and interaction between the two as well as for the maximum flexibility of use.

Emergent's characteristic use of biological thinking is employed at all levels and scales of the two buildings, but is most visually apparent in the facade patterning of the National Games Arena. The crystal inspired system is achieved using a steel frame that supports transparent, pressurized ETFE bubbles, as well as opaque aluminum panels. Part of the system's success comes from its ability to create a sense of movement from one section of the building to another, allowing for an architectural affect that influences both the direction and speed of movement due to the pattern gradient changing over space and time. This speaks to a complex understanding of what biological thinking can actually mean within the realm of architectural deployment; an understanding that allows traits and characteristics of non-

architectural environments, scales, and species to be researched, analyzed, and adapted in order to influence and challenge standard notions of design.

More importantly, this project serves as a reminder that there can be something of disciplinary importance at stake when building in Asia. In fact, Western architects looking to the east for opportunities to explore contemporary, Western concepts is nothing new. Through this project Emergent adds itself to a long list of designers, including Kahn, Corbusier and Gropius (to name but a few), that have been able to momentarily explore the possibilities of designing and building from a unique perspective in a context that, for all intents and purposes, has no western architectural tradition. Unfortunately, this has most recently led to a tremendous amount of figurative projects that take shape quickly under the guise of some immediately recognizable, superficial reference to objects found in nature, simplified cultural signifiers or both. This approach not only acts to prevent a robust discourse from evolving around these new projects, but also inflicts itself back on the West in a way that is currently neither slightly appreciated nor fully understood.

Emergent was able to avoid this pitfall by creating an intricate interplay between traditional, volumetric spaces and complex, contemporary geometries that attempt to abstract the Western architectural heritage that the former implies. This abstraction allows the firm to move past the typical figurative projects found in emerging Asian countries and explore the figural possibilities of an architecture that attempts to break habitual modes of communication and exchange. By framing the formal manifestation of the projects conceptual base with familiar architectural geometries, Emergent is at once bridging the disciplinary divide between East and West, while also allowing the project to act as a point of discursive infiltration into what could have otherwise been a purely referential exercise. The site, situated within downtown Shenyang, provides an exceptional backdrop for such a move due to the boarder condition that is created on the line between the urban center of the city and the adjacent Zhongshan Park – a line that this project sits directly on. By positioning the gradient of transition from familiar to abstract towards the park, the project conceptually links the two polar extremes. This move is further strengthened through the literal bridging between the two, allowing for pedestrians to experience the transformation of city to park as they move through the artificial sports landscape, over the elevated bridge, and into the park.

It could be argued that Emergent has produced similar projects that embody extremely comparable schemes with greater success. After all, many of their designs have been far more literal in the way biological thinking, transition gradients, and the integration of natural elements have been employed. But doing so would miss the point altogether. What is important here is not that the project should create a continuous transition from nature to architecture in a singular, literal gesture, or that the biological systems employed should be overwhelmingly heavy-handed in their use. Instead, what matters is that Emergent have gained the maturity and understanding to bring their expertise to the table in a manner that subtly pushes the boundaries of what Western architects are understood to be capable of building in the East, while simultaneously embedding contemporary systems of knowledge, use, and exchange into the thing itself.

Tom Wiscombe is a licensed architect living in the United States. He is founder and principal of *Emergent*, an internationally recognized design office operating at the forefront of digital design since 1999. *Emergent*'s work stands out in terms of its synthesis of form, pattern, color, and technology. In 2009, ICON Magazine named Principal Tom Wiscombe one of the "top 20 architects in the world who are making the future and transforming the way we work".

Benjamin Rice is a principal of the award-winning firm Matter Management, as well as a Visiting Instructor at the Virginia Tech School of Architecture + Design. His work has been published and exhibited widely including shows at the A+D Museum, Project 4, and the Denver Art Museum, as well as articles in On Ramp, Pidgin Magazine, The Huffington Post, and TARP. He received his Bachelor of Architecture from the Southern California Institute of Architecture and his Master of Architecture from Princeton University.

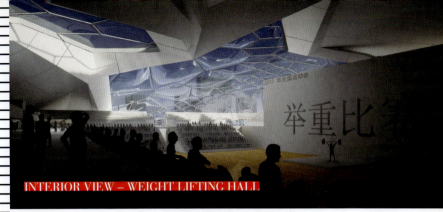

INTERIOR VIEW – WEIGHT LIFTING HALL

STRUCTURE DIAGRAM

SKIN TRANSLUCENCY

PLANS

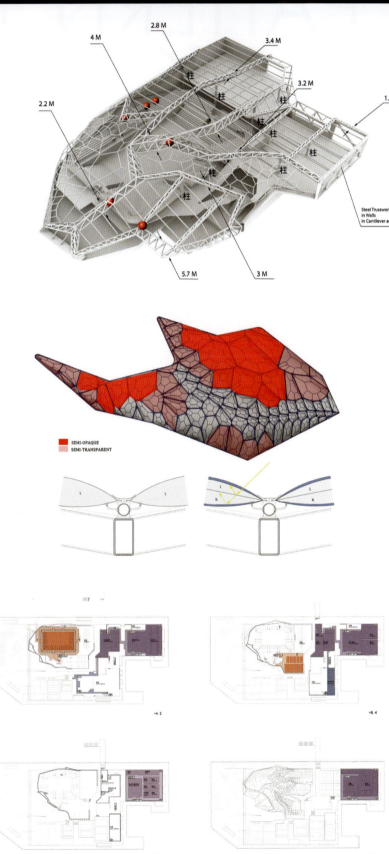

PATTERN + PERFORMANCE

DUNDEE, SCOTLAND
MOTIF AND SPATIALITY IN KENGO KUMA'S VICTORIA + ALBERT DUNDEE MUSEUM

TEXT: ELIE GAMBURG

IMAGES AND DRAWINGS: KENGO KUMA

If *ornament is crime*, what might Adolf Loos think of contemporary architecture's fascination with repetitive patterns?

Despite premature claims to the contrary, the rectilinear forms of modern architecture have not receded into the past. The reductive composition of minimal volumes remains a staple for contemporary designers. Yet the earlier, simple enclosures of high-modernism, rigidly derived from programmatic and construction requirements, have been displaced by an explosive cacophony of tessellated patterns, pictorial prints, warping screens, layered perforations, shifting grids, stuttering windows, or colorful cassettes. Vittorio Gregotti presaged this, discussing the post-modernist fascination with 'façade':

In the Fifties and Sixties the detail had some great and very diverse [modernist] protagonists… in which the analysis and displays of material, provided by the laws of construction and formation of the architectural object constituted its principal support… [while] the resulting eloquent aphasia, though with very different meanings, has been hastily taken over by a reawakening of interest in decoration, or the ornate.[1]

Depending on aesthetic tastes, some patterns may appear elegant, others gaudy; some may attract, others repel; some appear surprisingly boring despite their complexity, and others appear complex though formed from simple pieces. The best of Kengo Kuma's work from the past decade is often exemplary of the latter category: his projects typically consist of reductive volumes whose simple appearance is morphed by patterned assemblages of common materials.

The patterns used by Kuma and others to enliven otherwise simple arrangements of volumes rarely seem to penetrate projects beyond their surfaces. Overall forms remain unperturbed; interior spaces unaffected. Perhaps the truest way to categorize the multiplicity of patterns emerging in contemporary design is to differentiate between those that remain a motif and those that become spatial; in other words, between those that are

eVolo | Issue 4 | 2012

applied to and those that influence form.

Volumetric arrangements remain inviolate in most of Kuma's work; architectural character emerges from the interplay of material detail and pattern. In its stone details, Kengo Kuma's competition winning design for the new Victoria + Albert Museum in Dundee, Scotland follows this lineage. Formally, however, it is a striking departure from earlier projects: its patterned stone defines two twisting volumes containing vertiginous central spaces and public thresholds. The Dundee project is innovative because Kuma's use of materialized pattern gains an added spatial dimension.

Bamboo Sticks. Stone Slats. Travertine Tiles. Kuma has developed an entire oeuvre around the delicate repetition of multiple materials. His projects seem simple, initially, yet they are never simplistic. Their sophistication arises because the patterns are not merely pictorial; careful materiality inherently informs a tectonic understanding of surface. His Lotus House appears light because its checkered pattern of thin travertine tiles, delicately arranged corner-to-corner, forms a 'veil' that is clearly 'hanging.' The layered bamboo screens of his Great (Bamboo) Wall House provide visual and spatial transparency, allowing multiple spaces to be read from every vantage point. The walls of his Stone Museum are also tectonically rich: from the outside the apertures appear as singular elements within the matrix of stacked stone, while, inside, the walls de-materialize into platonic solids punctuated by a pattern of illuminated openings. 'In Stone Museum (2000), I even tried to transform stone, a massive material … into particles.'[2] This interplay of

negative and positive material readings conducts visitors through a carefully choreographed sequence of light and dark rooms.

Kuma uses these patterns to de-materialize project forms: 'I want to erase architecture. I have always wanted to do so, and I am not likely to ever change my mind.'[3] However, the patterns do not directly affect project form or spatial arrangement; rather, the de-materialized volumes typically derive from two operations: One group, such as his Hiroshige Museum of Art, Yusuhara Bridge Museum, or Forest/Floor House, is a re-interpretation of traditional Japanese building typologies; a larger group, such as Stone Museum, One Ometsando, Great (Bamboo) Wall House, and Museum of Kanayama Castle Ruin, consist of simple compositions of rectilinear volumes. In either vein, the purity of the initial forms is never compromised.

The twisted, rather than static, arrangement of the volumes in Kuma's Victoria and Albert Dundee immediately makes apparent its significant differences with his earlier work. Less obvious, but even more important, is that the scale of the stone slat pattern encompassing the project is significantly larger than other patterns that Kuma has used. This scalar shift enables the pattern to affect the volumes and better define the spaces of the project.

Formally, the project arranges two volumes on the site's edge, directly engaging the Firth[4] of Tay. The one closer to the city is subdivided into floors for small galleries and support. The other volume is almost completely hollow, except for a study center. This open volume functions as a 'Great

Hall:' an entry and gallery for exceptionally large art. The Great Hall serves as a covered public plaza terminating an outdoor public space sequence engaging the train station, a famous boat called the 'RRS Discovery', and Marketgait road, which runs to the city center. Conceptually, both volumes are initially positioned orthogonally about the main road to water axis. However, as they rise, both volumes fragment into independent slabs that twist to address the diagonal axis originating from the RRS Discovery. The extreme corners of the two twisting volumes touch at the top floor, allowing people to cross from one volume to the next. This creates a covered 'archway' over the river-walk and frames a view of the Firth – reinforcing the axial approach from the city even as the upper stories twist away from it. The result manages to be both crystalline and organic. The reading of the elevations changes dramatically as one moves around the project.

The twisting volumes are so dramatic that it is almost possible to dismiss the rhythmically patterned stone slat cladding as merely a residue of Kuma's typical design approach. Yet, the interior view of the Great Hall demonstrates that the stacked slats play a markedly different role here than in Kuma's earlier work. Whereas the slats in his Stone Museum remain proximate in size to roman bricks, the slats at Dundee are large enough to become benches, steps, even art displays. The scalar shift renders the pattern performative. More than mere visual texture or tactile surface, the stone slats become occupiable, and once inhabitable they become programmable. This lends the museum a surprising flexibility given the little actual exhibition space contained: the Great Hall's sloping surface operates simultaneously as gathering space, exhibition space, and circulation element. The stacking operates at a building scale at the upper level, where the connecting walkways sit simultaneously atop the sloping walls of the Great Hall and within the larger volume above this main space.

Seemingly minor, the scalar shift in the detail is, in fact, the project's critical innovation: enlarged, the slats change from motif to tectonic elements. Kuma's free-hand sketch clearly demonstrates how tightly spaced horizontal lines precisely 'render' the project's warped forms. Like the pencil lines, the shifting and overlapping of the slats is adaptive, precisely defining the curved/crystalline geometries of the twisted boxes. Visually, the sharp edges of the slats carefully delineate the warped surfaces, so they appear crisper and more refined, as can be seen from the close up view from the river-walk. REX's entry to the competition demonstrates the indeterminacy resulting from the absence of these lineaments. Though its form is simpler, the smooth surfaces do not define its volume as precisely as do Kuma's ribbed stone enclosure. The textural linearity also enhances the

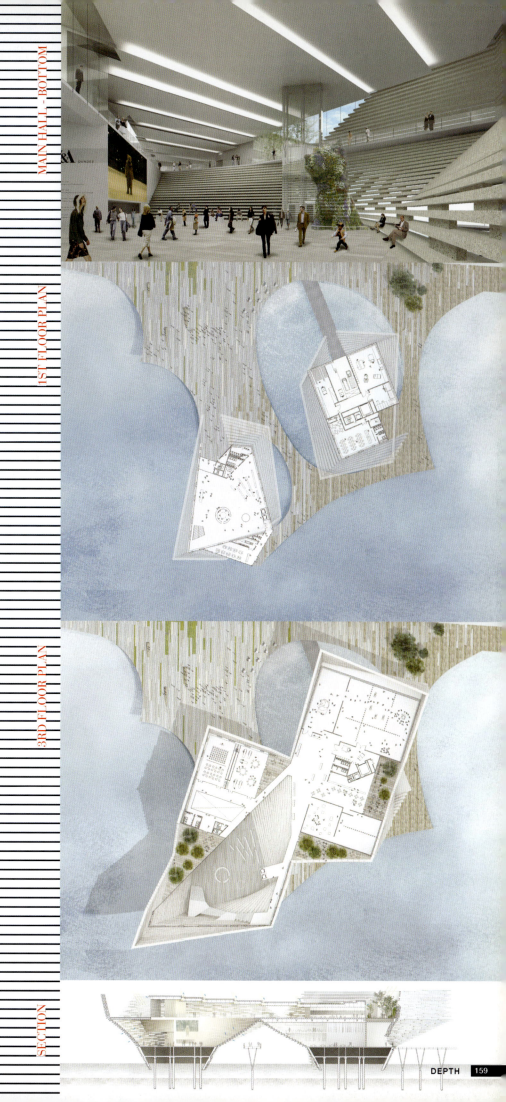

MAIN HALL – BOTTOM

1ST FLOOR PLAN

3RD FLOOR PLAN

SECTION PLAN

CONCEPT DIAGRAM

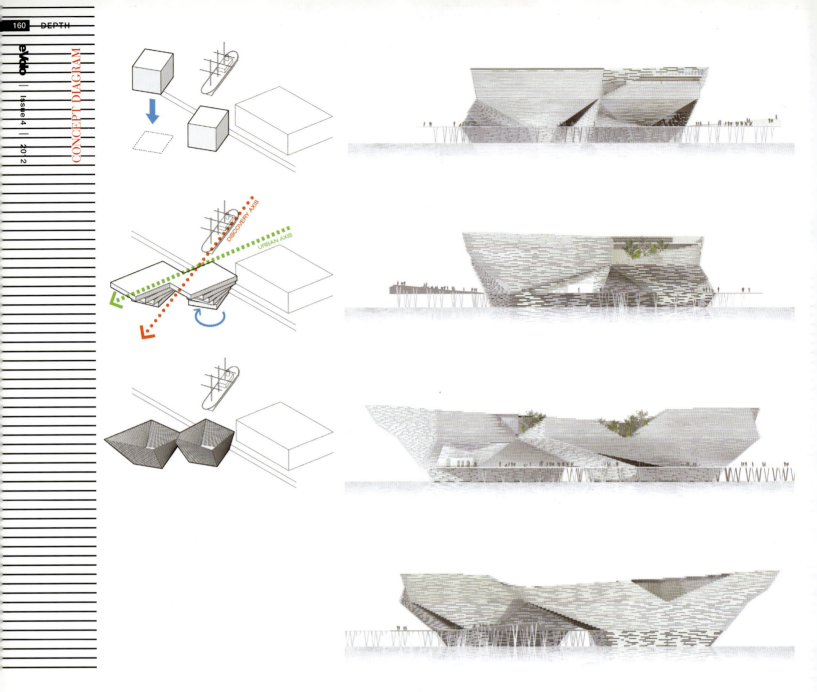

perspectival relationship from walk to water while visually elongating the project along the waterfront.

The stone also appears to conduct the 'weight' of the project's cantilevered upper story down to the ground, even though it is not structural. The heaviness of densely stacked stone in the museum precisely inverses the lightness of the delicately 'hanging' travertine tiles surrounding the Lotus House. This perceived weight visually drives the project into the soft bottom of the river below; while the precarious shifting of the slats above simultaneously renders the cantilevered upper stories more precipitous. Much of the weight of the stone slats derives from the proximity of their size with the size of our bodies. These larger slats function as larger 'components' rather than smaller 'elements.' Whereas all of Kuma's patterns break down the scale of his projects, the components of the Dundee project lend it a more human scale. Like the imprint of a Corbusian 'modular man' into concrete, the bench-size slats literally express the size and configuration of the users.

The shift to human scale facilitates the performance of the larger stone slat pattern. This performative development in Kuma's Victoria + Albert Dundee project is a substantial evolution: whereas other recent projects such as his Tamagawa Takashimaya department store are more organic than earlier work, and while earlier projects already explored the tectonic potential of patterned materials, none have actually spatialized or

programmed these patterns. At Dundee, Kuma's use of pattern drives its spatial development. More than adding visual interest to simple modernist volumes, his approach now offers designers a tool to more precisely develop contemporary fluid geometries. In both cases, it also has the added benefit of suggesting a human scale and providing both visual and tactile richness. Used to articulate complex surfaces, such a deeper use of pattern suggests a promising avenue to resolve contemporary design issues surrounding organic form.

(1) Gregotti, Vittorio. "The Exercise of Detailing." from Nesbitt, Kate (ed). Theorizing a New Agenda for Architecture. Princeton Architectural Press, NY. 1996.
(2) Kuma, Kengo. Watanabe, Hiroshi (trans). Particle on a Horizontal Plane. JA: The Japan Architect #38. Summer 2000.
(3) Kuma, Kengo. Watanabe, Hiroshi (trans). Digital Gardening. Space Architecture. Nov. 1997.
(4) Firth: a straight or inlet in lowland Scottish

Elie Gamburg received his B. Arch from Cornell University and his M. Arch II with distinction from Harvard University where he was also awarded the Kevin V. Kieran prize for academic achievement. He was the winner of the 2008 Evolo Skyscraper Competition, a 2002 Cornell finalist for the SOM travelling fellowship, and was a member of one six final selected teams invited to compete in the History Channel's "Engineering an Empire: Los Angeles" competition. His work has been featured in publications including GSD 08 Platform and Evolo: Skyscraper for the XXI Century. Elie is currently a senior designer at KPF, and teaches studio design at NYIT. He resides in New York City.

SOUMAYA MUSEUM
FREE / FERNANDO ROMERO

TEXT: BRIAN AHMES

DRAWINGS: FREE /FERNANDO ROMERO

VIEW FROM ENTRANCE PLAZA ©JAVIER HINOJOSA

The silhouette of Polanco, Mexico has been changed with the addition of the Soumaya Museum. Its challis-like gesture has made it a vessel not only for the art which inhabits its galleries but also for an urban cultural rebirth which is taking place.

All transformations begin with a gesture or idea, which translate to a positive result or negative impact on a city and its inhabitants. Just as Paris was reinterpreted in the mid 19th century by widening boulevards, creating green space and allowing a better public infrastructure, the process has changed today but conceptually has remained similar. The idea to reform an urban condition is not innovative, but the method, tools and resultants which shape the urban built are.

This large urban revitalization has occurred with the addition of the Guggenheim Museum Bilbao. The Spanish city of Bilbao spent an estimated $228 million on a new modern art museum which was to be located in an industrial site in dire need of revitalization. The new museum was only a piece of the entire city's facelift and much of the roots on the endeavor were new residences, business offices, subways and public infrastructure. The great success of re-urbanization in Bilbao was both the museum and the city's master plan for redevelopment.

The Soumaya Museum, designed by Fernando Romeo, is an example of planned urban transformation taking shape with an identifying gesture. The museum is a piece of a large mixed-use project in Polanco, Mexico which will serve as a keystone for planned future development. As an asymmetrical form twists out of the plinth it resides on, pedestrians and

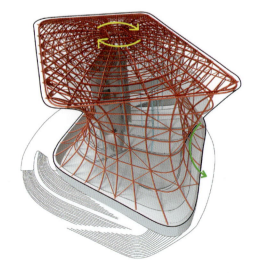

STRUCTURAL DIAGRAM

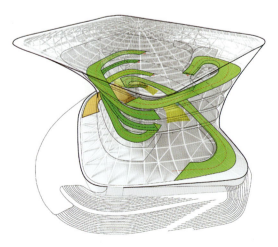

CIRCULATION DIAGRAM

STRUCTURAL DIAGRAM
CIRCULATION DIAGRAM

visitors alike will not overlook the museum as they pass by. The semi-reflective aluminum hexagons create a uniformly dense pattern which allows the museum to be seen at every angle creating soft reflections of light and form. One might view an artistic conceptual similarity in an urban sculptural presence to the Cloud Gate (Chicago Bean) designed by Anish Kapoor. The museum tries to capture the city in which it sits by providing art from many European artists from the 15th to the 20th century. Its galleries are large open pockets which have flexibility to change artist's pieces and showcase new works quite often if desired.

This private museum, funded by Carlos Slim, cost over $70 million with addition to the large development in that area still underway. Slim funded the museum and allowed free admission to its masterful paintings and world's second largest collection of Rodin Sculptures. All of the art is housed on six levels of exhibition space which has a natural circulation movement to the likes of the Solomon R. Guggenheim in New York by Frank Lloyd Wright. The spiraling access and non-linear transition volume create dynamic opportunities to experience the art and the architecture at the same time. The impressive form of the museum encases approximately 6,000 m2 of floor area and accommodates a 350 seat auditorium. Components of the program include a restaurant, offices, library, vaults and gift shop nested within the buildings framework.

The skeletal underlay of the Soumaya Museum is a web of curved steel columns and beams which twist and deform to create the museums unmistakable chassis. The tapered form and unique adapted structural members allow the museum to appear less volumetric and create more visibility around its midsection than a simple extruded shape. Each structural column has a unique form which contributes to the rotated shell of the museums non-uniform surface. As visitors make their way to the upper floor they are greeted by the first glimpses of daylight. This large open space is an umbrella by which the large cantilevered roof allows a naturally day lit environment to emerge into the museum. During the day, the top level of the museum creates a unique display of bounced light and color as the sun tries to puncture its way through every opening it finds. Throughout the rest of the museum, the gallery and sculpture spaces are lit by controlled lighting and the remaining spaces of the museum offer few chances for further daylight.

The Soumaya Museum's slightly twisted, curved and wedged volumetric design is a less complicated exercise in digital modeling than some other non-uniform buildings as of late. However, complex issues such as spatial configuration, circulation and constructability become the challenge with this design put forth by the architects and engineers. With the evolution

GROUND FLOOR PLAN - ENTRANCE

THIRD FLOOR PLAN – EXHIBITION HALLS

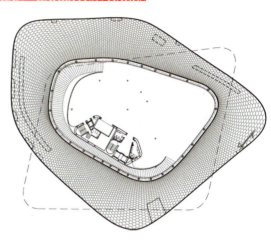

SIXTH FLOOR PLAN – EXHIBITION HALLS

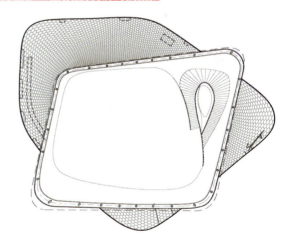

SECTION

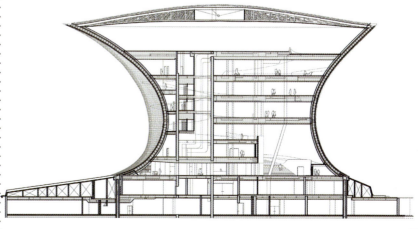

of the 3D digital tools, architects and engineers can communicate their thoughts and ideas on a more collaborative level. Much earlier in the design phase can changes be made to the form and program which cause significant alteration to MEP, structural and cladding systems further down the road. While the museum sits atop a concrete layered plinth, the height and scale do not overpower the buildings adjacent to it.

The residents of Polanco should view this museum as a symbol of art and culture in a public right. The museum was built and designed as a free amenity so all could share in what it stands for. The museums gesture of form, galleries of art and spaces inside and out will serve as a catalyst for urban growth and development for the future of the city.

Brian Ahmes received his Masters of Architecture from the Savannah College of Art and Design. His thesis on form generative surfacing was selected as "best graduation thesis" for that year. He has participated in numerous international design competitions and won AIA awards both locally and nationally. Currently, Brian is working for an international design firm designing healthcare facilities worldwide and conceptually believes that regardless of typology, architectural expression is imperative to performance, functionality and parametricism.

INTERVIEW WITH FERNANDO ROMERO[FREE]

BY ARVIN GARAY-CRUZ

New York, NY. October 5, 2011 - Fernando Romero is the principal at FREE (Fernando Romero Enterprise), one of the leading architectural studios in Mexico and New York. The practice is involved in the production of innovative architecture and urban planning with a diverse range of projects around the world.

Arvin Garay-Cruz [eVolo]: Having an array of projects worldwide gives you a special insight into the production of architecture in different countries. What would you say are the main differences in working in the United States, Latin America, Europe, or Asia, for instance?

Fernando Romero [FREE]: It is completely different to produce architecture in Europe and in the United States than in Latin America because the former have a larger middle class, their cities also have better infrastructure, and their economic system is sustainable in terms of cost of living versus earnings. Working in Asia represents a bigger cultural challenge for our studio. We believe that the only possible way to operate in the continent is by having local partners that understand their own cities and people.

Garay-Cruz: In a certain sense, you are conceiving and creating cutting-edge architecture in a country (Mexico) with certain technological constraints. Which have been your major challenges? On the other hand, what have the advantages been?

Romero: The main advantage would probably be that we are designing innovative structures that will become an important part of the city – landscapes conceived as new focal points and destinations. The disadvantages are that when you produce cutting-edge projects, clients tend to think that the studio is not interested in designing and building simpler commissions. This is a big challenge that we want to overcome by diversifying and working more on the base of the architectural pyramid. This means having more standard commissions where we can also deliver sustainable good design.

Garay-Cruz: It is impossible nowadays to talk about Mexico or with a Mexican architect without thinking about the current state of violence in the country. What has been your experience, as a person and as an architect?

Romero: This is a moment in the history of the country that will certainly change. It has been a huge challenge for all Mexicans but we are progressively winning the battle and remain optimistic about a prompt solution. Establishing a second office in New York has opened our doors to other markets and attracted new clients to Mexico. We do not remain isolated, but instead expand our interaction with the world. The political situation in the country is gradually changing and the studio is analyzing solutions from an architectural and urban point of view.

Garay-Cruz: Another related topic is the much-discussed situation of the border between the United States and Mexico. Since the publication of Hyperborder, what has changed? Would you make an addendum to the book?

Romero: In 2002 the studio designed a proposal for an inhabitable bridge between Mexico and the United States. The project is the first of many studies that analyze the current situation in the border and look at it as an opportunity to rethink social and urban conditions. In 2007 Hyperborder condensed and organized this research with a special focus on the contrast between the sister cities in the border. A year later the studio analyzed the city of Juarez. We are currently working on a proposal with one hundred initiatives that aim to transform the region, which is one of the most contrasted, unique, and dramatic borders in the world. The amount of people moving between the countries is unthinkable and it is very interesting to see the challenges that surface thanks to contrast between the number one superpower in the world and a developing nation. In truth, The Mexican-American border is the gate to the United States from Latin America.

Garay-Cruz: FREE has received a series of awards for the Museo Soumaya in Mexico City, your largest completed project tot his date. Which projects are now on the drawing board?

Romero: It is a very busy time at the office; we are designing a museum in the Southern part of Mexico and another one in Central America. The design for a hotel in Brazil is almost finished, and we are focusing our energy on the urban planning of a city in Central America. The studio just completed a new religious center in Mexico, next to the Villa of Guadalupe – one of the most important religious centers in the world. This new structure includes crypts, chapels, a market, and a museum. On a smaller scale, we are designing a very interesting series of community schools in Mexico.

Garay-Cruz: What has been the evolution of architecture since your early days at OMA? Where is it going?

Romero: It has been more than 10 years. At that time I had a very clear idea of the direction I wanted to take. It was the boom of the use of digital technologies in architecture – a period in time much more complex than the previous 30 years because of the instant access to information and the use of new technologies. It is strange, because the more we develop our career, the more we do not want to limit ourselves to a single direction, but instead want to be an open platform. This is the reason that we renamed the office FREE, because we are not only interested in architecture but in a wider range of challenges and opportunities.

Garay-Cruz: Do you see an evolution in the ways we teach architecture? What has been your experience as a professor?

Romero: I do not see a big difference yet, but I am sure that technology will allow for a more continuous organic flow in the way we teach it. At the moment I am more interested in continuing to learn and discover.

Garay-Cruz: eVolo just presented a new book at the Interior Design Show West in Vancouver, Canada. On our way there, the in-flight magazine featured the Museo Soumaya on the cover. We have been looking around and we have seen your projects published everywhere, there is a lot of information about your practice, but we also want to learn about the person behind it. What are other of your passions and goals?

Romero: I am extremely interested in technology and I am obsessed with music. I am becoming less interested in just talking about architecture, but instead I want to learn and discuss about other challenges of our generation.

Garay-Cruz: Thank you.

eVolo || Issue 4 || 2012

STEALTH
A NEW MUSEUM FOR MARIBOR

DAVID TAJCHMAN ARCHITECTS

TEXT: CHAD PORTER
IMAGES AND DRAWINGS:
DAVID TAJCHMAN ARCHITECTS

The Stealth, a concept for a new visual arts museum, was designed along the Drava River waterfront for the city of Maribor, the second largest city in Slovenia and soon to be the 2012 European capital. The site's location along the river is a popular local node of recreation, relaxation, and social occurrences. Stealth, as a concept, seeks to blend and become a part of this context – to the point where, experientially, it's relatively unnoticed, but encourages the city to exist through and within it. Stealth, in military technology, aims to reduce the recognizability of aircraft and missiles. In stealth's architectural vocabulary recognizability reduction happens by connecting the topographical differences between the neighborhood and river bank, replacing, creating, and preserving existing landscapes, and weaving environmental conditions with local traditions. In this design direction, the museum aims to physically and experientially become synonymous with Maribor's fabric.

With the site situated on sloped terrain between the neighborhood

and the river front, the museum has two basic massing options: excavate and extrude a mass or elevate the building's mass. Excavating and extruding can facilitate the planning process and efficiently maximize the buildable area. While it can practical, it also displaces public space and impairs the link between the neighborhood and riverfront. This edge concept is best represented in many ocean front condominiums found in Miami, Florida. Elevating the mass opens the ground floor allows the city to permeate through the building and blends the internalized program with the urban context. This allows the city to fluidly and effortlessly pass through the building. In the architect's words, the project connects the Drava bank with the upper side of the neighborhood. People pass through the covered ground floor, through an open space of protected outdoor activities. This gesture promotes activity and life within the project beyond the scope of the building program. Instead of this space being defined by articulated building structure, various autonomous program elements activate this level and can function

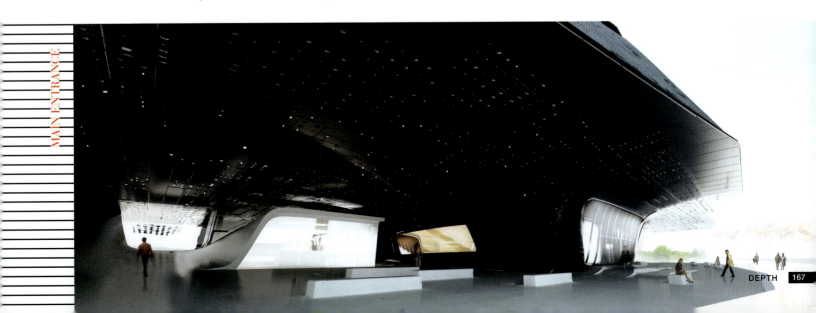

eVolo || Issue 4 || 2012

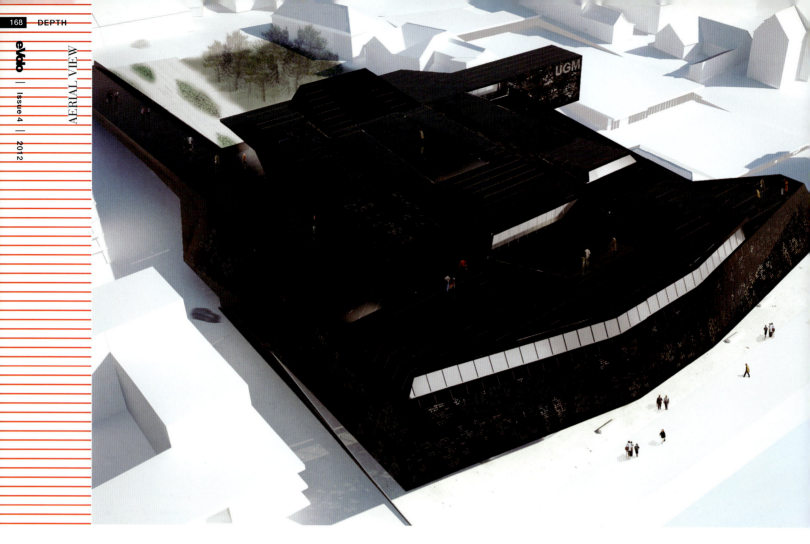

independently of the museum above.   The architect notes, the ground floor is freely accessible from the outside, permitting direct independent access, which intends to animate the Drava bank.   With these autonomous program components and spatial permeability, the building footprint becomes a sub-block within the city vs. a city block of building. In Maribor, a fine grain, porous building base is more synonymous with the urban fabric of smaller buildings on smaller lots – so instead of one building occupying the entire lot, it's perceived more as five independent buildings within the neighborhood. Important to this neighborhood link is the project's staircase, or architectural promenade that physically connects both levels of the city. Functioning as a spinal column, it is the cross sectional axis of the museum which links the riverfront, various museum programs at the landings, and the neighborhood above. As Tajchman describes, this inclined condition of the museum drove the organization and implementation of the project. The museum galleries are nestled between two points of the city: the riverfront and the neighborhood.

The staircase operates as a daily city space traversing the museum program.

The displacement of public and vegetated spaces is another result of excavating the site and extruding the building's mass. Stealth's incision of a minimally invasive ground floor facilitates urban flow and activities. Although different than before, the space still exists and with its new protection from the elements, promotes previously impractical events to occur. By preserving the space's existence and selectively improving the terrain the city assimilate this area into daily life rather than noticing its bruit existence along the water's edge. While mostly retaining the space below, the Stealth also creates a new landscape for the neighborhood node above. Its roof extends the neighborhood's edge toward the water – treating the roofscape as, in their words, a fifth façade. Inspired by the composition of Maribor's roofscape, which with the city's topography create an emblematic perception of the city; the designers seek to create a direct visual and morphological relationship with the context. More importantly than the visual relationship

to Maribor, the roof introduces new accessible urban spaces and previously unimagined experiences to city – giving it a public space net of plus one. Akin to the ground floor with autonomous program entrances, the roof-scape connects Stealth's restaurant, library, and creative industry center with the adjacent neighborhood syncing with the Maribor's urban grain – which adds urban program to neighborhood composition.

Programmatically and spatially the museum camouflages itself from standing out and becoming a burden on daily activity. However, because it is an important building addition to the city it must also be visually noticed and can be a photographic icon for Maribor. This can be a challenge for a building that wants to disappear. To do this, the design considers two important variables: sustainability and local tradition. If successful the building becomes iconic for both locals and visitors. Many buildings, such as the Royal Ontario Museum, are less considerate of local interest but are rather designed for books, design awards, and tourist. For Stealth, the skin is a composition of program driven fenestration, sustainability, and a conceptual patterning apparatus. Stealth's skin patterning is inspired by traditional Slovenian lacework. This idea is carried out though perforated and embossed panels on the exterior. The perforations selectively collect and diffuse natural light with the galleries while the embossed panels add both visual interest as well as traction on the roof's surfaces. While the panels allow selective natural light with the spaces it also filters and stocks rainwater which will be recycled for the building's needs. The skin's panels, a black aluminum surface, are designed to capture and store the sun's energy. For Stealth, blending the skin with the environment was not about matching materials or fenestration patterning and details but more about its conceptual device to place. This one off decision gives the locals a building that is conceivably there's even if the building has a locally strange form and color.

Going stealth is a bold concept for a culturally significant building. Through its massing and program decisions the museum almost disappears as one can move through it, around it, and on it without consciously paying attention the building. Also, the addition of a new landscape is an added amenity to the community. Much like the Oslo Opera House with its continuous roof of public space, the new museum not only creates new views and experiences of the city but also becomes a part of the landscape. The new roofscape and the relatively porous building program are the most successful stealth devices in this project. Although the skin does conceptually relate to the city's historic culture and effectively deliver's appropriate light with the space, it is also – for lack of a better term - a giant black box in the middle of a clay-tiled and white plaster landscape. Of course it shouldn't become an identical installation to its surrounding buildings, but perhaps with a different building skin material it would at least compositionally blend and disappear within the cityscape. However, regardless of skin – as an experience in Maribor, Stealth becomes and enhances its urban place.

Design: David Tajchman Architects. Intern: Luke Izri. Born in 1977 in Brussels, Belgium, David Tajchman studied architecture at Univerisita Libre de Bruxelles, The Institut Victor Horta, and at The Bartlett School of Architecture. He has been living in Brussels, London, and Paris. After having worked as project leader for several architecture and design practices including Dominique Perrault, Jacques Ferrier, Stephane Maupin and Patrick Jouin, he founded his own architecture agency in 2009 simultaneously in Paris and Brussels.

Chad Porter is an architect graduated from the University of Oklahoma. He is a member of the Cuban Chapter of the Council of European Urbanism. Chad is currently employed at HKS Architects working in both the United States and Mexico City.

ENTRANCE STAIRCASE

evolo | Issue 4 | 2012

THE COLLEGE OF ARTS AND THE COLLEGE OF EDUCATION AT THE SABAH AL-SALEM UNIVERSITY CITY

KUWAIT
PERKINS + WILL

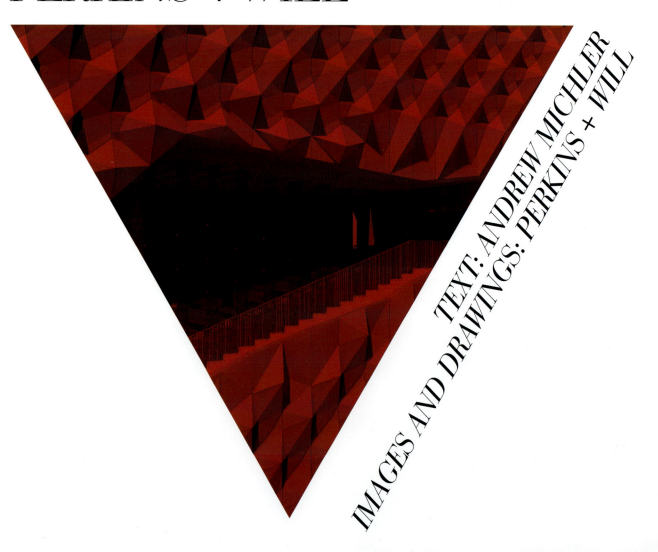

TEXT: ANDREW MICHLER
IMAGES AND DRAWINGS: PERKINS + WILL

The skin of buildings has taken on an iconic status in the rise of contemporary architecture. Think of shimmering titanium clad edifices from Libeskind, Gehry, and Hadid acting as self-congratulatory membranes wrapped around bulks of geometry. While plying awareness to the building the outer surface services are often limited to keeping out the rain, temperature, and atmosphere. As the notion of performance in building design focuses intently on site specific high performance shells, fenestration and opaque elements become more intertwined, attempting a goldilocks outcome: just enough daylight to satisfy the occupants without relying on artificial means or introducing unwanted heat and glare. That promise is tied intimately to the climate and to the aesthetic of the project which is where the aptitude of bold, high performance design can find its footing.

Sunlight can be both the worst enemy and best friend for building conceived as a world-class learning environment. The need to provide daylight into the social areas, core, and classrooms is now understood to be a vital characteristic of healthy design. No artificial sources of light can match the aptitude of sunlight to keep us alert and active, proven out by studies in both worker performance and increased student test scores. Keeping that light from causing glare and overheating has become as much art as science and with no hard formula to follow designers are learning by experience. The manifestation of that dichotomy is pushed to its limit in the Kuwaiti Desert where the new University of Kuwait expansion rests on the south western fringe of Kuwait City. The new 1200 acre Sabah Al-Salem University City will consolidate six different campuses which are currently dispersed throughout Kuwait City.

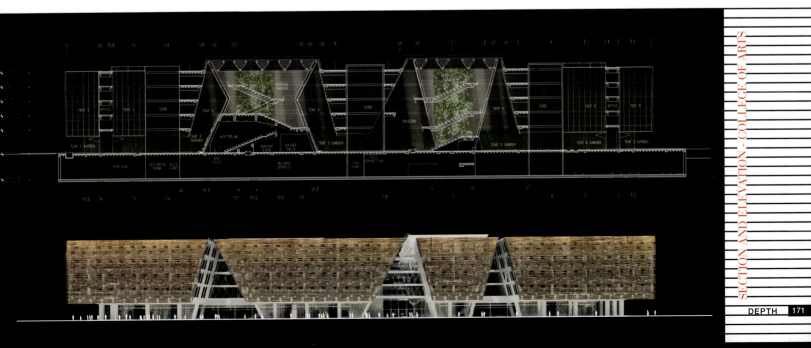

eNoto | issue 4 | 2012

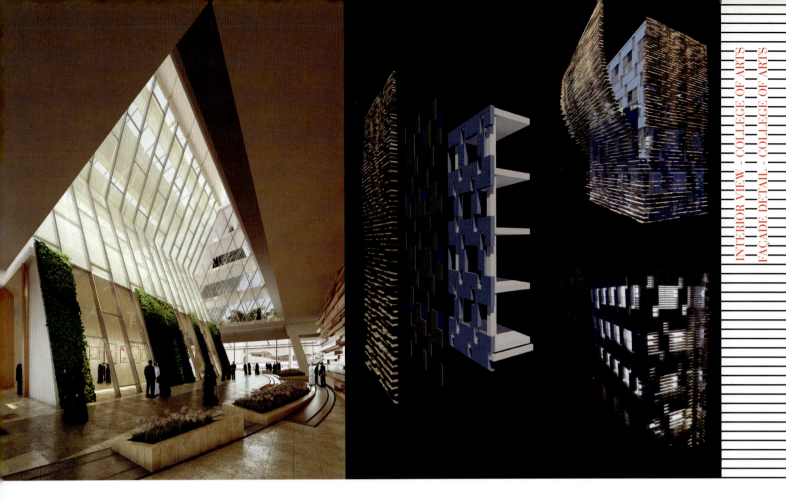

Here precipitation will rarely pass 12 inches a year but humidity can become stifling. The daily mean temperature for a July day is 101 degrees Fahrenheit with an average high of 114 degrees. Building design must accommodate temperatures that can reach an anesthetizing 140 degrees, a manifestation of nature that few of us will experience but a very real part of life for students and faculty of the University. Within that context Perkins + Will has designed two dynamic colleges for Sabah Al-Salem University. The College of Arts and the College of Education intend to foster a dynamic learning and social atmosphere that responds to the extreme environment not by force but by subtlety, and like two siblings the projects have some shared family characteristics but developed their own personality.

Sunlight is a central instrument of design for both buildings. Their common DNA is an introspection on how a building's skin, tasked to do two seemingly opposing things by eliminating heat while introducing light gives the projects their core identity, a complex and dynamic face to the sometimes shimmering, sometimes dust laden environment. The colleges rely on curtain walls of vertical strata, or anthropomorphically an epidermis where multiple functions are carried by individual elements.

The more restrained of the two is the College of Arts, a monolithic rectangular mass wrapped in a layer of limestone shelves. Triangular recesses, evoking Bedouin dewaniya tents, an ancient traditional space which has manifested into modern Kuwaiti architecture as a greeting room and social space (1), cleave the entire program and

SPATIAL AND PROGRAM CONCEPT - COLLEGE OF EDUCATION

CIRCULATION - COLLEGE OF EDUCATION

A1: DESIGN SPACES FOR "PRODUCTIVE COLLISIONS"

CLASSROOMS:
MODULAR, REPETITIVE, LEARNING ENVIRONMENT

COURTYARDS:
MAJOR PROGRAMMED AMENITIES

BOARDWALK:
CIRCULATION PATH W/ PROGRAMMED SECONDARY LEARNING/ SOCIAL FUNCTIONS

COLLEGE OF EDUCATION
KUWAIT UNIVERSITY

COURTYARDS + BOARDWALK = PRODUCTIVE COLLISONS

BOARDWALK
CIRCULATION PATH W/ PROGRAMMED SECONDARY LEARNING / SOCIAL FUNCTIONS

1. ENTRY
2. AUDITORIUM
3. STUDY/ CAFETERIA
4. STUDY HALL
5. FACULTY LOUNGE
6. FACULTY CAFE
7. FACULTY DINING
8. EXHIBITIONS

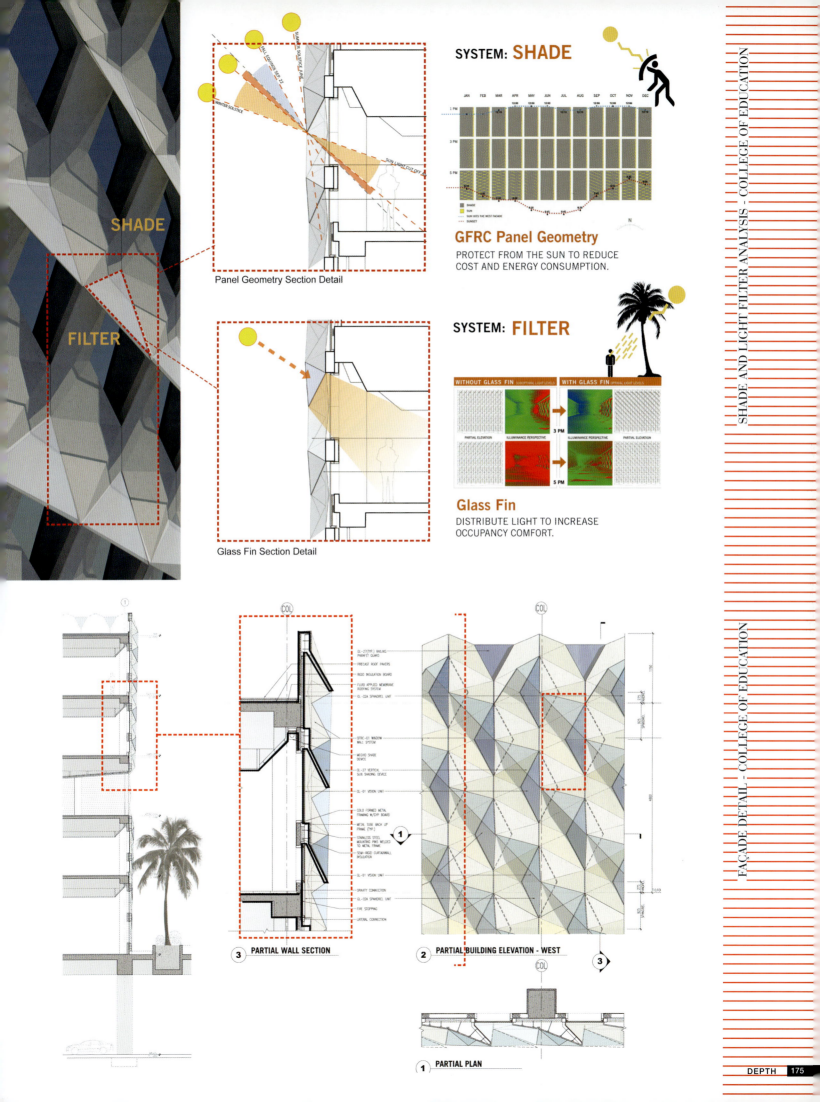

SHADE

FILTER

Panel Geometry Section Detail

Glass Fin Section Detail

SYSTEM: SHADE

GFRC Panel Geometry
PROTECT FROM THE SUN TO REDUCE COST AND ENERGY CONSUMPTION.

SYSTEM: FILTER

WITHOUT GLASS FIN *(SUBOPTIMAL LIGHT LEVELS)* | WITH GLASS FIN *(OPTIMAL LIGHT LEVELS)*

Glass Fin
DISTRIBUTE LIGHT TO INCREASE OCCUPANCY COMFORT.

GL-27(TYP.) RAILING PARAPET GUARD
PRECAST ROOF PAVERS
RIGID INSULATION BOARD
FLUID APPLIED MEMBRANE ROOFING SYSTEM
GL-02A SPANDREL UNIT

GFRC-01 WINDOW WALL SYSTEM
MECHO SHADE DEVICE
GL-27 VERTICAL SUN SHADING DEVICE
GL-01 VISION UNIT
COLD FORMED METAL FRAMING W/GYP BOARD
METAL TUBE BACK UP FRAME (TYP.)
STAINLESS STEEL MOUNTING PINS WELDED TO METAL FRAME
SEMI-RIGID CURTAINWALL INSULATION
GL-01 VISION UNIT
GRAVITY CONNECTION
GL-02A SPANDREL UNIT
FIRE STOPPING
LATERAL CONNECTION

3 **PARTIAL WALL SECTION**

2 **PARTIAL BUILDING ELEVATION - WEST**

1 **PARTIAL PLAN**

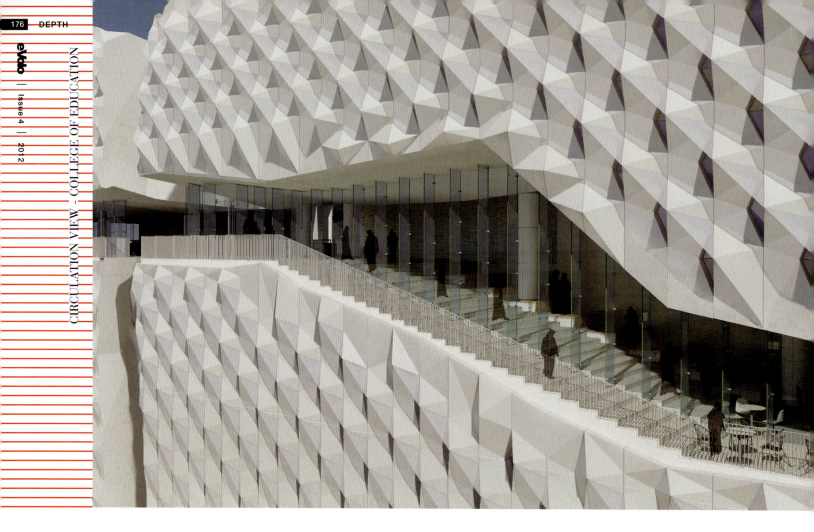

open the interior to a synthetic oasis. The College is to be a self contained environment whose open, cavern-like core is the social hub of the school. The outer entrance spaces are to be primarily naturally cooled with vegetated walls and stack ventilation, and the inner core's latent heat loads cooled conventionally. Filtered daylight from above illuminates the trafficked space which expands at the ground floor by the sloping internal walls. The triangular formulation also presents a natural draft that can be taken advantage of during more moderate seasons. Studios, offices and classrooms all open to the internal communal zone. The simple massing of the building becomes a blank slate for the ceaseless horizontality sliced by the triangular egress. The College of Arts close cousin resides to the west where the LEED Platinum King Abdulla University has used a very similar strategy for coping with the harsh sun. Strips of parallel facade elements wrap the

glazing, providing relief from the noon time solar exposure and from aesthetic tedium.

The College of Education has a more aggressive taste in façade experimentation and delves into an almost molecular binding of elements to achieve the allusive goal of gentle light but not heat. The façade formulation reflects the language of Islamic Art's complex geometry, born from symmetry and repetition that adorns classical architecture throughout the region. The geometry of intersecting planes integrates with the diamond shaped windows, allowing only a sliver of direct daylight into the classrooms. Each grouping of façade elements holds a plane of frosted glass which, angling away from the windows, diffuses the incoming light and cuts glare to a minimum. During summer noon hours the sun is completely blocked, in which angular nodes reflect indirect light inwards toward the ceiling. The resulting reduction

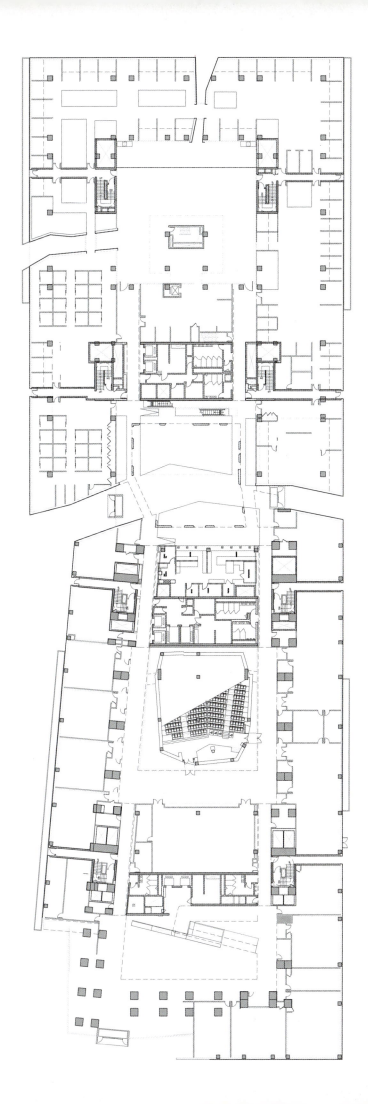

in electrical lighting has the cascading effect of a reduced cooling load.

The integration of program is equally experimental where patterns of traffic flow and social interaction becomes a distinctive quality to the learning environment. Perkins + Will seems to be channeling a Northern European sensibility this time (think of UN Studio's trademark internal winding walkways or BIG's bike path through 8 House) by introducing an internal sidewalk which feeds the public and private spaces on all five floors. The 'boardwalk' rises along the perimeter of the entire building both inside and out, breaking the face of the building into tapering quadrants with floor to ceiling vision glazing tucked under the building's mass. The familiar 'oasis' on the upper floors is the natural gathering place with an auditorium tucked underneath in the core of the building. On the other end is a full story day lit atrium with a standalone library collection towering in the center. The building's layered egress also allows for a mix of traditional classrooms and offices to be interspersed with nontraditional and support spaces like study zones, recreational spaces, lounges and computer stations which fill niches in the floor plate.

Sharing elements with the College of Arts, vegetated walls, self-shading mass and natural ventilation gives Sabah Al-Salem University City environmental bragging rights with the anticipation of contented occupants. Both projects are seeking a LEED Gold plaque, a worthy accomplishment, but considering the extreme design climate the real exam is pass or fail.

Andrew Michler, LEED AP BD+C, is a consultant and writer, and has been living off-grid in Masonville, Colorado since 1995. He is the owner of Baosol LLC Adaptive, a sustainable building consulting company that specializes in design, education and advocacy. His formal education is in the fine arts and focuses primarily on conceptual art installations. He is currently chair of the Northern Colorado Renewable Energy Society. Writing extensively about sustainable building projects, theory and practice, his efforts are directed at helping develop a low entropy society.

References
My Travels My Experience
http://mytravelsmyexperiences.blogspot
com/2010/04/diwaniya-in-q8.html

eVolo || issue4 || 2012

PIER MUSEUM OF LATIN AMERICAN IMMIGRANTS

MIAMI, FL
MACIEJ JAKUB ZAWADZKI

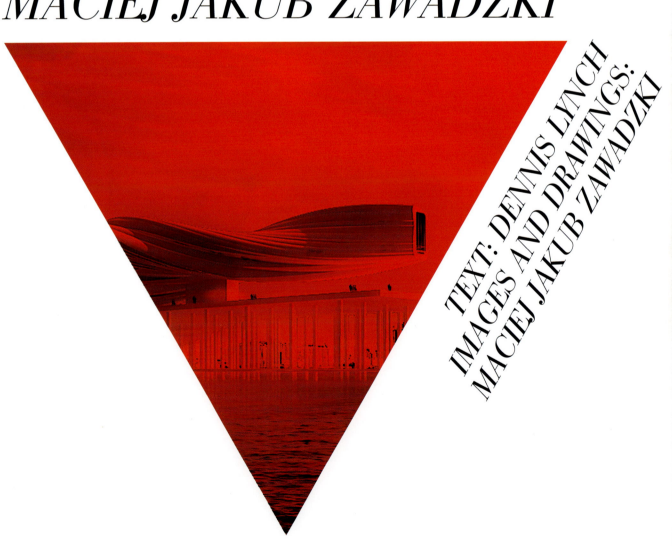

TEXT: DENNIS LYNCH
IMAGES AND DRAWINGS:
MACIEJ JAKUB ZAWADZKI

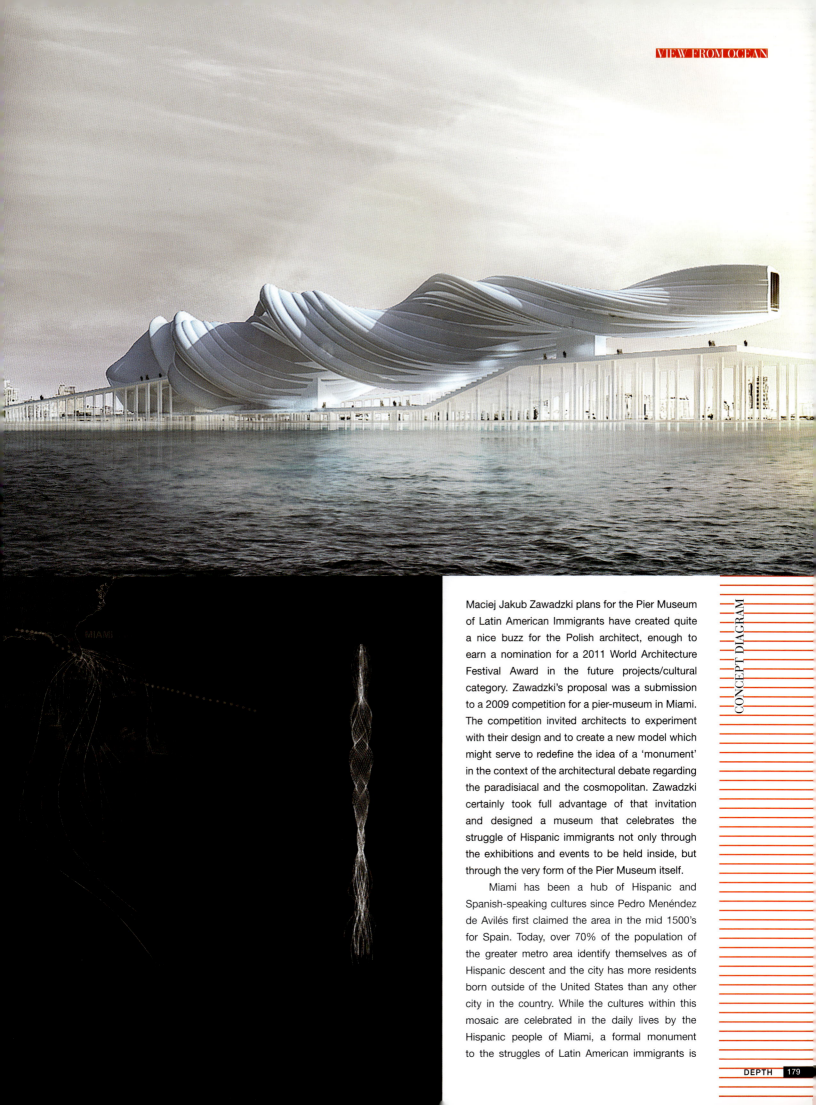

Maciej Jakub Zawadzki plans for the Pier Museum of Latin American Immigrants have created quite a nice buzz for the Polish architect, enough to earn a nomination for a 2011 World Architecture Festival Award in the future projects/cultural category. Zawadzki's proposal was a submission to a 2009 competition for a pier-museum in Miami. The competition invited architects to experiment with their design and to create a new model which might serve to redefine the idea of a 'monument' in the context of the architectural debate regarding the paradisiacal and the cosmopolitan. Zawadzki certainly took full advantage of that invitation and designed a museum that celebrates the struggle of Hispanic immigrants not only through the exhibitions and events to be held inside, but through the very form of the Pier Museum itself.

Miami has been a hub of Hispanic and Spanish-speaking cultures since Pedro Menéndez de Avilés first claimed the area in the mid 1500's for Spain. Today, over 70% of the population of the greater metro area identify themselves as of Hispanic descent and the city has more residents born outside of the United States than any other city in the country. While the cultures within this mosaic are celebrated in the daily lives by the Hispanic people of Miami, a formal monument to the struggles of Latin American immigrants is

eVolo | Issue 4 | 2012

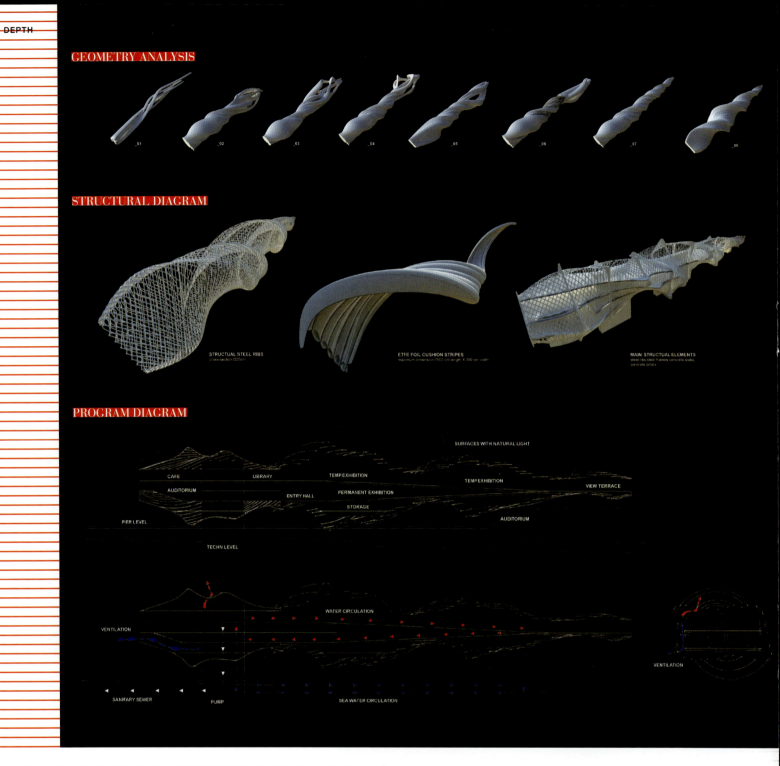

GEOMETRY ANALYSIS

_01 _02 _03 _04 _05 _06 _07 _08

STRUCTURAL DIAGRAM

STRUCTUAL STEEL RIBS
cross-section 125cm

ETFE FOIL CUSHION STRIPES
maximum dimension 7500 cm length X 360 cm width

MAIN STRUCTURAL ELEMENTS
steel ribs, steel frames, concrete slabs,
concrete pillars

PROGRAM DIAGRAM

SURFACES WITH NATURAL LIGHT

CAFE   LIBRARY   TEMP. EXHIBITION   TEMP. EXHIBITION   VIEW TERRACE

AUDITORIUM   ENTRY HALL   PERMANENT EXHIBITION

STORAGE   AUDITORIUM

PIER LEVEL

TECHN LEVEL

WATER CIRCULATION

VENTILATION   VENTILATION

SANITARY SEWER   PUMP   SEA WATER CIRCULATION

lacking in the city. The Pier Museum of Latin American Immigrants would offer a true monument of the people who made the journey from their homelands through south Florida.

Zawadski's primary goal in design was to represent and honor the literal and emotional turbulence so many immigrants endured in their journey to the United States. A horizontal orientation composed of multiple energetic waves brings to mind the universal goal of happiness and prosperity of all migrants, but discovered by each through unique paths wrought with emotion.

To actually form the dramatic exterior, he merged the geographies of two phenomena: the immense natural power of the local environment and the equally turbulent journeys so many immigrants embarked upon. Aggressive irregular shapes mimicking the diverse paths of immigration come to form a kinetic and dramatic shape; a paradoxical fusion of beauty and the unrelenting power of nature twisting and rolling like the ocean waves that brought hopefuls to American shores. Visions of prosperity, mixed emotions of parting with home, and images of tangible maelstroms are all present in the outward form of the Museum.

There's a saying in literary communities: "show, don't tell"; to create

an image, to make a reader feel as though they are experiencing what you write and not just being told about it. The concept certainly spills over into architecture in the practice of special formation. Fellow Polish architectural scholar Amos Rapoport has said of architectural space: "…space is the three-dimensional extension of the world around us, the intervals, distances and relationships between people and people, people and things, and things and things". Space, and particularly interior space can be approached to echo the role and contents of the building itself.

In this case, the interior space of the Pier-Museum is a spatial representation of the complex emotional journey immigrants endure in passage. Twisting elevations remind visitors of the confusion and challenges encountered by immigrants and soft interior lines play with the paradoxical feelings of hardship, somber beauty, and hope. What results are spaces that create this almost uneasy feeling of being lost, adrift in an endless ocean. Typical notions of order are cast aside in the Pier-Museum for this atmosphere of subdued turmoil.

Visitors enter into a hall near the shore-side of the Museum. Moving back towards the shore are a library, auditorium, and café. The exhibits are to the seaside of the horizontal space, where natural light is allowed in through the roof to light the spaces. A visitor experiences the exhibits, learning the history of immigration and is slowly moved along a path that ends with an open-ended ocean-view terrace. Visitors come to this terrace to find a striking view of the waters so many immigrants braved to pursue life in the U.S. The pier-level is also open to visitors to enjoy magnificent open-air spaces over the water.

The Museum is set to host events year-round and so was designed to adapt to changing climate conditions. Of course what is most concerning is the extreme weather phenomena the very Museum resembles. To deal with hurricane force winds and thousands of pounds of water pressure, aerodynamics and water load were accounted for in the formal design process to minimize direct forces on the building. The pier is to be held by concrete pillars and the base for the Museum made of slabs. Steel and concrete will be used to support the Museum structurally. The Museum fluid shape is formed by ETFE strips surrounding a strong steel mesh, offering the flexibility the Museum will need to withstand the extreme conditions.

Where wind and sea are a danger in extreme conditions, in average day-to-day conditions the sea breezes and surrounding ocean water offer a natural cooling system as an environmentally friendly way to help cope with average temperatures in the 80s F (30 C). Cool air blown in from the ocean will be circulated through pier-level vents while hot air is expelled through vents on the roof. Seawater is circulated through a pump running down through a pillar to the ocean.

The Museum will be located on a pier extended out from Miami Beach along the axis of 5th street, perpendicular to Ocean Drive. The dramatic shape and bustling location is prime to attract visitors and garner public interest into the history of immigration.

Dennis Lynch is a senior at the University of Massachusetts Amherst studying Journalism and Legal Studies. Dennis has been a contributing writer at eVolo since 2010.
Maciej Jakub Zawadzki is an award-winning Polish architect with a Masters Degree in Architecture from the Warsaw University of Technology. Maciej has previously collaborated with Bjarke Ingels Group (BIG) in Copenhagen, Denmark. His proposal for the Latin American Immigrants in Miami is currently shortlisted for Building of the Year at the 2011 World Architecture Festival in Barcelona.

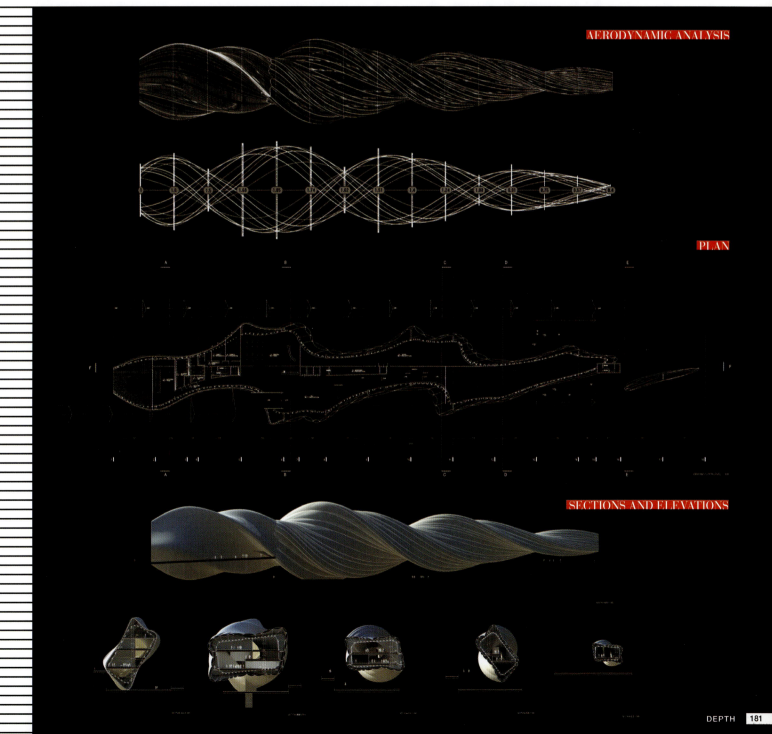

AERODYNAMIC ANALYSIS

PLAN

SECTIONS AND ELEVATIONS

eVolo | Issue 4 | 2012

MUSEUM OF IMAGE AND SOUND

RIO DE JANEIRO, BRAZIL
DILLER SCOFIDIO + RENFRO

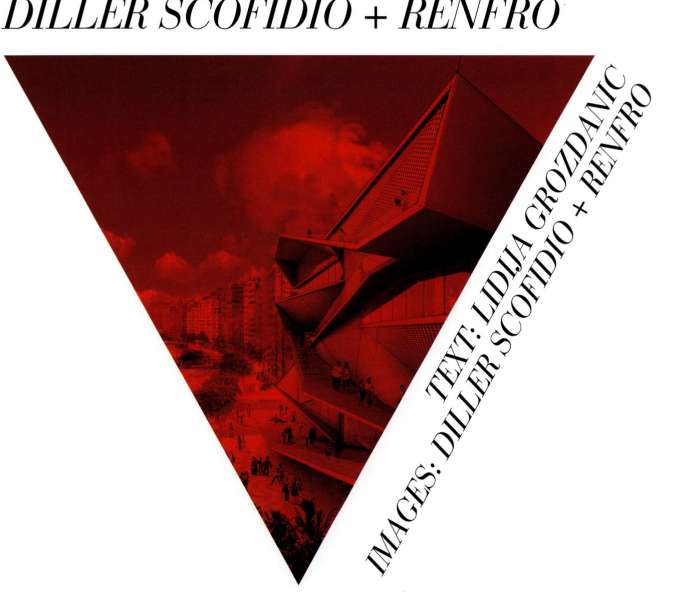

TEXT: LIDIJA GROZDANIC

IMAGES: DILLER SCOFIDIO + RENFRO

The first thought that comes to mind is: "Yes, this is a DS+R building". Given the problematics of branding in contemporary architecture it is reasonable to expect one's reductionist attitude towards architecture of signature gestures. Often uninventive and predictable, it provides justification for observers and readers to quickly move on or turn the page. The Museum of Image and Sound in Rio de Janeiro possesses that distinctiveness in form, to some extent noticeable in the studio's previous work on National Music Center in Calgary and the Eyebeam Museum of Art and Technology in New York. However, DS+R's interdisciplinary provenience and constant investigation into performance spaces suggest that there might be a revealing subtext behind the building's strong visual rhetorics.

Winning a competition among six other architectural studios, Diller Scofidio + Renfro produced a project that seemed to be most responsive to the site requirements. Set within a wall-like strip of Rio's waterfront, the building engages in issues of public accessibility and social integration, creating a thick interface between galleries and the boulevard. Although loosely considerate towards orthogonal geometry of surrounding buildings, the context within which the Museum is positioned pertains to the horizontal, instead of the vertical narrative. Deriving from the trajectory of the Burle Marx walkway, a public path meanders back and forth through six stories of museum content. It traverses indoor and outdoor spaces and branches to make galleries, education programs, spaces of public leisure and entertainment.

PANOPTICON

With its beachfront elevation in constant state of flux, the building aims to deconstruct social mechanisms of museum culture. Deliberately compromising the inherited elitism of exhibition spaces, the architects introduce a "subversive" element of multiple public access points. It is an act of creative rebellion that establishes a physical field of user-content interaction as surrogate for the absent cultural dynamics of the city's waterfront. Transposing the principles of beach culture, or what the architects would call-unified democratic space, into the vertical plane, the building redefines the spatial distribution of positions of power. The vertical circulation sequence translates the social patterns of the beach and creates a fresh interpretation of the urban panopticon. The previous panoramic view, overexposed to tourist and restricted for many residents, is given back to the public. The

structure constantly generates activity and stimulates the creation of a new social coordinate system with the common man (possibly in a swimsuit) at its center.

MIRROR-MAZE

Except for the purpose of providing a view, the architects introduce a vertical path in order to enhance a gradual detachment from external influences. The climb itself establishes a sense of self-awareness, a crucial step in reaching an optimal level of perceptiveness. Further north, along the coastline, one can find similar treatment of the museum entrance. The Niteroi Contemporary Art Museum by Oscar Niemeyer introduces a kind of promenade cinematique, providing an almost ritual experience of entering a museum. It delivers a 360 panoramic view of the surroundings but remains essentially introverted. Along with the example of Rio De Janeiro Museum of Modern Art, situated across the Bay, this type of modernist approach to cultural spaces seems to be anachronistic in face of contemporary art. The new Museum of Image and Sound expands the concept of communicating art by establishing a two-way interaction with the city. Much of its east elevation will be a punched grille, creating partial transparency with an effect of inclusiveness, particularly valuable at night. Because of its precedent features and public accessibility the Museum acts as an anomaly within the uniform fabric of Rio's waterfront. Its engaged façade creates a psycho-geographical effect of self-awareness, both of architecture and user. It is a relationship of reciprocity; the public flow activates the building while the latter draws focus on the individual, at the same time providing a desirable model for the rest of the coastline. This sense of mirrors-reflecting-mirrors reminds of Charlie Chaplin's film, "The Circus", often interpreted as one through which Chaplin turns the mirror towards himself. The main character, the Tramp, unwittingly becomes part of the circus performance. By not being funny when he's supposed to and vice-versa, he dazzles the audience. The literal expression of self-discovery through spatial intervention is found in the chase scene when the Tramp escapes the cops by dashing into a funhouse Mirror Maze. Its walls kaleidoscopically reflect many images of the Tramp, which creates an effect structurally more significant as a parable than a vessel for delivering comic relief. As if holding each other's mirrors, the visitor and building create a symbiotic relationship that propels the story forward, and keeps the Museum's mechanisms in motion.

eVolo

| Issue 4 |

| 2012

EXHIBITION-IST

The new museum will house a large amount of material dedicated to cultural history of Rio, currently stored and exhibited in two small buildings in the downtown area. Over a thousand interviews and about 4 000 hours of recordings, along with movies, posters and manuscripts will be at one point available to the public. Organized around a large glass atrium, the exhibition spaces culminate with a 300-person outdoor cinema, overlooking Copacabana Beach. Ramps and stairs connect split-level exhibition spaces and a projection gallery. The intermingling of these display spaces with retail and entertainment areas creates a vibrant atmosphere that seems to be derived from the city itself.

Recalling Brazilian art in general, a sense of exuberance and sensuality emerges. The blurring of the line between architecture and display creates an impression of continuous performance, expressing the very nature of the artifacts stored within the building. The Museum seems to follow the cultural impulses of Rio de Janeiro and is simultaneously transformed into an architectural voyeur and exhibitionist.

"Architecture is nothing but a special-effects machine, that delights and disturbs the senses. Our work is a cross-media", says Liz Diller in her TED appearance in 2007. The correlation between the name of the Museum of Image and Sound and the cinematic effect generated by the moving image along its elevation, empirically confirm DS+R's interdisciplinary attitude in designing. There is a genuine recognition of architecture's immanence to all other disciplines which enables a constant interflow of influences. Whether it's characterized as over-intellectualized or exceedingly theatrical, DS+R's work is versatile and playful. The ephemerality of the Blur Building, the paving of the Highline and floating galleries of the ICA in Boston, among other projects, are examples of challenging the conventions of space. A bit like Chaplin's Tramp character, DS+R simply don't seem to perform in a way the public would expect from Starchitects.

Lidija Grozdanic is an architect based in Montenegro. Lidija studied at the Univerzitet u Beogradu and worked for Bonico. She has been a contributing writer at eVolo since 2010.

Diller Scofidio + Renfro is an interdisciplinary design studio that integrates architecture, the visual arts, and the performing arts. Based in New York City, Diller Scofidio + Renfro is led by three partners who work collaboratively with a staff of 65 architects, artists and administrators.
Elizabeth Diller, a founding member of Diller Scofidio + Renfro, attended The Cooper Union School of Art and received a Bachelor of Architecture from the Cooper Union School of Architecture. Ms. Diller is a Professor of Architecture at Princeton University.
Ricardo Scofidio, RA, a founding member of Diller Scofidio + Renfro, attended The Cooper Union School of Architecture and received a Bachelor of Architecture from Columbia University. Mr. Scofidio is Professor Emeritus of Architecture at Cooper Union.
Charles Renfro, RA, joined the studio in 1997 and became partner in 2004. He attended Rice University and received a Master of Architecture degree from Columbia University. Mr. Renfro is currently a Visiting Professor at Parsons New School for Design.

ENTRANCE FROM BEACH PROMENADE

NIGHT VIEW

THE TIMES EUREKA PAVILION

LONDON, UNITED KINGDOM
NEX ARCHITECTURE

TEXT: DANIELLE DEL SOL
IMAGES AND DRAWINGS:
NEX ARCHITECTURE

eVolo

Issue 4 | 2012

EXTERIOR VIEW

PANELS DETAIL

INTERIOR VIEW

A skeletal addition to London's lush Kew Gardens brought an unusual architectural form this summer and fall to a space already rich with visual stimulation: Kew's grounds, which are listed as a UNESCO world heritage site, are littered with ancient glass greenhouses, exotic foliage and landscaping, and even a Dali sculpture of a melting clock.

Adding to that rich mass of artful form is the Times Eureka Pavilion, an intimate outdoor room constructed from connecting wooden polygons. Designed by London-based Nex Architecture, the transparent honeycomb cube is pieced together with spruce panels that hold shapes within shapes: hexagons within hexagons, which are nestled within large rectangles. In the ample free space left by the large spaces, curled plastic shapes connect to the wooden planks to fill in the structure's exterior. This additional design element adds to the powerful shadow show that shifts throughout the day inside of the Pavilion as the sun moves through the sky and the geometric shapes and curls are projected onto the ground.

Nex Architecture was commissioned by and collaborated closely with landscape designer Marcus Barnett for the pavilion's design. This

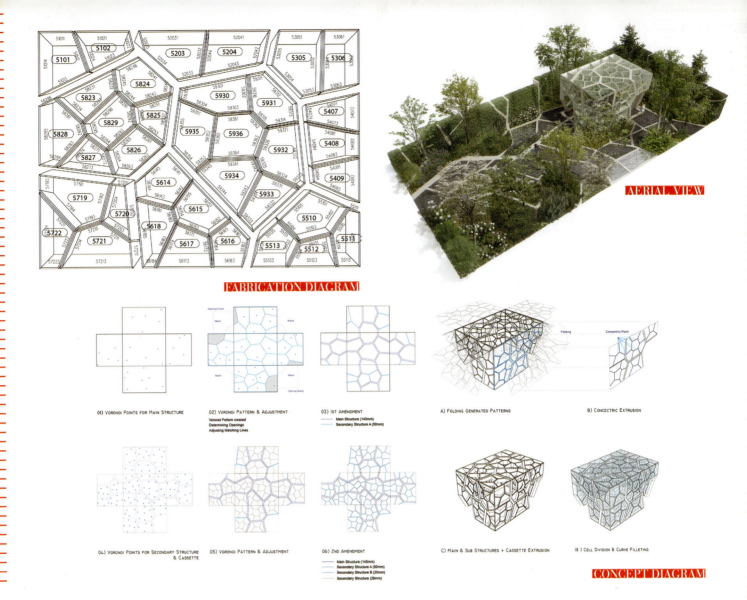

FABRICATION DIAGRAM

AERIAL VIEW

01) VORONOI POINTS FOR MAIN STRUCTURE

02) VORONOI PATTERN & ADJUSTMENT
Voronoi Pattern created
Determining Openings
Adjusting Matching Lines

03) 1ST AMENDMENT
Main Structure (140mm)
Secondary Structure A (50mm)

A) FOLDING GENERATED PATTERNS

B) CONCECTRIC EXTRUSION

04) VORONOI POINTS FOR SECONDARY STRUCTURE & CASSETTE

05) VORONOI PATTERN & ADJUSTMENT

06) 2ND AMENDMENT
Main Structure (140mm)
Secondary Structure A (50mm)
Secondary Structure B (20mm)
Secondary Structure (20mm)

C) MAIN & SUB STRUCTURES + CASSETTE EXTRUSION

IB) CELL DIVISION & CURVE FILLETING

CONCEPT DIAGRAM

partnership inspired the firm's architects in two key ways: First, it provided a specific context in which the structure would be placed. The Pavilion is hugged snugly by shrubs, wildflowers and small trees, and its design, with its light brown shade and stark shapes, is at once both a startling contrast to the soft landscaping and also a logical, organic presence. As the Pavilion nestles within the landscape, so are its own shapes that define the exterior nestled within one another; everything in the patch exists individually but relies on the support of its surrounding elements to reinforce its placement and beauty.

Additionally, Barnett's garden design inspired the architects' concept for the design as a whole: As they began to consider the natural setting and context for their pavilion, they began to think about plants on the cellular level. This micro-scale visual provided the basis for the geometric design. "The garden explores the significance of plants to science and society," the firm states on its website. "The design approach is inspired by the cellular structure of plants and processes of plant growth and formation.

"Using computational genetic algorithms, the plan of the garden was grown by capillary branching and subsequent cellular division. The timber and plastic pavilion…will allow visitors to experience the patterns of biological structure at an unfamiliar scale."

Solid wood benches inside the pavilion allow visitors to linger and rest, experiencing the design elements and shadows at play. A glass roof keeps the interior dry, allowing the pavilion to function as a rain shelter as well.

Barnett's heavy placement of plants that are used for medicinal, commercial, and industrial purposes was meant to emphasize plants' never-ending importance in our every day lives. This underscores the

symbiotic nature of the pavilion's existence within the garden, and the design of the pavilion itself, as explored earlier. The designers purposefully broadcast this message: "The garden…demonstrates humanity's symbiotic interdependence with natural ecosystems," they stated.

The garden's design was commissioned by the London Times, the city's leading daily newspaper, and the Royal Botanic Gardens at Kew for the 2011 RHS Chelsea Flower Show. Barnett was chosen by the Times to design the garden, which is meant to support the paper's dedication to science, as shown by their monthly publication of Eureka science magazine. Barnett then chose Nex to design the pavilion to fit within his garden.

The structure is "green" in every sense: The spruce panels were sustainably harvested, and the plastic used within each "cell" is made from recycled materials.

The garden was awarded a silver medal by the Royal Horitcultural Society.

NEX Architecture is based in London, UK at the center of an international network of the world's leading design consultants and specialists. It is a new breed of multi-disciplinary design office that focuses on the intersection between architecture, infrastructure, and urban design. NEX pursues innovation both in the design processes and in the environment they create.

Danielle Del Sol is a New Orleans-based writer and deputy editor of Preservation in Print, the monthly magazine of the Preservation Resource Center, one of the nation's leading historic preservation nonprofits. She hails from both Miami, Florida and Fayetteville, Arkansas — two very different, but equally inspiring worlds — and holds a master's degree in preservation studies from the Tulane University School of Architecture. She writes for national and local publications on architecture, urban planning, policy and culture, and is passionate about reporting on the impact that land use decisions have on our everyday lives.

eVolo || Issue 4 || 2012

SAMARANCH MEMORIAL OLYMPIC MUSEUM

TIANJIN, CHINA
HOLM ARCHITECTURE OFFICE (HAO)
+ ARCHILAND BEIJING
+ KRAGH & BERGLUND

TEXT: LIDIJA GROZDANIC
IMAGES AND DRAWINGS:
HAO + ARCHILAND BEIJING
+ KRAGH & BERGLUND

There is something essentially disturbing about circular buildings. They deny us the familiarity of corners, and fail to fulfill our primordial need for finite spaces and concluded beginnings. We are left with the ambiguity that confuses course with direction, and the unease in realizing that the process of moving will lead us back to the point of departure. The awareness of time is anesthetized, as the building's configuration continuously recreates the experience of journey.

It is this quality of psycho-geographic mapping of time that Samaranch Museum explores. It becomes an exaggeration of the concept that interprets architecture as "a time collecting machine". The visitors are exposed to a kind of subtle subversion, as they are able to see the past and future projections of themselves across the patio. It is not a conscious thought, but an instinctive need, that of retracing our own movement in space. That prescribed paradigm of gradually mastering built space is overthrown by evoking the experience of temporal continuum.

In the case of Samaranch Museum, what should have represented the physical barrier between the inside and outside is gently lifted, inviting visitors into the first internal patio, where the entry to the building is located. The circular ramp lifts and guides them through a continuous loop of exhibition and memorial areas. The use of framing and negative space is inverted so that the juxtaposing of artificial and natural creates an unexpected relationship of forces. With the building constantly generating movement, the space it encompasses seems to take on the role of crucial importance. The patio becomes a place of stillness, an eye within a vortex of human motion, with its dynamics amplified by the changes in height and occasional divergence of floor plates. The building becomes a visual provocateur, instead of a calm refuge. The archetypal roles of artificial and natural are curiously reversed.

By winning the first prize in a competition, Holm Architecture Office (HAO)

CONCEPT DIAGRAM

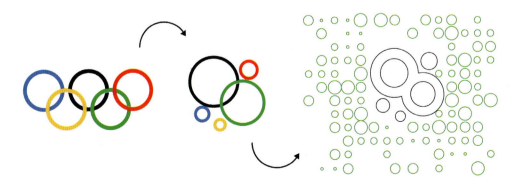

GEOMETRY ANALYSIS

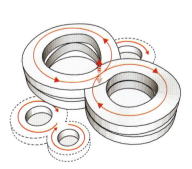

and Archiland Beijing with Kragh & Berglund landscape architects gained the opportunity to build in Tianjin, a site of several Olympic events of the year 2008. Holm Architecture's work includes large scale planning projects as well as smaller experiments such as editorials and interior design. Their approaches to specific tasks seem to be diverse, ranging from parametric design to modular environments of high-density housing.

The predictable referencing to interlocking circles of the Olympic symbol is further developed by creating a structure of two above-ground undulating rings with three sunken courtyards. The movement trajectories merge two typologies: the memorial and the museum. The memorial part of the endeavor was to create a facility that will honor the life of Juan Antonio Samaranch, the president of the International Olympic Committee from 1980 to 2001, and a strong supporter of China's bid as host city for the 2008 Olympic Games. The building design also incorporates green technologies,

from the installation of energy-producing solar cells on the building's roof to climate control through geothermal heating and cooling. The treatment of the surrounding park is consistently devoted to the circle: the 80 000 square meter area is embroidered with a network of public paths, interconnecting the 204 differently landscaped circles which represent each of the member countries of the International Olympic Committee. By overlaying of circulation, vegetation, topography and activity diagrams, the final design of the park establishes a seemingly random pattern of engaged public space.

It is to possible to compare the Samaranch Museum to BIG's Greenland National Gallery and even SANAA's Rolex Learning Center, as they show similar formal attitudes in use of circular layout schemes. There is always a risk in engaging with such potent geometry, as it tends to overtake the complete project. It is a tyrant that, if the rhythm it establishes is not obeyed by the rest of the design, can devour the whole thing. In that light, there is little

room for debating on authenticity. The architectural intentions may match, leaving room for assessing the execution, while the experiences of space remain unique. Similar formal premises and use of circular navigation through space are simply frameworks for developing specific architectural narratives.

The obvious fact is that the shape itself is not new: the zero, the number eight and the Möbius Band, weather representing the idea of the Infinite or Jung's Road to the Unconscious, all have strong symbolic meanings. Translated into the language of built environment they recreate the principles of journey as "microcosmic instances of a macrocosmic pattern". Buildings become road movies, with characters transformed by the specific encounters that occur on the margins of the road. The visual stimuli along the path aim to transform the traveler, as he/she navigates through the exhibitions. The informative and didactic nature of the museum experience is merged into a mesmerizing flow of impressions. The investigation into temporal determinants is similarly conducted in Aleksandr Sokurov's Russian Ark. A road movie through the Russian State Hermitage Museum, depicting 200 years of Russian history, is created in a single unedited shot, running uninterrupted from first moment to last. By using a first-person perspective and never cutting, never cheating time, it brings architecture and cinema as close as they can get. As a technical experiment, the film, above all, attempts to create a narrative immediacy. The camera swoops and glides, drifts, pulls in, and sails through space creating choreography of spatial assemblies similar to the architecture of the Samaranch Museum. The two mediums are driven by the same essential desire to express themselves "in one breath".

Through the erasure of conventional architectural editing, and by dismissing the vocabulary of visual barriers and intermissions, the Museum is able to present its contents as a continuous image of Olympic heritage.

Lidija Grozdanic is an architect based in Montenegro. Lidija studied at the Univerzitet u Beogradu and worked for Bonico. She has been a contributing writer at eVolo since 2010.

Holm Architecture Office (HAO) is an international design collective founded by Danish architect Jens Holm. HAO focuses on creating strong working collaborations with clients and designers through an open and inclusive design process. HAO believes that collaboration on all levels of the design process leads to better ideas and exciting projects.
Holm Architecture Office Team: Jens Holm, Niklas Thormark
Archiland Team: Morten Holm, Tian Kun, Chen Pu, Adam Chapulski, Camilla Bundgaard, Yuxiaomin, Liulingling
Kragh & Berglund Team: Jonas Berglung, Hans Kragh

LANDSCAPE DESIGN DIAGRAM

  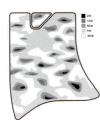 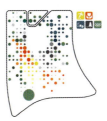

SUSTAINABLE SYSTEMS DIAGRAM

PLANS

LEVEL -1 / RESTAURANT, AUDITORIUM & ADMINISTRATION

LEVEL 1 / COURTYARD & ENTRY

LEVEL 2 / ENTRY, CAFE & EXHIBITION

 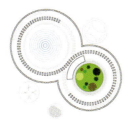

LEVEL 3 / TERRASSE & EXHIBITION

LEVEL 4 / EXHIBITION

LEVEL 5 / ROOF

dezeen watchstore

Watches by boutique brands and named designers

www.dezeenwatchstore.com